I Laura,
The Story of a Kansas Family

Memoirs of Laura Margaret Schmid Hogan
Edited by Stephen D. Webb

My best wishes.
Laura X. Hogan
2013

1st Edition

First Edition 2010

Published by:

Ammons Communications
Western North Carolina
SAN NO. 8 5 1 – 0 8 8 1
29 Regal Avenue • Sylva, North Carolina 28779
Phone/fax: (828) 631-4587

Library of Congress Control Number: 2010934507
ISBN: 978-0-9827611-4-4

OUR LOVING MOTHER
A tribute to my mother, by Laura Margaret Schmid

Our Mother could not write a speech
I guess she never tried
She would just talk our tears away
When our puppy died

She never sat and wrote a book
Did not have time to try
But, boy! Could she make clothes that fit
And calm us when we cried

At games of scrabble, Mom was sharp
At golf she would be a flop
But, My, Oh My, how she could cook
And sweep, and sew, and mop

No history book records her deeds,
No poet sang her fame
But all the needy, near and far
They blessed my Mother's name

Her mode of life was tried and true
Her methods never failed
And though her brood no honors drew
Her love, life's work, prevailed

Dedication

This book is dedicated to my descendants. May it shed some light on the background of poverty and hardships of their parents' lives. May it encourage all of you to live life one day at a time, and to dedicate yourself to honesty, integrity and kindness. May it give to one and all assurance that perseverance and dedication to your life's goals will, in the end, bring to you happiness beyond your fondest dreams. This is the wish of the last remaining member of the Schmids from Atwood, Kansas, your Aunt Laura Schmid Hogan.

Forward: Why Write This Book?

Because I, Laura, have not forgotten.

Having been born on the high plains of the United States in the early twentieth century, when the grasslands and the mercy of God represented our existence, I developed something of an awareness of life, different from the life we all know now. As the youngest female in a large family, experiencing life and death through the harsh reality of farming in the central United States brought me to something few others have experienced. Growing up was an existence sparse with amenities. We did not know what lie ahead, and we lived each day as it came.

I remember the serenity of a home-life supported by my Father, dedicated to building a home for his endearing wife and children. Back then a good home was how you survived, how you existed; not a luxury like it is today. In those days, an endearing wife and MANY children (18 born, 15 that lived) were necessary for simple existence in that meek environment, over which we had little control. My Father's faith and commitment to life through the poverty of high plains farming is the root of this story.

Did my parents know a different life than you or I? I don't believe they dreamed as we do, that life is ours to live and to love, as we do today. All they looked for was survival, and enjoying their family as the Lord gave it to them. They learned early to be kind, honest, to work hard, and to learn to appreciate each other no matter where you came from or what your purpose was for being there. They counted only pennies, looked for no recognition, and accepted life on a daily basis. Faith in God, trust in God, and a deep commitment to life was what got them through.

I dedicate this book to both my Mother and my Father. Lucky for me I was part of this family. This book details my life in its developing ways, my triumphs and tragedies, my life experiences as the years rolled on. Let it be a tribute to all my brothers and sisters young and old, far and near, and a story for the world of a life and a lifetime that I, Laura, have not forgotten.

Acknowledgements

The following people have contributed significantly to my life and to this book:

Janis Bryson
Sister Marylou Cassidy
Lorrie Covert
Daniel Hogan V
Janet Krause
Diane Mettler
Laura Olifiers
Eva Pochop
Threasa Rippe
Charlotte Sekulich
Joseph Schmid
Wendi Schmid
Bernadine Smith

Photos – Family Collections

Cover Design and Family Tree – Mary Webb

Edited by – Stephen D. Webb

Table of Contents

LAURA S HOGAN

THANK YOU FOR BEING HERE

Life offers us times of joy, and times of stress

Time to work and time to rest

Time to share because we care

Time to love and time to dream

Leaving memories that do not end

Remembering me, as a friend

Know I love you, one and all

When you need me give a call

You are a special person

Walking through my life leaving

Flowers of kindness in your path

Thank you for your many flowers!

Love, Laura

Chapter 1

A TREE GROWS IN KANSAS

Going back some 86 years takes some thought and doing. I have such grand feelings of childhood, yet to remember all the things that took place is not easy. There were 15 of us that grew up in the Schmid family. I understand that my mother actually had 21 pregnancies, 3 miscarriages and 3 stillborns. My father always said he had two baseball teams, so that meant the three stillborns would have been girls, but were they named? Where were they buried? I was never told. I do know that my mother used to take us to a tree in the cow pasture and would tell us there were some graves there. For some reason I always thought they were Indians, but I do not know if there were any in our locality. None of my sisters or brothers ever mentioned anything about those graves. Recently, I asked my remaining brother if he knew who was buried there, but he did not know either.

My mother took us to that tree in times when she needed strength. It sounds funny for me to say that! I, Laura, the 12th child of 15 brought up by Eva and Martin Schmid, Midwest farmers of the 1920s, never knew Ma to show *any* weakness. But I know now that Ma drew strength from accepting life's ups and downs with heart and effort. It wasn't a choice, really. Death, hard times, and hard work were what you could expect from life, and she never felt cheated or overwhelmed. Making the best of what you had was her way of life, not for livelihood but for simple survival. Enjoyment of the family and all the tasks that went along with it, including grieving, was the way you made the best of life. You did the best you could. – Mom: you did the best you could and it turned out to be the best for our family and me.

It took five to six adults and three children hand in hand to circle the trunk of that cottonwood tree in the cow pasture. That was about the size of a typical group of us Schmids that would go out into the world to find what we could find: Ma and four or five grown kids, and as many children as were needed in the field that day. I remember well the fun we had trying to circle that big old

1

cottonwood tree. It grew from strong roots, was thick, knotted and gnarled. It lifted up its branches and seemed to embrace the world with a glory of many stretching arms, beaming with leaves and reaching out in all directions. That tree was the most visible life for miles in that prairie, and it seemed to greet the prairie, from which it grew from nothing, with reverence and tenderness. From afar it seemed to bend its attention to the green grass of the prairie, tending to the very earth that gives it life.

Perhaps we should start from what I know and remember about the early beginnings. My father's life story is one of early responsibility and achievement, and self-imposed adventure. Martin Schmid was born in the little town of Solbock, Germany on February 17, 1872. The church registry reported that the date may have been his christening date. We always believed it was his birthday. He was one of six children but there was one boy and one girl who died at birth, and later children were given the same names. At an early age (15 years old) he joined the army and was assigned to a Horse Drawn Artillery Battalion. He was rated as being very superior, intelligent, and proficient. In June of 1892, at the age of 20, he was assigned to Company 2 in Amber and trained to be the driver of the Horse Drawn Artillery. He moved from town to town and eventually developed "wanderlust." He arrived in Hamburg in 1897, a young man of 25 looking for adventure. He decided to become a stowaway on a ship. The captain of the ship befriended him and he began working as a cook's apprentice. He learned much from the captain. He crossed the ocean 52 times, and would always state that as one of his greatest personal achievements.

Around 1899 the captain told him he was tired of crossing the ocean and that he heard you could homestead out in the Midwest in the United States.

He asked my father: "Do you want to go with me?"

Martin Schmid thought for a moment. He had heard that his cousin had gone to America, and was somewhere in Kansas in a town that began with an *A*, so he decided to go. They boarded a train out of Newport, Rhode Island and when they got to a town beginning with an *A* and my father was out of money, he said good-bye to the captain who went on to California. That town with an *A* was Atwood, Kansas, where my father obtained a homestead.

He did not find his cousin, but met a man named James

Sramek who owned a meat market and gave him a job in Ludell, about seven or eight miles east of Atwood. He lived in Atwood and traveled to Ludell by horse for three years learning the meat market business. Then Mr. Sramek offered to sell him the market.

He had met Eva Haller, my mother, while working for Jim, and married her on October 13, 1903. On November 12th of that year, Martin Schmid became a United States Citizen.

--

My mother's grandparents were born in Dittelbrunn, Bavaria and immigrated here to Haubstadt, Indiana. My mother's parents, both born in Haubstadt, were poor farmers and decided when they met that they needed a better life.

My mother was born on Independence Day. Eva Marie Haller was the second oldest of seven children, born on July 4th, 1884 in Haubstadt, Indiana.

As he and his wife had talked about earlier, my grandfather, Paul Haller, left home with 50 cents in his pocket to find a better life, and traveled to Atwood, Kansas. He left my mother, my uncle, and my grandmother in Indiana and they joined him later.

Paul Haller was a very hard worker and was dedicated to his family. Despite having very little schooling, he became the Justice of the Peace in the little village of Atwood. He made a home for his family, a dugout some 15 to 17 miles north and east of Atwood. He could not make it back and forth to work on a daily basis as he had only a horse for transportation. So he would spend the week at work. He would leave early Monday morning and ride his horse into town. He kept the horse tied in back of his office where he would sleep during the week and returned home every Friday night. His son Adam and his daughter Eva, my mother, carried a lot of the family burdens since they were his oldest children.

My mother was raised in that dugout, a house made of grass and dirt. Remains of its site were still there in the years that my family traveled back home to visit my mother's family. There was of course no electricity and no water. My grandmother and her oldest son Adam would take a sled, hitch a horse to it and go up the hill to a neighbor who had a well. The neighbor was very kind and helpful. They would pull the water up from the well on a bucket with a rope, and then take it back home in big milk cans.

More children came along and the family grew. Times were hard and food was scarce. My grandfather planted a beautiful orchard, but when things were growing nicely a prairie fire destroyed all but three apricot trees and one crab apple tree. Thank God for those trees or the family would not have survived! Those trees remained growing and fruitful for years to come. Then in 1891, when my mother was seven, the grasshopper invasion took everything, even most of the grass! They had only a cow and a few chickens left. At that time a few of the men in the area helped Grandpa dig a well so they could have their own water for the family and the stock. The family survived!

As the family grew, the dugout was made into three rooms divided by curtains. There were seven children. The children really took care of each other. The only way they could travel was to either walk or take a wagon. Even with the wagon it would take days to go anywhere.

Kansas Today, Looks much like it did in the early 1900's:
Wide Open Spaces

Kansas was indeed a prairie, you could see for miles and miles. No trees, no houses, just grasslands (the only viable plant at the time). Cattle lived on the land. The wind blew across the plains like the people would like to, but blizzards blocked any movement. Times were very, very rough. The grass died, and hunger reined on people and animals alike. It was famine without any outside help, like you could get even in my day.

My father met Eva when she was nineteen years of age in 1903. They married in that same year, and then Mr. Sramek decided to sell his shop to Martin. They moved into the two-room building attached to the meat market in the village of Ludell. My father would butcher the meat. My mom brought nine babies into the world during that time, and helped to run the meat market.

The Meat Market in Ludell, and the Attached Home for Eleven

Dad would carve the meat, make sausage, bologna, wieners, blood sausage and anything else that could be concocted. Ludell was their home for fourteen years. I wish I knew more about that existence, a family of eleven, living in two rooms, with no electric power, no running water, and only an outside toilet known as *the closet*, but that was long before I was born. The children old enough to go to school walked a mile to a one-room schoolhouse and there was only one other family who had children in the school at the time. That old building held class for over 70 years and was always known as *The Ludell School House.* It is still standing today, although the little town of Ludell has been mostly deserted.

They saved every penny they could, and in 1919 Dad purchased 320 acres of farmland about 2½ miles East of Atwood and

½ mile north. On the land was a three-room house: kitchen, dining room and bedroom. Outside were three sheds, a small one-roomer, a two-roomer and a chicken house.

One-Room Schoolhouse in Ludell

As the nine children grew into fifteen, the small shed became the girls' bunkhouse, and one of the rooms in the two-room shed became the boys' bunkhouse. There was no heat or electricity in any of the sheds. So Pa bought two coal/oil stoves so he could warm the rooms before we went to bed. Because we were small we actually slept five kids sideways in the beds. Sleeping this way was cozy, and necessary in the dead of winter. Pa or Ma would go out about 10:00 PM and turn off the coal burning stoves. Today, we know we could have died of carbon monoxide poisoning had they not remembered to turn off the stoves. Of course in the summer, 100 to 120 degree weather brought a different kind of coziness!

During the winter it would be so cold after the heat had been turned off that our breath would freeze on top of the feather beds. Ma made these feather beds from the feathers of the ducks and geese that she plucked to make them ready for eating or for selling. The feather beds were about six feet long and two feet high. We had a lot of fun jumping up and down on those feather beds and yes, they were *so* warm because Ma had made them. She made flannel covers over the ticking so the covers could be washed when winter was over. The feather beds then landed in a trunk for the summer. It was so hot that it was more comfy to sleep on the floor, away from your siblings. We used only sheets for cover in the summer.

Threasa and Annie, Two of Laura's Older Sisters

One of John Denver's most beautiful songs is "Grandma's Feather Beds." I still play it often today because it brings back so many memories.

In those days we wore long winter underwear that we only got to change once a week. The long legs would stretch and we would have to wrap them around our legs, and pull up the long cotton stockings to hold them down. You can imagine what your legs looked like if you were a poor wrapper!

The cold was not our only problem. We had bed bugs! They were small red bugs that found a home in the mattresses. There were lots of them and they would get on your body in the middle of the night and suck blood from your skin. You would itch like crazy. Ma used to give us cans with some kerosene inside; we would take a stick and pick them off the mattress and kill them in the kerosene. They were hard to find as they lived in the seams and in the buttons. So you can see why it was good back then to have a close sibling. It took weeks to get them all, but eventually we did. Then "Fly Tox" came into use and you would spray the mattress with that. Sometime, a long time after, we seemed to have conquered them.

The girls' bedroom had two beds and when we got too tall to sleep sideways, we moved one by one into the other bed, where three could sleep together the long way. The boys' bedroom had three beds so only three had to sleep in each bed. If a hired hand had no place to sleep, one of the boys would wrap up in blankets and sleep on the floor.

Fields of Alfalfa and Wheat

The second room in the boys' shed was turned into the washhouse, which served for washing the bottles, washing the clothes, making lard and heating water. Pa installed a large iron kettle that held about 30 gallons of water and had a firebox under it. All the water used for the family was heated in this kettle, and each night each kid had to pump water and carry it into the kettle. It normally took 10 to 12 buckets, and would take all night to heat. Ma would get up in the middle of the night and place more wood in the firebox.

All the hot water needed for the family, other than a full teakettle in the kitchen of the house, was heated in this *Lard Kettle*.

The milk bottles had to be washed on a daily basis. The clothes needed hot water for washing. Baths taken by the older kids needed heating. The water pump was about ten feet from the door of the washhouse. We had to pump water every night to make sure the older girls had enough hot water to wash the bottles for the next day. The lard kettle had many other purposes as well: cooking lard, cooking blood sausage, boiling horses hooves, pigs feet, and making soap. It was definitely *multi-purpose.*

Chickens On the Farm

Soon after moving there, Pa built a big barn. After that he started buying, fattening and slaughtering his own animals on the farm. Mom and the kids that were old enough milked umpteen cows by hand. I remember how small my hand was to try and go around the cow's teats. It would take me a long time to milk one. Each kid had their own cow to milk. Ma would know which cow would not kick. We got to name our own cow. I called mine Violet. I loved that name. The cow recognized us and was always nice to her milker! As each kid became more efficient, we would milk two or three in order to get it all done.

Ma bottled the milk and separated the cream. Each day Dad took the slaughtered cattle to the market along with the milk, cream and eggs that had been packed for selling. Mom was never at loss to know what needed to be done. I remember well her 4:00 AM rising time because it showed how much had to be done before the children had to leave for school. By this time her oldest son, James, was able to help slaughter the animals and help Pa in the meat market. He was a dedicated, smart son who was faithful to Pa all his life.

Verneda and Joe

After the move to the farm, the family quickly grew to 13 children (6 boys and 5 girls). There were James Paul, Katherine Mary, John Joseph, Threasa Louise, Annie Catherine, and twins Frank George and Fred Andrew, Verneda Frances, and Joseph Henry from the days of living at the meat market. Agnes Elizabeth was born the year the family moved to the farm, and Paul Albert arrived shortly after the move. There were approximately one to one and a half years between them so there was a lot of camaraderie and close affiliation, brought on by jobs assigned. *Everyone* had their assignments; Ma ran the house like clockwork, assigning tasks to each of us kids and keeping up with all the work every day without relief. There really was no time for us to fight or goof-off. You did what you had to do because you had so much to do.

The Midwest suffered tremendously in 1918 when the flu and pneumonia epidemics developed. Diseases and deaths were unbelievable. Mom said people were dying like flies. The neighborhoods and families were devastated by the impact. Many of the Schmid neighbors died. Ma's cousins died. It didn't matter if you were young or old, rich or poor, there was no help. Pneumonia was devastating. Ma remembered Dr. Henneberger traveling all day and all night trying to help. He worried about Ma and Pa's large family. Fortunately, the Schmid family escaped those tragedies.

In 1922, however, my sister Annie contacted Diphtheria. She was 13 years of age and newly confirmed in the Sacred Heart Church in Atwood. They put her in the master bedroom and no one was allowed in the room but her mother and Ms. Harrison, the nurse. The doctor, Henneberger (called by his last name) came every day. The other children living at that time, Jim, Johnnie, Katherine (known as Toots), Threasa, Fred, Frank, Verneda, Joseph, Agnes and the baby Paul Albert had to be vaccinated with a shot in the back! All of them remember how painful that was. The doctor came to the house and put them over the back of a chair, told them not to move. The needle went in and that HURT! They were quarantined for months.

Annie Catherine in Her Confirmation Dress, 1922
Annie improved and finally after 31 days alone, she asked if

she could come out to eat supper with the family. Everyone was so excited and thrilled. She ate quickly and then said she was tired, so they put her back to bed. That night, on October 25, 1922, Annie Catherine Schmid died in her sleep in the arms of her father.

They had her body in the house one day, then the undertaker came and took her away to the graveyard at St. John's Church, near where Grandpa and Grandma Haller lived. The last picture taken of Annie was her Confirmation picture, which was taken on the steps of our catholic church in Atwood. She was buried in her confirmation dress.

I, Laura Margaret, was born on April 9, 1923, five months after Annie's death. Annie's birthday was April 3, 1909. Mom always said the Lord sent me to help take her place. Mom loved Annie so dearly. She called her a little pal always at my side.

Baby Laura, August 1923 with her brother Jim

As I was growing up she would say, "You're a lot like Annie, she was so beautiful. She was God's little angel and he took her home and sent you in her place."

I truly believe I was beautiful as I weighed 13 pounds when I was born, 30 pounds at 6 months. I had dark brown hair and beautiful brown eyes; still have them today (only the hair relies on the bottle). My older brothers and sisters loved me dearly, but I don't think in any way I ever filled Annie's shoes. My brother Johnnie nicknamed me *Cupie* at 6 months of age. He died still calling me by that name. Later in life Pa started calling me *Skippie*. Those loving nicknames lasted throughout our lifetime.

For some reason my brothers Joe, Paul, and I grew taller than any of the other kids. We seemed to stay thinner as well, though the other kids in the family were not overly heavy. We all had large German bones, so our weight hinged on the body frame. I must add, however, that every one of the children had a very different personality. In the following years, Charles Martin, Louis Frederick, and Andrew Bernard joined the family. My mother used to say she had her own apostles. With 14 names to sort through, when we were all together she would try calling one or the other and then would say, "Whichever one you are, come here!"

By the time we were five years old we had to learn how to milk a cow, Mom taught us all. Those big old buckets were heavy to carry! And we were given a limited time to get the chores done because we had to get off to school. The one-room schoolhouse was three miles away down the road north.

Milking cows was not an easy thing to do as your hand had to go around the teats with your thumb bent so you could get the milk to come out of the udder. Mom could milk a cow in a minute! Sometimes a *little* longer, and when the cows were fresh they might give two buckets of milk. You called the cow "fresh" when the little calf was born. She would let it feed on its mother's udder for two weeks. Then we had to teach the baby calf to drink by first putting our fingers in its mouth and then placing the calf's mouth in the bucket with the milk. I never did like that routine.

The mother's udder was often very sore from the calf, and she would try to kick anyone who came near it! Mom was the one who knew how to handle them. She would strap the hind legs, or they would have caused serious harm with the kicking! Mom always knew how to solve the problem.

When I was just starting to milk my brothers Joe and Paul (known as Spuds) tried to trick me by offering me a nickel if I would crawl under the cow's udder and suck her teats!

The Lord was with me as I was just about to try it when Ma saw us and yelled "What are you doing!?!"

I told her everything and she was so upset with my brothers, she told Pa! He took care of them that night! That was the one time I saw him use the sharpening strap from his razor! That cow had just had her calf; I could have been killed! Of course, they never tried that again.

In those days my oldest sister Katherine Mary (known as Toots), just 19 years of age, had to have her appendix removed. That meant she had to be in the hospital three weeks and could not do any work for one year, especially not lifting. I was the baby at that time. So Toots' new job was to take care of me in the buggy! Mom would put the bottles and the diapers in the buggy, so Toots could reach them from the bed and if I cried she could rock the carriage.

She always said, "I am your mother! I love you so, you are so beautiful!"

Laura, Paul, Verneda, Joe and Agnes, 1926

My brother Johnnie loved me dearly. Jim always loved me as well and kept in close contact with me for the rest of his life. So, you know I was spoiled rotten! They all showed love for me, but you know babies love to be loved. And they all loved having a distraction from chores!

I do remember my brother Andrew being born as there was a midwife in our house. She came out as we were coming home from school one day to tell us we had a new brother. My mother never went to the hospital to have a baby; a midwife would come and I understand she stayed for two weeks. I don't know if she was paid, I assume something.

Many years later, Toots told me where babies came from, but even at 15 years of age I never realized when someone was pregnant. Families that I worked for added children and it would always be a surprise to me. I would wonder where that baby was hidden.

By the time I was four years old, my next older brother, Paul Albert (known to us as Spuds because of the shape of his head) was to start school. He was five years old. He had been sick a lot and my mother was concerned that he would need extra help so she asked Ms. Rose, the teacher, if she would allow her to send me along with him, even though I was just four.

So I started school when I was four years old, and a little on the timid side. How well I remember having to go to *the closet;* (today it would be known as the toilet). You indicated this necessity by holding up your right hand and putting up two fingers. Ms. Rose as we called her wasn't watching and I had waited too long, so Liberty School had its first flood! Ms. Rose was upset with me and made me take a pan of water and wash up the mess.

A few months passed when Paul Albert (Spuds) got sick again and wasn't doing so well. He was always weak and tired and would fall asleep in school. Ms. Rose told Ma to keep him at home and have him do his homework. The older kids could bring the homework to school the next day. That left me as the only one in that class. Ms. Rose didn't want to mess with me so she double promoted me to the third grade! I was the littlest girl in the school and the boys were always hard on me.

The Liberty School was three miles down the road north and we always had to walk. The only time we got a ride was when it snowed, Pa would have to put us in a wagon and take us to school. Then he would have to come back to pick us up each day until the road was clear.

Ma would pack us lunch by making syrup sandwiches. She

would put them in a fourteen-quart kettle, give us another kettle of apples, and we had two gallons of milk to carry! Well, you have to know those sandwiches became mush. We would just grab into the kettle and get a handful. To this day I am not a syrup lover, but will eat it on pancakes.

Freddie, Verneda and Frankie in Front of the Bunkhouse

We used to have a marker in the road and we had to take turns carrying the kettles. When we got to the marker, down the kettle would go and we'd run, then another kid would pick it up.

On occasion a farmer would come down the road either in a wagon or a Model T Ford. We learned that if we lagged behind the group, two or three of us could catch a ride. It was such fun teasing your siblings from the back of a truck as it sped by.

You have to know that the boys all wore "Oshgosh" overalls that were always too big, so they would chug the straps up to their neck to make the overalls last longer. They had these big brass buttons and they were dangerous! We would play ball and hide-and-seek around the building. One day, I ran smack dab into Paul Albert and the button cut my lip open! The scar is still there today.

Paul Albert (Spuds, my friend and brother) and I often pulled off things we should not have done. We would hide the Schippert kids' lunches, or pull on their overall straps so their lunches would fall and then they would trade food with us (they always had better food). They would pick on us and we would pick on them; that was the way.

Because Spuds was so weak, he would pick up a cold, fever or disease like it was there waiting for him. He was always the first one to get sick. Poor Ma was always at a loss trying to keep the sickness from spreading. Most of us usually managed to get sick with what Spuds brought home no matter what Ma did.

Then there were the Shippert boys, Ernest and Everett. They were always making me do things a little girl didn't want to do! They would pull up my dress and then giggle like crazy. I soon would not go out to play; I would sit in the room for the 15-minute recess.

One day I got wise and snuck one of Paul's overalls out of the house and hid it in the weeds in a ditch. On the way to school I put it on over my dress and when I came back I would put it in the weed again. Now that I am older, I wonder why I was not concerned with spiders or snakes getting into the overall! I wasn't, and because it rained so seldom, it never got wet. I don't think Mom ever knew what I was doing, but Ernest and Everett couldn't lift my dress because of those overalls. Both of them have since gone into eternity. I wonder if they still look up dresses!

Louie Frederick was just a baby at this time, around 1926 and was always vomiting. Dr. Henneberger decided that he had to be put on goat's milk. That meant that Pa had to buy some goats and the girls had to milk them, to have milk for Louie. Spuds and I would tie the goat up by its tail just to see it jump and kick. Well, we didn't get away with that for too long. Ma told us that if we did that again, we would have to milk the goat. We didn't want to do that, so we quit pestering the goat! Pa had bought two goats, a male and a female. So it wasn't long before we had six!

As we grew older, Paul Albert, Charles Martin, Louie Frederick, Andrew Bernard and I, Laura Margaret had to walk home from school together. Naturally we were thirsty so when we got home, without anyone knowing it, we would sneak up to the hayloft in the barn. During the summer, Pa would make beer for the hired hands (Pa did not drink himself). Kansas was a dry state, so when Pa went out to buy cattle he would go across the line into Nebraska and buy hops and the other ingredients to make the beer. He would put the mixture into a very large 50-gallon stone jar and kept it up in the hayloft where it was warm and out of the sun, to ferment. We kids would sneak up there almost every day after school! We would have been playing in the schoolyard, playing ball, throwing dirt, whatever (you know how dirty kids get) and had very dirty hands by the time we got up to the hayloft. There we had hidden an old rusty tin can under the straw and would take our dirty hands and we would push aside the heavy foam on top and sneak a drink of Pa's beer!

Fred and John in 1928
Butchering was a daily event on the farm

Then one night at the supper table, Pa said to Ma, "I guess I have to change sights for the beer, because I checked it to see if it was ready to be bottled, and over half of it is gone! It must have evaporated!"

All of us kids were kicking each other under the table, trying hard not to laugh! I am not sure if he every figured out what we were doing, but from then on we were very careful and cut down our sipping.

There were nine Schmid kids in the school, one Constable, an adopted boy, and three Schipperts, one girl and the two boys mentioned earlier. My older brothers and sisters had already graduated from the eighth grade. Pa forced them to go back a second year in the eighth grade, and then leave, as he did not like high school. He did not believe you needed any further education past the eighth grade.

His strong belief was, "YOU CAN BE WHAT YOU WANT TO BE WITHOUT THAT STUFF!"

The Schmid Clan, 16 plus 3 Neighbors
Laura is on the right end of the front row

He was adamant: "No kid of mine is ever going to high school!"

My dear sister Verneda was a very smart, brilliant girl and while she missed seven months of school in her eighth grade, she ended up having the highest grade in the county! That meant you could go to high school on a scholarship (in those days you had to pay an entrance fee and purchase your own books to go to high school). The priest at Sacred Heart Church obtained that scholarship for her, but my father would only allow her to go three months, and then made her leave school to work at home! She would always talk about this most of her life, wishing she had been able to go on.

Not one of the children was allowed to go on to high school. If you ask any of them, they would all say they've always regretted not being able to go. My second oldest brother, Johnnie, was a brilliant mechanic. Mom used to say at 6 months he would tear a toy apart, put it back together then throw it away! As I reveal their lives, you will find how so many of them became successful.

Johnnie and his New Car, 1930

As the years rolled on into the early 1930s, the dust storms and the depression changed everyone's life. Poverty was unbelievable! My mom's garden saved our family, she raised enough vegetables for our own use, and then had some to sell to neighbors for a pittance: 5 cents, 10 cents. She would give them anything they wanted, good soul and community-minded that she was. And every kid in the family over four had to work on the farm to raise enough food to survive. We weeded the corn, pumped and carried the water, chopped the wood, milked the cows, fed the pigs, and did our own schoolwork as well! Eggs and milk were sold so cheap. Eggs 10 cents a dozen and milk 15 cents a quart. People were starving, begging for help and my mother and father would give away food goods for free if someone came in without any money.

Ma and Pa would share extra butter or eggs, milk or cream, or vegetables that we had with any neighbor in need. They would send us kids with a basket down the road to neighbors they knew needed help. We remember the neighbors crying when we showed up, they were so happy to see us.

Food was limited by the government in an effort to ration rare supplies. They limited every family to ¼ pound of butter every two weeks, no matter how big your family was. We Schmid kids were lucky, because we had the products of the land and the animals.

This was a time when Ma and Pa would tell us all, "You don't waste anything! You will eat what you get whether you like it or not. You waste not, you'll want not!"

Gypsies would come and beg. Ma had a hard time sharing with them because she knew how badly the neighbors needed the same things. Eggs and milk were sold so cheap, but some could still not afford them.

Every day we said *Grace* before the meal and *Grace* after the meal and asked God to send us rain, and everyone my family knew who had died were remembered as well, there was always a long list. It was not unusual for the whole town to pray at Mass for rain. After all, life depended on the products of the land.

We couldn't afford new clothes or new shoes. We lived on hand-me-downs. We wore shoes that were too small, too big, no soles, whatever was available! We would glue on cardboard so we didn't get hurt on rocks or sticks. We managed. That life made the few-and-far-between good parts that much better.

I remember my first *boughten* dress. I was only seven years old when I was to be confirmed in the church. Mom ordered me a red silk dress with a white collar, from the Montgomery Ward catalog. It cost her $1.19.

When she placed it on me, she said, "Oh honey, always wear red. You look absolutely beautiful in this dress!"

Time has not changed that for me, as I often wear red and friends, relatives, all those close to me will always comment, "Man, you look great in red!" Many would always say "Here comes the Lady in Red!" I loved the song *Lady in Red*. Maybe I should be buried in a red one, but I wouldn't want to scare the angels taking me home!

There was little money to buy clothes. It mattered not whether you were male or female. The oldest one got the new clothes and then they were handed down from one to the other. Flour came in white or printed cloth, sometimes colors, so Ma would rip the bags apart and match them up. The girls got dresses made from the sacks, or if they were not what she liked, they were hemmed into dishtowels. Mom made all the dresses, how she found time I can't imagine, but along the way she taught all of us girls to mend and sew. Mom showed us younger girls how to cut pieces of cloth into little squares and make pillow tops. I made a pillow top out of scraps when I was only five years old! I have it in my memoirs.

Mom wore printed dresses and a hat with elastic around it to cover her hair. She also made aprons to wear while cooking and cleaning the house or washing the bottles. The apron had many uses. She would lift it up, fill it with eggs, vegetables, little chickens, anything that needed taken care of, to move them from one place to another. Or if her hands were dirty, she would wipe them with the apron; or if one of the kids cried, she would wipe the tears away! I never saw her with a *new* dress. The only place you could buy clothes was from the Sears and Roebuck, or Montgomery Ward catalogs.

With no money for toilet paper, the catalogs supplied the paper we used in the outhouse. Pa would sit and look at the catalog prior to ripping the pages, and pry the door open with his foot so he could read the catalog. The road to Ludell passed right close to the end of the house. If anyone came down the road, they would see him sitting there. It probably was his only quiet time with so many kids in the house. It never bothered Pa that they would see him, but it bothered Ma a lot.

In order to keep the garden growing we had to carry buckets of water from the well and Mom would take a can of water from the bucket to pour it on the plant so we did not waste water pouring it over the ground. There was a windmill near the house that would pump water up from the well beneath it. But if the wind didn't blow, the well would go dry. During the depression, the wind did not blow as it did during the dust storm years. The older boys would have to pump water by hand for the cows, pigs, house; every drop that was used and that was a hard job!

The well went dry once and I remember them taking the horse and wagon out to the well in the pasture to get water. There was a second windmill in the pasture, but if the wind did not blow, no water was in the tank, so they had to tie a rope on the bucket, lower it into the well and pull it up by hand. They would fill large 10-gallon milk cans with the water, load the wagon full and take it back for the animals. Then they'd go back for another load for the house. *Waste not, want not* was the slogan for the day and it hit hard when the very water you drank to survive was in such short supply. It was months before water returned to the well.

Most of the time our drinking water came from the pump that was about 100 feet away from the house. My father had installed a wood plank walk to make the walk easier. The rule was if you emptied the water bucket, you had to go fill it. We used a water dipper and it didn't take long for us to figure out that if you didn't drink all the water in the dipper you would put it back in the bucket and it would last longer and you wouldn't have to refill it. Perhaps this is why when one kid got sick, all of us did; all of us except Johnnie. For reasons never discovered, Johnnie escaped almost every illness in our house.

We would all wash our hands in the same water in the wash pan. Talk about dirty! That water would be so dirty it was almost like mud! But if we dumped it, and the water bucket was empty, you knew it was your job to go fill the bucket; so we rarely did.

There was an open pipe in the sink and under the pipe was this 10 gallon bucket that caught the dirty water, so if that bucket got filled, you had to go empty it down in the yard. If it overflowed, you had to wipe it up with rags, so emptying it wasn't a job we tried to avoid. We all used one towel to wipe our hands and after it got black it would have to be changed. Our towels were sewn together like a circle and put into this holder so you rolled it around and when it got really dirty one of the older kids would change it and put on a clean towel.

How did we take baths? Well, you got to change your clothes once a week, and on Saturday night beginning at 6:30, Mom would fill the wash tub one half way in the kitchen, using the hot water from the tea kettle to warm it. The youngest child was bathed first, on to the next, to the next, to the end. Then the adults took baths after the little ones were done.

Fortunately, Pa needed more water for the animals, so they sold enough milk, vegetables, and eggs to raise enough money to have a big cement tank built. It was 5 feet deep, 20 feet wide, and 30 feet long. As long as the windmill ran, water filled the tank. Then the boys dug a ditch and put in pipes to run water to the garden and to siphon water to the cow tanks.

Pa added goldfish to the tank so they would eat the algae. That meant the older kids could jump in the tank to take a swim, so now the washtub had less use. In those days, no one questioned the water quality. Of course, in the winter that was out of the question. Eventually, the older kids bathed in the washhouse and heated the water in the lard kettle. The girls would go first, then dump their water and then the boys would take over.

The Gang Takes a Dip in the Water Tank

The goldfish became the talk of the town as they grew, many of them 12 to 20 inches long. Pa recounted that he believed some of them lived to be 10 to 20 years old. After Pa died they withered away with the rest of the farm. They were all gone when it was sold.

The garden was easier to water after that. Ma had rows and rows of cabbage, beans, peas, cucumbers, beets, celery, dill, asparagus, lettuce, carrots, onions, and any vegetable available! We had choke cherry trees and raspberry plants. Coming home from school we had to weed at least 1/2 row every day. There was a wicked weed called *bindweed* and it would crawl under the ground and under the roots of the plants, so they had to be weeded every day. Mom could never figure out how to kill it. As long as I was home, that weed was a pain in the neck.

Also, the gardens had snakes! Some were garden snakes, little ones that just ate bugs. But there were also bull snakes, big ones that usually did not bite, they would just run off and go somewhere in their holes. The big problem was rattlesnakes! They could be found in the garden at times; mostly they lived in the cow pasture under the soap weeds. Fortunately they would rattle before they bit.

Ma Sees a Snake in the Garden

They were deadly dangerous! One day Mom went to the pasture to bring home the cows, she tripped on a rock, fell on a soap weed and there was a rattlesnake in that weed! He raised his head, rattled and bit her. Thank goodness she had a belt on her dress, and knew that she had to cut off the flow of blood to her body. She tied the belt above the bite and cut her leg open with the hairpin out of her hair to let out the blood! She went home, and one of the boys took her on a horse to the doctor. He congratulated her because she saved her life by what she had done.

Later, one of the boys went out to the pasture and located the snake and shot it with a gun. When he cut off the head, fourteen tiny snakes came running out of the body! Snakes would swallow the little ones when they faced danger. He cut off the rattle; I have it along with another in a little box of mementos. Mom always said it could be made into earrings. Not for me! But I did save it, as it is one of my most vivid memories.

The Snake that Bit Ma

Then we had these extra pests, prairies full of Prairie Dogs. Simple little animals, adorable to look at, but smart and clever about escaping human interruptions. You could blame these cute little millions of rodents for destroying the grasslands, so needed for cattle raising. They caused trouble on the farm for many, many years. They were fertile to say the least, and knew enough to dig their homes below the ground with several exits. This made exterminating them next to impossible. Once they were driven from their homes or moved on, the burrows were perfect refuge for the deadly rattlesnake. Love 'em or hate 'em, there was no middle ground. All farmers hated them. They aggravated farmers and morticians alike; they loved cemeteries too! The prairie dog problems were never solved.

I remember well how one dog always acted as a guard while the others worked or played. If he sensed danger, he would throw his head back and give a sharp, two-toned bark. Then they would all drop into their burrows to save their lives. They have lived on the prairies for millions of years. Will they go away? Probably not! They were all over the countryside and eventually moved into towns.

Other pains were bugs; those big long green tomato worms

that had horns were the worst! We battled turtles, rabbits and ground hogs in the garden as well. Every day we would have to pick off those gross green tomato worms. We dropped them in kerosene cans and we could watch them squirm and die.

Prairie Dogs

Rodent pests were our prey. We were able to trap rabbits and then we could have them to eat! The boys would skin them and save their skins to sell, clean their bodies and Ma would cut them up and fry them like chicken. We never ate the ground hogs, but we used to have turtle soup!

Coyotes were a real threat, so we always had three or four dogs to protect the animals. During this time we were allowed to trap coyotes, skunks and raccoons. The boys would skin them and they could sell the hides for 25 to 50 cents a piece! That was big money in those days. I still have a coyote coat made from one of the coyotes my nephew trapped. He tanned it himself, and then sent it to me as a gift. I had it made into a jacket and it was the talk of the town! I only wish I could wear it today without people frowning.

Rats and mice loved living on the farm, and why not? There was always waste food somewhere. But humans we were and we did not like their presence. Ma and Pa had some 30 or so cats living in the barn and the granary. They had their stomachs filled at all times catching the mice.

Prairie Dog Burrows

We kids loved it when kittens were born and we would play with them for hours. To take care of them was such an enjoyable and empowering activity for a kid, good practice for the kind of responsibility we saw in our parents and that was needed to survive as an adult. We would feed them fresh cow's milk every morning, then we'd come back for a second feeding every night as well.

Tom, a black and white cat, would follow Ma around every time he saw her because she would have something in her apron pocket to feed him. One would term him *obese* today, as he weighed over 30 pounds. However, this was a cat that was used to long nights of hunting, and all of the hazards and happenings of farm living, so he was a *stout* 30 pounds! He never needed to meow because of his stature; *everyone* knew he was coming. He and the other cats would line up in the hayloft after a long day of resting. We loved watching them; to see so many cats stretching and sharpening their claws for a long night of hunting was quite a sight to behold.

In total the garden was probably one half acre. We had corn

from the farm as it was planted to feed the animals, but we could eat as much as we wanted during the corn season. That created another job for us kids. Pa would tell us to cut across the field as we came home from school and pull the weeds out of the rows, until the corn was big enough to outgrow the weeds. We had a lot of fun in the cornfields, hiding from each other and playing games, more play than work. But Pa didn't know that, and we managed to weed enough along the way to play.

   We had rows and rows of potatoes, watermelon and cantaloupe plants to weed as well. We would stomp on a watermelon and break it open, and then eat it with our dirty hands. What a great feast that was when the watermelons were ripe! We knew how to tap it with a fist and listen for a sound, which would indicate if it was ripe or not ready. Through the knowledge passed down from older siblings, I doubt that any of us younger kids ever cracked a 'green' watermelon because we knew exactly when they were ready.

The Farm in Kansas, (Picture taken in 1987)
Ma's home from 1919 to 1972

   People coming down the road would try to find the watermelon patch and steal them, so Pa would hide it in the cornfields where the watermelons could not be seen. That kept *our* watermelon patch nice and safe, and we kids knew that and guarded it. What Ma and Pa didn't know was that at night, we Schmid kids would go down the road to the Argabright's watermelon patch for fun and break open the watermelons there and eat them. Mr. Argabright was pretty aware of what we did and all he would do is shoot a shotgun in the air to let us know he knew we were there. Then we would run like crazy to go home. If Pa ever knew about that, he kept it to himself. Years later, Mr. Argabright would laugh about how he scared us.

My brother Spuds remembers as well as I that a man in town had purchased a new pair of shoes. He was very proud of those shoes and apparently had shown and bragged about them to Pa in the butcher shop. This one night there was someone stealing watermelons in the watermelon patch. So Pa shot a gun in the air to scare them away. When daylight came, Pa and some of the kids checked the patch to see what had happened. They discovered many watermelons broken open, and a new shoe that Pa recognized. The gunshot had indeed scared the thieves away, *right out of their shoes,* you could say. Pa took the shoe to the butcher shop. When the customer came into the shop again, Pa questioned him as to why he wasn't wearing his new shoes. The man finally confessed that he had been in the watermelon patch, but he really would like to have his shoe back to complete his pair! Pa said he would gladly return it, but the man would have to go down to the farm and "apologize to the Mrs." The man came back to the butcher shop many times, but Pa remained adamant and said he could have the shoe only when he went and apologized to Ma. That apology was never offered, so the shoe was never returned.

In order to have a garden there were six beehives off the end of it. They had to transfer pollen for the plants so they would produce fruit. In return they got the plants' nectar. They also provided honey for us to eat! We were never allowed to go near the hives; they did not respect human beings if you threatened their lives, and kids playing could easily be confused for a threat. There was a queen and once she left, the whole hive would leave to start somewhere else. That's when Ma would go out and collect the honeycombs full of honey. She would have enough combs for selling and to give away to anyone of us kids that wanted one or to the neighbors too. One year she collected twenty-four combs. She would keep them in the cellar where it was cool, and that year we always had combs down there waiting to be used. That time of the season was when we would get a break from the syrup sandwiches at school and get honey sandwiches instead! We loved it because it wasn't so mushy. Ma and Pa kept the hives clean and ready through the winter, so the bees returned every spring.

The Old Hand Washer

How did Ma do the wash? Well we had a hand stick on a washer that had a dolly inside and we had to pull the stick back and forth for 15 minutes. Mom would fill the washer with hot water from the lard tank, add the soap, and then assign us to do the pulling. Then the wash went into two big washtubs filled with cold water for rinsing the clothes. There was also a hand wringer. When the washing was finished, we then would have to turn the wringer so Ma could rinse the clothes. That is why three kids were kept home from school every week on Monday, because the washing had to be done. We started at 7:00 in the morning and we were lucky if we finished by 5:00 that night. Sometimes, we'd have to break for dinner and then continue afterwards.

We had seven aluminum lines in the yard for hanging laundry to dry. I remember poor Ma out in the dead of winter hanging clothes on those lines. The clothes were freezing in the basket, but she managed to put them out and hang them up on those aluminum lines. The clothes would freeze, but Ma would take them off the lines, bring them into the dining room and hang them on the chairs. If they were not too wet, she would roll them up for ironing the next day. That saved sprinkling them. They were always removed in time to set the table to eat.

One time those aluminum lines brought lightning into our house! One night my brother Andrew Bernard (Andy) was frying potatoes on the iron cook stove. There was a terrible lightning and thunderstorm. The lightning struck the aluminum clothes line, crossed over to the telephone in the kitchen and since Andy was using a steel turner to cook the potatoes, it hit the turner! It went through his body and melted the rubber soles of his shoes onto the wooden floor! He always said he was "scared to death!" Thank God for those shoes because he would have been electrocuted had he not had the rubber soles. The rubber could not be removed from the floor, so it was there until the house was sold and destroyed years later. Anyone who came to visit would question the black spots on the floor. So Andy became famous among our visitors as the boy who was struck by lightning. For sure he never forgot that night!

We had a weekly job as well churning butter, taking turns if we got tired doing it. On Saturdays Ma would have at least five gallons of sour cream that she had saved during the week. We had a hand churn that you had to sit and pump up and down until the cream turned into butter. This would supply not only butter, but buttermilk that Ma used in cooking as well. She also kept heavy cream that could be made into whipped cream for toppings on desserts; now *that* was a treat we loved. Treats like these, as well as food were plentiful on the farm. Was weight a problem? None of us kids were ever overweight, I guess because we walked three miles to school and back everyday and also worked in the garden.

Pa, James Paul (Jim) and the other boys who worked in the meat market wore full white coats (like the doctors used to wear) and they also wore white aprons. Because they were always full of animal blood, on Sunday nights they had to be soaked in cold water so the blood would not stain them, another complication in getting the washing done. In the summer those white clothes would bleach from drying on the lines in the sun. In the winter they would freeze on the lines but the sun would still bleach them white. They also wore starched shirts.

Usually, there would be 12 bushels of clothes to be ironed. The older girls had the job of sprinkling the clothes the night before so they could start ironing on Tuesday. It would take three of them three days to get the ironing done because they would have to stop and clear the table for meal times.

My sister Threasa hated ironing shirts. She and Joe used to squabble all the time because Joe would say his shirt was not ironed right.

Threasa would holler at him, saying, "I hope you marry a lazy slob and then you can bitch at her." The rivalry never destroyed their friendship. He married and she never heard another word. Threasa moved on from the farm for a better life, but it was cut short in the end.

The irons that were in use at the time were solid iron with removable handles. They were heated on the kitchen stove, but by 11:00 AM food had to be started for dinner and the irons would have to be put in the warming oven to make room for the food. When the meal was over, the irons and the ironers returned to their job.

Some years later, a gas iron was created that heated itself. It was expensive, but Pa bought one for the family to use. Toots was the only one allowed to use it, as she was the oldest girl. It functioned on two gaskets that would break easily if you touched them. The mask would be lit because the gas would fill it like a balloon. As long as the gaskets were lit the iron worked great. The heat could be adjusted by moving a little gadget on top of the iron. That made ironing easier because it would always stay hot, and you did not have to keep running to the stove to get another iron.

Shortly after we got that iron, they made a gas powered light fixture similar to the iron. There was a switch to turn on, then Ma could light it with a match. That existed until they finally put a transformer out on the road and brought electricity into our house. *Glory, Hallelujah!*

When electricity came in, Pa bought an electric iron. I was only about six years old when one day my sister Verneda told me to come do my ironing.

I didn't feel like it, so I said, "No, I ain't going to do it!"

She said, "You come right now and do it, or I will tell Pa!"

My answer: "I'm not doing it, I'm running away from home!"

She replied, "Go ahead. See who cares!"

I was so upset, I went out of the house and went down the road about ½ mile. There was a bridge there and I decided to crawl under the bridge and hide. *Then they will have to look for me!* I thought. Well, after about five minutes, I looked up and there were spiders, there were mice and probably even rats in the weeds where I was sitting! Then I thought, *Oh man! There might be rattlesnakes under here!* So with trepidation, I crawled out and tried to sneak home down the long ditch that ran beside the road to our house. I figured that I could sneak in the north door and Verneda wouldn't see me, then I could hide under the bed.

My assumptions were pretty far off, as Verneda saw me coming and locked the door, then opened it and said, "Ha! Ha! You had to come home, didn't you?!"

I said, "Leave me alone!"

That night she told Pa and because he loved me, he just gave me a talking-to and told me: "You have to mind your sisters and your Mother!"

Years later I took my future husband out to meet the family.

When we got on the train to return to college I asked him, "So who did you like the most?"

Holy Toledo, his answer was: "I loved your sister Verneda!"

Well he got an ear-full on the train ride back!

Time, however, erased my harsh feelings and as the years rolled on, Verneda and I became the best of sisters. All these memories came back to me as she was called home to God. Her children gave me the cross off her coffin. It hangs on our bedroom wall reminding me of many memories, good and bad, and also to ask God to let her rest in peace.

You have to know as well, that all the overalls, socks and shirts for the family would get holes from wear and tear. When the clothes were ironed, the torn ones had to be mended either by hand or by a sewing machine run by hand. Poor Ma used to be up all hours of the night mending! Old worn out overalls were used for patches and what was left was put into mops for scrubbing the floors.

Years later, after I married, I went back home. My sister Verneda was now a widow with eight sons and only one daughter. She had so much patching to do: seven bushels of overalls that needed mending! I spent two days mending for her. She cried when I left because she was so grateful for the help. I hope that erased my orneriness towards her when I was a child.

Our dining room was a fairly large room where we had a wood burning stove and a table that had four extra boards. Most of the time there were twenty for meals: all the kids, Ma and Pa, and three or four hired hands. The little kids were at the bottom of the table and we got what was left over, as the adults needed lots of energy for working all day in the fields.

We were never allowed to leave anything on the plate. If we did, we got it for the next meal that came along. We had to eat the leftovers before we could eat anything else. We lived on the rule of *waste not, want not!* You have to know as well, we had no refrigeration, and so if food was left over, we had to eat it soon anyway. Also, we did not get a choice on what we could eat; you ate what was given to you. That's why we developed a taste for any kind of food.

The only way you could get out of eating what you had was to get the kid next to you to eat it off your plate. We used to steal off each other's plate if we liked what they had. Then that kid would holler, "He (or she) stole my food!"

My mother had a regular routine. She made homemade bread, usually 14 to 20 loaves at a time. She used 50 pounds of flour every week! She would make the bread in a washtub. On Fridays we got a real treat, she made homemade doughnuts, or fried bread; treats I will always remember. We loved the centers that were cut out and we would fight like crazy to get them. We did not eat meat on Fridays, so Ma made lots of special treats, like homemade dumplings. They were made with flour, baking powder and sometimes eggs, cooked in hot water and we ate them with syrup and/or butter. The only fish we could get were sardines in a can.

On Saturdays she would make homemade noodles. She was known throughout the country for her magnificent, hair-thin noodles. She would roll out the dough on the table and watch it dry to the point where she could cut it without the stems breaking. Chicken noodle soup was the mark of the day every Sunday for as long as I can remember. Sometimes she made so many noodles she would sell them at the meat market. If her sisters found out, however, they would come begging and, of course, they got what they wanted. The people in town lost out.

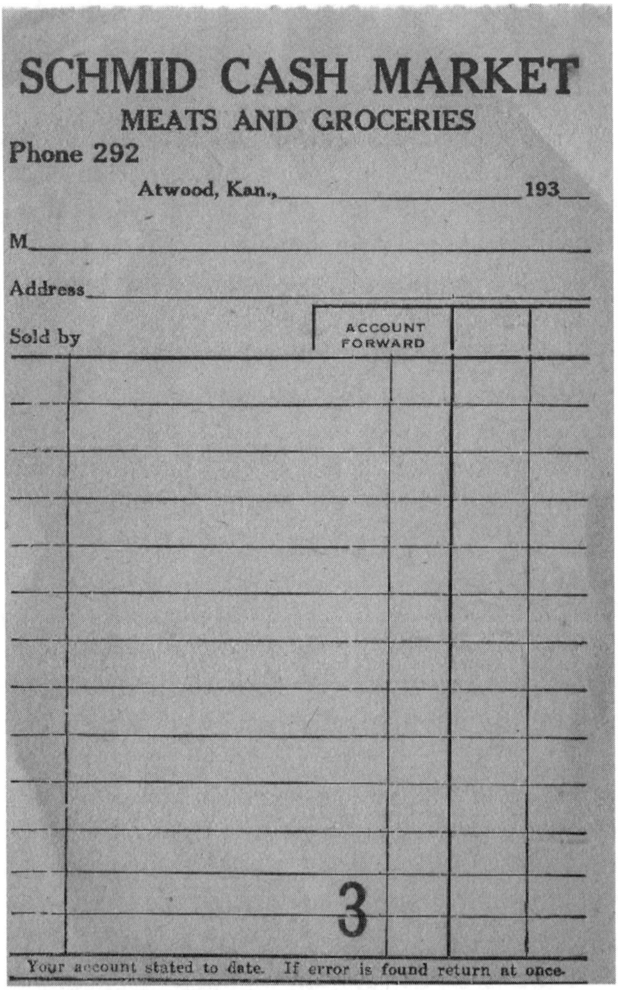

SCHMID CASH MARKET
MEATS AND GROCERIES
Phone 292

Atwood, Kan.,_____193___

M_____

Address_____

Sold by		ACCOUNT FORWARD		
		3		

Your account stated to date. If error is found return at once.

Pa's Business Stationery

Another specialty every Sunday was homemade ice cream!

Ma would mix it up and put it in the ice cream freezer. It had a place inside for the ingredients, a bucket on the outside to hold the ice, and a handle to turn it. The boys would go down to the haystack and get the ice stored there and break it up. Then we took turns turning the freezer until the ice cream was frozen. Not one member of our family ever forgot that wonderful routine. I still like to make homemade ice cream for our family.

Speaking of food, because there were so many to feed, Ma did not have time to peel potatoes. She would put them in a 14-quart kettle and cook them with the skins on. In those days, we didn't eat the skins. Now you can't get me to eat a "red bliss potato!" Forget that!

Ma fried a lot of meat with the lard she made. She made corn bread with sour cream topping that was out of this world! She would add a little sugar to the cream, then put it back in the oven to brown. It was a delectable food, loved by every kid in the family.

Ma's Vegetable Garden

My mother could do anything you could dream of. Her garden was her lifeline and every time extra vegetables were available she knew how to can them. She canned corn, beans, peas, tomatoes, and made salt-brine for the meats. She even made homemade sauerkraut. How could she do this all? We kids had to fill in where we were needed.

We would be assigned to pick the cucumbers for pickling: sweet, dill, and relish. There were days when the girls had to help can tomatoes, a job they hated. They picked five or six bushels a day. Ma would scald them in hot water, put them in cold water and then the girls had to peel them. It was not a hard job, just messy and tiring. It was not uncommon for Mom to can 40 to 50 bushels of tomatoes throughout the harvest season. By spring they were all opened and eaten.

I do remember well when she stopped canning green beans and peas. Our neighbor, a girl that lived down the road about a half-mile had opened home-canned green beans and died of food poisoning. That ended all the non-citrus canning for the Schmid family.

The other hard job was grinding cabbage and pounding it for making sauerkraut. We had to fill a 25-gallon stone jar! That job was hard, but we all loved the sauerkraut. We ate it all up and always asked for more! I still love sauerkraut today.
Peeling corn was assigned to the younger boys. Then they were given a brush to brush off all the silk. Spuds hated doing that so he used to try to get me to do it for him. Sometimes I would, sometimes I wouldn't.

We were not allowed to eat meat on Fridays. Our catholic religion was stringent at that time. We would have milk gravy and homemade bread. Often we would have rice with milk, sugar, or cream on it and ate that as the main meal! We always had lots of eggs as we had about 150 hens who might lay three to four eggs a day. That meant we had more than Pa could sell. Ma had Leghorns, Rhode Island Reds, Brahmas, and Wyandotte. The Leghorns laid more eggs than the others. We had two chicken houses with a lot of nests for the chickens to lay their eggs. Farmers knew that you could only have one rooster for every 14 or 15 hens, so there were 15 roosters that did their job of crowing every morning at 4:00 AM. So you could say Ma had alarm clocks coming out of her ears, as the roosters crowed and the coyotes howled!

The family ate chicken almost every day. They were often sold in Pa's market, however Ma raised hundreds of chickens each year for the family's use. Nearly every day we had to get chickens ready to eat. Ma would call us and we would go to the chicken house. She had a long wire that had a hook on it to catch a chicken by the foot. She would then lay its head on a stump of wood and chop off the head and drop the body on the ground. We would watch it jump around until the heart stopped, then we had to pick it up by the legs and dump it in the bucket of hot water and pick off the feathers! We got pretty good at that. The usual number needed was 14 to 16 chickens per meal.

Ma and the girls made the finest fried chicken you ever ate! They would have been great competitors for *Kentucky Fried Chicken*. Calories were needed in a farmer's diet. When you work twelve to fourteen hours a day in the heat and the sun, you don't have to count calories. I picked up the technique of frying the chicken, but I no longer work long days on a farm, so I try to resist making it.

Pa had a connection where he would buy barrels of apples, probably up in Nebraska. They were put in the underground cellar and we would have them all year long. Ma would make apple pies as well. Her specialty was apple pie with sour cream and sugar!

Lemonade was a staple and a favorite in the summer months. Lemon helped you through the heat of the day, so we used to take milk cans filled with lemonade out to the men in the fields. It was made from well water, and so was not very cold, but they drank it anyway, appreciating every drop. We kids were the lemon squeezers! We used to squeeze three or four dozen at a time.

Summertime Brought Fields of Sunflowers

Summers did not mean vacation for any of us. It meant getting ready for winter, and Ma and Pa needed us to help carry the load. We had to hoe the garden, bring in wood to stockpile for the winter, rake the yard, and get the cows out of the pasture. Work was always plentiful on the farm, but even more so in the summer and fall.

Ma would send us out to gather eggs. We liked doing that as long as we didn't find a *sitting hen*. If the hen was sitting on her eggs when you went to get them, she would peck you so hard you would bleed! So if there were any *sitting hens*, you left them alone. Hens would sit on their eggs for 21 days, hopping off only long enough to eat or drink. That was our only chance at getting the eggs from a *sitting hen*! There were usually ten to fifteen eggs from each hen.

One of the biggest problems on the farm was flies. They multiplied by the millions! They lived everywhere! Our dining room had to be fly-toxxed before every meal. Mom would have hanging stickers to catch them, but you could not eat because they would swarm all over your plate. They would bite too, if they were hungry. The milk house and barns were loaded with them as well, and before we could milk in the summer, the barn had to be sprayed. The cows and horses would switch their tails to keep them off of their bodies and if you were in the process of milking the cow, you would get swatted by the tail.

The School Gang (Laura: front center, age 7)

Who did the work around the house? I remember Toots and Threasa having to cook breakfast every morning: fried eggs, bacon, toast, cereal and pancakes by the dozen! All on the table especially early for the hired hands, so they could get off to the fields.

We were all assigned jobs. At five years of age you could set the table, put on the knives, forks and spoons. The next year you put on the plates, cups and saucers. After the meal was over the five-year-old picked up the spoons, forks and knives, the six-year-old took the plates and cups and saucers to the kitchen. The seven-year-old sorted them, the eight-year-old would start to wash them, the nine-year-old would dry them, and the older ones would put them up into the kitchen cabinet; no one was left out! The dishwater was poured out into the ditch in the yard that ran down to the pigpen for them to drink. (Yes, they drank it and they loved that slop!).

The Closet, **in Winter**

The children were assigned to making the beds in the bunkhouses, sweeping the floors, cleaning the main house and other assorted household chores. One child was assigned each week to do the bunkhouses, another to the main house, and a third to the milk house. That was a tedious and dreaded task! We always had to work fast so we could get to school on time.

Well, the other assignment which every kid tried to get away from was to empty the pots by the beds. The water closet was outside and quite a distance to walk, especially at night in the winter.

So a white pot with a lid was kept by the bedside and if you had to go in the night, you got up and used it and put back the lid. In the morning the last one out of bed was supposed to go empty it in the water closet and go to the pump and rinse it out, but every kid would deny that he or she was the last one out. Well, because I was the smallest one and too young in those days to milk cows, I was given the job of emptying them out. This didn't just mean in our bunkhouse, but in the boys' bunkhouse and in the main bedroom as well. Boy, I hated that job! So I used to try to get out of it by saying I forgot. Of course my older sisters knew better and they would squeal on me. So, I soon learned to just do it.

My mother had an Uncle Jake, an Aunt Eve, and an Aunt Emma that lived in Louisville, Kentucky. Uncle Jake was an entrepreneur of sorts and became a millionaire. They used to come to Kansas to see the family, and even at three years of age I remember looking for them to come as they gave every niece, nephew, cousin, whoever, a two-dollar bill! I had those two-dollar bills until I married. Unfortunately, when the stock market crashed in 1929, Uncle Jake went down the tubes hook, line and sinker. Within the following years they lost everything; his business, his home, his money and even his friends. Uncle Jake died of despair.

It took less than three weeks for the stock market to crash. Over 35 billion dollars were lost. Many people lost it all. No one could afford washing machines or other appliances, and there were very few amenities available. To add to their desperation, in 1929 a hailstorm dropping hail as big as grapefruits pounded all the grasslands into the ground. Everyone lost all of their crops. By 1932 it was said that over two million Americans had lost their jobs. Within three months one fourth of the banks were forced to close. Herbert Hoover was president and his career ended as Franklin Roosevelt took office.

President Roosevelt was very intent on trying to save the economy, the people and the country. He started commissions to organize plans for revisions and give hope and promise to the people. But it didn't happen overnight. Three commissions were started: the Civil Conservation Commission, the Work Project Association, and the Public Works Administration.

Most of the men were out of work and were desperate to make a living. The prairie land and the vacant land in the Midwest, especially Kansas, Arkansas, Oklahoma and Nebraska seemed to offer them a haven where they could start over. The jobs were not easy, and they were allowed only to work so many hours per day. That gave others who needed it a chance to work as well. They would hand-plow the fields, dig ditches to make roads, and sleep in tents on the ground.

The Windmill in the Pasture

Pa, still holding onto the meat market, made bologna every Friday. People came from miles around to buy it, so there was usually very little left for the family. The Schmid kids began to move on for better lives.

My brother Fred Andrew (Fritz) and my sister Threasa Louise had moved to Kentucky to get jobs through Uncle Jake. My father loved Threasa so much that he cried when she left. Fritz worked with Uncle Jake and when Uncle Jake went down the tubes after the stock market crash, Fritz had a hard time finding a job. After some time though, Fritz got a job with A & P. When the war started, he joined the Navy. Then Threasa left Kentucky and went to Detroit to work in a factory.

During the years of the terrible dust storms (the early 1930s);

you could not believe how we had to manage to live. Usually about 11:00 AM you could see the cloud of dirt growing in the sky. They would form into huge black clouds. Within a few hours, the wind and dirt blew so hard you could not see your hands in front of you. The dirt blew into any crack in the house. We had to hang wet towels and sheets over the windows and they would turn into mud. They had to be changed three or four times in a day. The windowsills would gather three to four inches of dirt, so we had to take a brush and bucket to clean them off. We did that three or four times a day as well! The air was so heavy it would smother out the coal oil lamps and the fire in the cook stove. In order to have anything to eat or drink, we had to cover everything with towels.

We lost many cows from dust pneumonia in the pasture. The dirt blew so hard it piled up to cover the barbed-wire fence. The cows would then walk over the fence, fall into ditches and lose their way. Most of them suffocated from the dust, or died of thirst or exhaustion. They would try to find the creek for water. If there was water there it was muddy. They would drink it anyway trying to keep cool!

Storms Rage in "Dust Bowl"

May 12. Another dust storm has struck the Great Plains. Experts estimate that 650,000,000 tons of topsoil have been blown away by this storm and the ones before it. The "Dust Bowl" farmers of Kansas, Nebraska, Oklahoma, Texas, and New Mexico are seeing tremendous crop and livestock losses.

Months of drought and the poor condition of soil from years of overproduction are at the root of the problem, agriculture experts say.

Dust Storm, Western Kansas Highway

Source: Frank N. Magill, *Great Events from History*, American Series, Englewood Cliffs, NJ: Salem Press, 1975.

Dust Storms Hit Kansas

The temperature was often 120 to 130 degrees in the shade. Crops were non-existent. Animals would die, and my brothers would have to dig a hole with shovels to bury them. Then the hungry coyotes would dig them up to have something to eat.

The dust got into the engines of the cars and trucks and ruined them. Very seldom could they be started again. The dust would also short the lights in the car, so if they did start, you could not use them at night. The years were noted as the *Dirty Thirties, the era of drought and economic depression.*

The simple good life had gone away, and Martin and Eva's oldest children could no longer hang on so some time beginning around 1932 and the following years, the kids left to find a better life. As I understand it, seven of the kids left home in the span of one year's time. Some married, others went on their way. There was no way they could make a living on land that produced nothing, no crops, no water. Just dust.

In these hard times James Paul (Jim) became ill with dust pneumonia, so he left the meat market and went to Manitou Springs, Colorado to try to get well.

On *Black Sunday*, April 14, 1935, the telephone rang 14 times; it was the general alarm. The operator announced that the worse dust storm ever was to arrive by 11:00 AM.

"Get your family in! We are predicting that it could be the end of the world!"
My mother made sandwiches fast so we would have something to eat, knowing the fire in the cook stove would smother out. The sandwiches were peanut butter and jelly. They brought apples out of the cellar so we would not starve.

The dust storm arrived as predicted! It was dark as midnight starting at 11:00 AM and that darkness lasted all day long. Even in the house you had a hard time seeing your hand in front of you! My brother Johnnie who was working in the fields when it hit started immediately for home when he saw it coming. There were people driving on the road who could not see a thing, they landed in the ditch. On Johnnie's way home he followed the barbed-wire fence and in doing so ran into five people. They all were crying because they had also found the barbed-wire fence and had severely cut their hands. He told them to take his hand as he had gloves on, and that he would take them to our house. They got to our house at 11:00 PM that night!

Back at the house, Mom tried to make coffee. We held tin cups over a kerosene lamp trying to heat the water. It was so bad;

everyone thought it was the end of time! All of us were in the dining room just trying to breathe. We held wet washcloths over our faces.

Mom then said, "We need to pray. We must say the Rosary so that the Lord will know we need him."

She said the rosary three times. Then eventually everyone fell asleep either on the floor or in a chair. That storm lasted a full three days and when it did begin to clear up, we were all alive and able to have some real food. The dust storms persisted for three years.

During this time President Roosevelt set up the W.P.A. (the Works Project Association), a committee to figure out how to overcome the problem. They sent trees to the farmers to plant and told them to plow hills to stop the dirt from blowing across level land.

Agnes' House

Then finally the rains came! During these next few years, tornados were very common. We had a cellar deep in the ground where our food was stored, because it was cool underground. This provided emergency shelter. Of course, it was also a great place for spiders. Many times we found black widow spiders there. They were deadly if they bit you. Mom would take a match and burn them in the web.

When a storm was brewing in the sky, the operator sent out the general alarm telling everyone to go underground. My older sister Agnes's home was hit once. Fortunately, it missed her house, but took all the sheds. It picked up an iron fence post and drove it right through a cow's stomach! It pulled all the feathers off 40 chickens! It lasted only minutes, but that meant the cow had to be slaughtered and the chickens killed. Since there was no refrigeration, they had to cook them. So they had plenty of chicken for the farmers who helped clean up the mess.

Agnes' Sheds Destroyed by Tornado

But that meant my sister Agnes Elizabeth and her husband Steve lost long-term food supplies for their own family as well as for selling. They ended up eating pork that had been salted in a barrel for months. I had to help Agnes in this period as she had her third child and needed me to take care of the other children. I got sick of eating pork sandwiches and dill pickles for breakfast, dinner and supper!

Finally they sold enough eggs so Steve could go to town to get flour and coffee as the flour barrel was empty and so was the coffee pot. Steve got into the wagon, went into town and returned about five hours later. We were anxious to see him, thinking he would bring us back some great food. Words will not describe the anger of my sister Agnes when she found out that he had spent $1.50

of the money to buy a bottle of liquor! He felt he deserved it after all that had happened. At least the flour barrel and the coffee pot were replenished, but that was it. It took a long time for them to regain their losses.

The one thing people could count on was personal concern for everyone, the homeless, the neighbors, and even sometimes the gypsies. Sharing was something you willingly did. Neighbors became friends, friends were to be found anywhere if you wanted them.

However, times were so bad many families just gave up. They loaded up their wagons and took off to the west. I never knew why they didn't go east, but California became the destination of many (maybe because there was a lot of talk about gold being found there).

The gypsies then posed a big problem. They would come down the road, loads of them at a time and steal food. One particular time Spuds (Paul Albert) and his son, Dennis, came to visit Charles Martin (Bushy), Andrew Bernard (Andy) and Ma, who were living on the farm at the time. They saw all these wagons full of gypsies coming down the road. They lined the road for one full mile from Toot's house to the highway! Spuds, Dennis, Bushy and Andy immediately went to Ma's house and started shooting tin cans and stuff so they would know we had guns. Then they stayed up all night playing cards with the lights on and showing activity in the house. Periodically they would go outside to check the farmyard. They were worried that the gypsies would steal everything they could get their hands on.

Gypsies were very cunning. They would always have a lot of people in the wagon and if you were home, one would come and knock on the door to buy a chicken from you. While one was at the door, the others were out at the chicken house catching chickens as fast as they could. They could easily steal three or four dozen chickens in minutes as they had their own wire catchers and knew exactly how to use them! Ma also worried that they might try to kidnap a child or hurt them. There was no way of catching them as the Sheriff was in town three miles away and by the time he would get there, they would be gone. When daylight came the next day, they left and went off somewhere else.

At this time, Toots, the oldest girl, and the younger boys

were helping Pa in the meat Market. Charles took over slaughtering the animals. In 1938, when Pa was 66, he was injured while helping to get a steer slaughtered. The steer took after him and struck him to the ground with its horn (I still have the horn today). Pa broke his hip and ended up at the Henneberger hospital for over six months! Recuperated, he returned home with one leg four inches shorter than the other. He tried keeping the market open. Although it was called "Schmid's Cash Market," the cash flow was only a trickle at this time as anyone coming into the store with children and no money never went away without meat.

President Roosevelt started the Civilian Conservation Corpse (known as the C.C.C.) and sent the men out to build Highway 36 during these hard times. The men would come into the market and tell Pa that they hadn't gotten their check.

"Will you let me charge it and I'll bring in the money when I get it?"

Pa was goodhearted and generous, but too many transactions like this, plus the crippling hip injury forced him to close shop in 1938. He had given credit to these people that amounted to over $75,000. The banks took his small savings and he lost the market. He retired to his home until his death five years later on October 25, 1943. He was 72. It was exactly twenty-one years after Annie Catherine had died in Pa's arms of diphtheria.

Around 1937 and 38, the girls found partners and went on their way. The war came and its harsh reality was devastating! Seven of Ma's sons had to register.

World War II had started. Five of Pa's sons, Frank George, Fred Andrew, Joseph Henry, Paul Albert, and Louis Frederick were called to war. Frank, living in Chicago joined the Navy. Fred, living in Kentucky also joined the Navy. Paul (Spuds) joined the Navy from Denver and Joe and Louis were both drafted into the Army. The older boys, Jim and Johnnie, were drafted but then were sent back because of their age. Charlie, one of the youngest boys, was given a reprieve because there was no one else at home to work on the farm. All of our soldiers were overseas. The results of their experiences changed everyone's life forever. Thank God, no one was killed in action, but the experience changed their lives either in failing to re-adjust or ending up in complete despair. Louis committed suicide and Frankie became a recluse.

Due to censorship not one of my brothers in the service received the word that Pa had died. They never knew until the war ended. Mom received an award from President Roosevelt after the five Sullivan brothers went down on one ship. He realized that because they were in different services, the total number of her sons serving in the military was not recognized. All of the boys remained in the service until the war ended.

The Barn (Picture Taken in 1987)

When the boys returned home they were all attentive to Ma's needs. Spuds would drive out from Denver at least once a month to make sure Ma had food in the refrigerator. Jim used to sneak home to Ma without his wife knowing to give Ma money and help Charlie out. Charlie had started a family and had a hard time feeding them. The boys never let Ma go without food. Agnes would come once a week and clean her house for her. Andy, living in the bunkhouse at the home place, would come every morning to have coffee.

Charlie, Andy and I were left at home to save the farm. Occidental Life Insurance of St. Louis was foreclosing on the farm and all our household possessions! We appealed to them and promised we would do everything we could to produce money on the farm. Because I had gone to high school they decided to give us a chance. Shortly after that I left to go to college, so it took Charlie and Andy many years to redeem the farm, but they did.

Mom remained on the farm for 27 years after Pa died, milking cows and taking care of chickens, ducks and geese, and growing vegetables in her garden until she fell and broke her hip. That ended her stay at the Schmid farm. Her new home became the Good Samaritan Center in Atwood. She was 86 years of age. Her severe injury and arthritis put her in a wheel chair. Dr. Henneberger informed the family that she could no longer live on the farm. One of her youngest sons, Charlie, begged her to come live with him.

Her answer was, "I do not want to be a burden to any one of my kids! Just let me go where I will be taken care of."

She was happy at the Good Samaritan Center and called it home. My mother accepted life and its problems, and seldom cried except when a loved one died. Her husband, five children, four in-laws, and three grandchildren preceded her death. She went into eternity on January 25, 1976 at 91 years, 6 months and 22 days of life. In the end Ma joined Pa and her children that had passed before her at the graveyard at St. John's Church.

The Graveyard at St. John's Church
Annie's tombstone is in the foreground

That graveyard stands as a beacon to the past, with the prairie winds still blowing. Oil wells now surround the area, and vacant farmlands give home to Mother Nature's little animals. Grasslands are hardly visible, but remains of old stone walls remind visitors that once there were farms, towns and people there. Now it is only peace that lives on the prairie.

Vacant Farmlands in Atwood, Kansas

Chapter 2

THE ROOTS OF THE KANSAS TREE

This tree in Kansas planted by Martin and Eva Schmid had strong roots with a life of many branches, from the seeding to the very end. This tree was not dependent on sunny days, weathered many sudden storm clouds, and stayed standing sturdy through the hardships of an unforgiving world. It grew with many branches, some broken, some strong and some weak; but they all took their cues from the strong roots below, whose rugged beginnings taught the basis of survival. As of 2010 only two branches remain.

MY FATHER MARTIN (Pa) – "YOU CAN BE WHAT YOU WANT TO BE!"

Pa, as we always called him, was a short, heavily built man, who weighed somewhere around 250 pounds. He had a head of dark black hair and a mustache that we called a strainer. He would sit at the table and always used his hand to wind around the ends of his mustache. Obviously, he did not want to get it full of food, but yes, sometimes he would lick it off.

Everyone who knew Pa recognized his integrity, his stoic outlook on life, his honesty, his dedication and his staunch belief that he was right in any decision he made. He was stubborn and determined. That describes his life. Although he was stubborn, charity, kindness and hard work were continuously evident throughout his 72 years.

Both my mother and father could speak fluent German. My father refused to teach any of us kids the German language, and would not allow Ma to teach it either.

"You are an American, living in America! No way do you need to know how to speak German!" he would say.

My sisters Toots and Threasa and brothers Jim and Johnnie caught enough from Ma and Pa's conversations that they could understand what was being said. Ma would speak to her cousins on the phone in German so the other people in the neighborhood (listening on the party line) could not understand. Toots could speak a little. But none of them ever let Pa know what they had learned or they would have gotten a whopping!

Pa had a goal, to be somebody. He was so brilliant with arithmetic, you would not believe he had such little schooling. No one could ever challenge Pa on his mathematical skills. He could add numbers in his head faster than you could write them down. It didn't matter whether it was a one-digit number or a five-digit number. He would simply say within seconds what the total was. I don't believe he *ever* made a mistake. I always thought he was another Einstein.

Pa grew up in poverty and hardly talked of his family. My mother used to ask him about his brother and sisters, but he never heard from them. He would refer to home as the pear tree in the yard, and a lumberyard in the back and that was about it. Sometimes he would say he had a cousin that he liked a lot, the one he set out to find when he and the captain took to the road out of Newport, Rhode Island. A picture of that cousin showed up and it had been mailed from Atchison, Kansas. To my knowledge, that reunion never took place.

I also know he would mention a brother named August, and years later I set out to meet him. In the 1960's there was an August Schmid who opened a 'Schmid Statuary' in South Boston. I thought he might be my father's brother so I called. The man did not speak English. Through an interpreter on his end of the line, I told my story and we three arranged to meet at a restaurant in South Boston, Blinbstrub's (a very prominent restaurant at the time). That day the interpreter called me and said that August had dropped dead the day before.

When Ma and Pa were first married they had their first baby, James Paul, born in August of 1904. James was only six months old when they traveled in a wagon to St. John's Church in Beardsley, Kansas, for Mass. It was very cold that Sunday, and the baby was crying hard while Mass was being given. The priest at that time was very old, had to cover two parishes and slept under the altar because he could not make it home after the last Mass. Obviously he was tired as well, and when he was giving the sermon he spoke out.

"Will the woman with that bawling brat get it out of here!"

My father stood up and said, "The woman *and man* with that bawling brat will get out of here, but I promise you, as long as I live, I will *never* enter another catholic church!"

They left, my mother cried and cried, and begged and begged for Pa to forgive the priest.

"You can't blame him, obviously he is overworked and probably has not had anything to eat since yesterday."

All her pleading was in vain. Pa would not set foot in the church, though he made sure we did. Only on his deathbed did he answer Ma's plea and return to the catholic church.

Ma and Pa's Wedding Picture

When we had to go to church, Pa would get up, harness the horses, hitch them to the wagon, and bring out the hot bricks to keep our feet warm. Then he would load us all up and take us three miles into Atwood (usually 30 to 50 minutes) to get to church on time. Pa would sit out in the freezing cold, no matter how cold it was while we went to Mass. He would be there to take us home.

Ma used to plead with him, "Why are you so stubborn?"

He never changed. The people in the town knew he would not go to church. My sister Verneda wanted him to give her away when she married.

"No way! I'll be there outside," and he was.

Toots' First Communion, 1918

We were never allowed to miss Mass, never missed catechism, never missed summer school, never missed our monthly confession, we all made our first communion, received confirmation, and only three of the boys married out of the church.

There were very few catholic families in the area and the priest asked for boys to be servers at the daily Mass. Prayer was a vital part of every farmer's day and if it was possible, they would go to Mass to pray. Pa would get up in the morning and harness the two ponies, Bill and Don, and get Joe and Spuds out of bed to ride the three miles into town to serve at the daily Mass. This went on for years until the boys were self-sufficient and got up on their own and harnessed their own ponies.

Joe, Spuds and the Ponies, Bill and Don

When did Pa change his mind? In the year of 1943, he became ill, the war was on and he was diagnosed as having stomach cancer. He ended up in the hospital, went into a coma and the doctor said death could occur anytime.

I, Laura, said to mom, "Why don't we call Father Flavin, 'cause he could give Pa the last Sacraments."

She said, "Oh, child, Pa is in a coma and he won't even know he's there."

I said, "Well, let's see what Father Flavin says."

I called Father and he said, "You and your mom go home,

and I will go up to the hospital."

When he arrived at the hospital Dr. Henneberger discouraged him saying, "He is completely out of it, why go in?"

Father said, "Well let me see."

Within an hour the phone rang. Father Flavin was on the line and asked to speak to my Mother.

When she got on the phone, he said, "Mrs. Schmid, do you want to hear the bad news or the good news first?"

She replied "The good news."

"Well, the door was closed to your husband's room, and when I opened it, your husband sat up in bed and said, "I've been waiting for you Father." I asked him "Would you like to go to confession?" He replied, "Yes." Then he said the finest Act of Contrition I have ever heard from anyone's mouth. I gave him Absolution, he closed his eyes and passed away."

Pa's Funeral

Because the people in the town knew he did not go to church, and because he was taken to the church with the casket closed, they started the rumor that they had to keep the casket closed so the devil wouldn't get out. Then the paper announced that Butch Schmid returned to the catholic church on his deathbed. I am sure the Lord welcomed him with open arms. Father Flavin had written the paper and asked them to please clear up Butch Schmid's name.

My father never drank liquor, never smoked, never cussed, and never took the name of God in vain. He was recognized as one of the hardest working men in the county of more than 60 families.

Holidays were never forgotten in all the years. Even in the worst years, Santa would arrive on Christmas Eve with a bushel of oranges. Every kid waited for that knock on the door. In good years, Santa had a few toys and would only leave them during the dark of night. Each kid got one toy, no more. If you wanted to change with someone else you could, as long as you both agreed.

Easter was another big holiday as Ma would save onion skins for coloring the eggs. On Holy Thursday she would cook 6 dozen eggs in the water with the onion skins and they would come out colored orangey-brown. On Holy Saturday all the older kids had to help color the eggs with Easter egg coloring. They made enough to fill a 10-gallon bucket.

The Easter bunny arrived sometime in the night and would hide all those eggs in the yard. We knew he was there because we would find bunny footprints all along the walkway outside the main house. When we kids would find the eggs on Easter morning, if the bucket didn't get filled, we were sent back out until it was. *The bunny* knew all the eggs had to be found.

At dinner Pa played a game called *Sparkle*. He would pick an egg and for some reason or other he knew how to pick it. He would then challenge each kid to 'pick your egg and sparkle with me.' We would hit the two eggs together, one end and then the other. Pa's egg would seldom if ever crack. Once your egg cracked on both ends, the next challenger took over. I only remember beating Pa once. This was a tradition I carried on with my own family for years and now I teach my grandchildren to play. I also hide eggs and lay down bunny footprints when I can.

You could not talk education with Pa. He never went beyond the third grade, but he had tremendous mathematical skills. He could add numbers in his head without writing anything down or using any device. He did this all day long in his meat market, totaling orders for his customers and he was never wrong. There was a lady, Mrs. Ratcliff, who was a very successful organist and pianist and was very well-to-do. She took pride in her education and looked down on my father for his disdain for it. She loved my father's products, but would always question when he would tell her how much the bill was. Pa would add figures in his head faster than you could write them down.

She would yell at him... "Put those figures in the cash register!"

Irked to say the least, he would say, "Do it yourself and if you find I made a mistake I will give you a whole double order free of charge."

She would grab the packages and go out the door mad as a chicken!

My sister, Toots, who was helping him in the market would say, "Pa, she has the right to know that the figures added up right."

Pa replied, "She can go to ----! I'll put them in the cash register if I feel like it, and I'm not going to if I don't want to."

Even with this controversy, Mrs. Ratcliff was Pa's biggest supporter of his business for all his years.

When Pa broke his hip in 1938, he was hospitalized for six months. When he returned home, his broken hip had caused his left leg to shrink by four to six inches. He could walk, but it took a lot of effort.

My brother Fritz came home one time to see him and promised, "When I go back, I think I can get a shoemaker to make a shoe with a big heel for you."

Well, it took about six months and Fritz arrived for Christmas with this big shoe, a heel about five to six inches, with a sole built up as well about five inches. Thank goodness, the shoe fit and Pa, with a lot of help, learned to walk with that shoe. You need to know, however, the shoe made a loud, heavy noise as he walked down the wooden plank walkway between the main house, where he and Ma slept, and the bunkhouses where us kids slept. Even with his handicap, he kept track of the kids getting out of bed to help Ma milk those 50 to 60 cows every morning. When we heard that walk, *out we got!* We knew that you get out of bed darn fast or Pa will come in and jerk you out of bed, and he'd whop you on the butt, so you didn't wait!

When I returned home when my mother died, my sisters had saved Pa's big shoe for me. I had it for years and years, but then the water tank in our house broke. The shoe got wet and was all moldy and I had to throw it away. I always dreamed of saving it to use as a planter to remind me of Pa.

When the stock market crashed, Pa's meat market began to go down hill. Toots, Charlie and I tried so hard to save the business, but the banks closed. Pa had no money; the bank took his $3,000 savings and then he lost the market. The bank took the money from him. I honestly think he died of despair.

Where did Pa get his meat? He would get up at the same time as Ma, at 4:00 AM, hitch up two horses onto the wagon and travel miles and miles, trying to find someone raising cattle, pigs, goats, sheep, then would bid for them. If they took his offer, they were loaded into the wagon and he would come home to slaughter them. Usually he would be back by 7:00 AM, just as Ma and the kids had finished milking. All the boys learned to butcher, but Jim and Johnnie were the king butchers at this time. It would take them about one half hour to shoot the animal in the head, stab the neck so the blood would run out, hang the animal by the legs and then skin it with wicked sharp knives. They would have a bucket of water to dip the knives in to keep them clean. They were so good at skinning, they became area champions and would hire out to slaughter any animal for $1. The blood was saved in a bucket. Pa would sometimes drink it as warm as it was, but mainly it was saved to make blood sausage and other goods.

The intestines were ripped out, saving the heart, lungs, brains, liver, kidneys, and tails to be washed and marketed. Usually, the intestines were fed to the pigs and they would devour them like dessert. If Pa needed them for sausage the kids were assigned to wash them out. After washing the body of the slaughtered animal with several buckets of water, they would wrap the whole animal with cloths, put it in the wagon and off to town Pa and the older boys would go. Pa's meat market would open by 10:00 AM and would close by 8:00 PM. The farmers would come in after sundown, so he would stay open to accommodate them. No one ever questioned sanitization or worried about spoiled meat.

While the boys were butchering, Ma and the older girls had to separate the milk, and bottle the whole milk and cream. Bottles had to be washed every night and turned over to dry. They were filled the next morning, hand-capped and put into wire baskets for Pa to take to the market.

These were days before *pasteurization*. Skimmed milk was necessary food for the pigs, chickens, cats and dogs. Cats were a necessity to keep mice out of the barn and dogs were needed to keep away any unknown intruder. They would chase away foxes, and bark at any unknown human intruders, however, coyotes were a real threat. Mom called them her alarm clock, because they would come to the top of the hill in the pasture in the early morning about 3:00 or 4:00 AM. They had a howl that would scare anyone and of course, if the dogs didn't scare them off, they would completely kill all the chickens, geese, ducks and the few turkeys we had.

The county organized a coyote hunt once a year. This kept the population under control. You were allowed to shoot them.

There were about 60 families in the town, so they butchered two to four large animals a week. What wasn't sold in the meat market was the food brought home for the family. Yes, we had to eat the brains, the liver, the kidneys, the tails, *and* the tongues, because most of the good meat was sold in the market.

In the summer Ma made sure the men always had fried steak, chicken, pork chops or the like. Pa could make bologna, blood sausage, wieners, headcheese, and smoked ham. Pa's bologna and wieners were sold so rapidly, we kids hardly ever got to have them. Pa would reward us though. After church on Sunday we would all go to the meat market and get a wiener. All the kids at church knew this, and Pa would give them each one for free, as long as they lasted.

After Pa died, my older brother Jim held the recipe for the bologna, blood sausage and the other fine meat products. His wife would not share it with anyone and what happened to it, no one ever knew.

Where did the water come from? We had a windmill that would pump up the water from underground into a tank. Pa and the boys hand-drilled a well nearer to the house, 200 feet deep and a yard wide. Water pumped by the windmill would go into the house well after the tank was filled.

That well was about 100 feet from the house and we had to hand-pump all the water we got from it. All the water we used in the house had to be carried in by us. In addition, the milk house was about 10 feet from the pump, and we had to pump the water and put it into a huge lard kettle with a burner below for heating. Every night, the bottles coming home from the market were brought to the milk house to be washed by the older girls. Toots and Threasa, and of course any other girl who was old enough (usually anyone older than 5 years) had to help. They were washed, rinsed and turned over to dry. This stage in time was lucky for me, because I was too young and little to have to work that hard.

In addition to butchering, Pa taught the boys to plow the fields, plant the corn, mow the alfalfa and chop the wood for heat. Where did the wood come from? There was a crick (now known as a creek) about a half a mile west and north of the house. Cottonwood trees were in abundance there and they would cut them down to dry for a summer before the wood would burn. Pa would often let the gypsies cut the trees down and give them food for the days they worked. They would sleep in the haystacks. When there was not enough wood to burn, they were sent to the pasture with a wagon to pick up dried cow-chips. They could be burned to provide heat as well, and there was always a joke about how much a *cow-chip picker upper* would be paid. Many wagon loads were brought home and piled for use.

Pa taught Ma how to use the fat of the hogs to make lard. She would have to do that about every two months, as he would keep the fat in the icebox in town so it would not spoil. After it was made, it was poured into large five-gallon metal cans and sold at the market. Any lard that was left over was known as tallow. Pa would take it home and Mom would heat it up, and add lye to make soap. It would have to cook four to five hours. That would be put into large washtubs, and set out in the yard to dry and harden. Then she would cut the soap into squares so she could use it in the hand washer. She was so good at it that the neighbors would come to buy soap from her. Pa also taught Ma how to cook the blood sausage, headcheese and liverwurst. We had loads of that hanging in the milk house to cure. Then he would sell them in the meat market.

It was very difficult to run the market at first, because they would have to freeze water into ice chunks, take the ice to town and store it in a shed covered with straw so it wouldn't melt. This ice was used to keep the meat fresh. Then finally, a man came and opened an ICE STORE. That was a blessing. The church even thanked God for sending this man. The man made a good living because everyone needed ice.

Having ice available brought competition for Pa's market. A man named Anton opened a market across the street. He was never able to beat Pa in quality of meat, however. My father knew that cattle fed on corn and good alfalfa made the meat the best in town. He would not sell his cattle to any competitor. Another thing we kids had to learn to do was to wash out some of the pig's intestines, because that was the skin used to make the bologna, wieners, sausage, and other meats Ma had to cook. We would even help Ma grind the meat for Pa to take to town.

This was before refrigeration, so ice was *so* important. In the winter the men had to cut the ice from the crick, and from the big water tank after it was built. They cut it into squares weighing something like 75 to 100 pounds. They would bury the squares in the haystacks to keep them frozen well into the summer. In the summer the hired hands would sleep on top of those stacks because they were cool. Temperatures in those days were unbelievable! Zero to 20 and 30 degrees below in winter, and in the summer it was not unusual to have 120 to 130 degrees *in the shade!* At times, it was so hot the men could not work in the fields in the afternoons for fear they would die of heat exhaustion.

Most of the summer, when the sun rose in the morning around 4:30 AM, the men would head for the field. They saw the morning sky every day on their way to work. In those days the heat could cause terrible tornados, thunderstorms and lightning that could be deadly if you were caught in the fields when they hit. But they knew the sky's various colors and moods, and they could always see the clouds forming in the sky. When they looked bad, they immediately headed for home.

There was always so much work that Pa had to hire men when he could to work in the fields. This was a big help to my brothers who worked in the fields, since they also had so many chores to do. One time he hired a man (where he found him, no one knows) who claimed to be an Atheist.

When the weather would get bad the boys would say, "Boy, we'd better pray," as was the custom for Christian farmers at the time.

The Atheist would yell at them and say, "There is no God! Who do you think you are calling?"

Well, one day out of a clear blue sky, a black cloud seemed to arrive out of nowhere. A dangerous lightning storm swelled up and immediately started firing bolts. The lightning was terrible. A lightning bolt would kill you in an instant, set fire to any structure it hit, and was known to blow up things like trees, cars and wagons. They jumped off the wagon and got under the load of hay for protection. The thunder shook the wagon full of hay.

Then the Atheist said, "Holy God, get us out of here!"

After that the boys never let him get away with saying he didn't believe in God.

In the 1930's Pa had a Model-T Ford. An old guy that sold him cattle traded cars with him and Pa got an *Oberlin*, a larger car that seemed more compatible to Pa's needs. He didn't have it very long, when one day he wanted to check on the boys to see what they were doing at the North Place. He came home from the shop earlier than usual that day and headed the 2½ miles north of the house to the North place. The trouble was there was a very narrow bridge about one half mile down the road. Only one car could go over it at a time. There were very poor iron rails on the sides. Pa was not paying attention and was going as fast as he could when he saw another car coming from the other side. He thought, *I'll beat him over the bridge*. Well, he didn't! The other car stopped, but Pa veered to the side and hit the iron rails. The *Oberlin* went half way off the bridge! Pa had to crawl over the seat and go over the back to get out of the car. The neighbors could not believe that he wasn't killed.

Pa's Car Wreck at the One Lane Bridge
The Oberlin was wrecked, so it turned into a kid's play car

for us. It gave us years of fun and, of course, it holds a little history. I was playing on it once with my brothers and fell out of it and broke my collarbone. Pa had forbidden us to go near that old wreck because he knew that it harbored snakes and spiders and the metal was all torn; but that didn't keep us off. My brothers concocted a story about breaking my collarbone in the cornfield because they would have gotten the strap for messing around in that car! *They* would have gotten the strap, not me! Pa liked Laura.

Pa worked so many hours that he usually didn't get home until around 8:30 or 9:00 at night. We kids were put to bed once he got home, but if we were naughty or bad that day, he was given the report by the older brothers and sisters and Pa would then deal out the punishment. He had a leather razor strap about a foot long and if he felt they deserved it, he would strap the boys. I don't remember him ever using the strap on me. I don't know if any of my sisters every got the strap. I know that I didn't.

One time on a weekend, I remember Fritz getting pushed up against the shed by Pa and then he hit him because he went out the night before and didn't come home. Fritz had a hang-up for a girl named Gertrude Shattuck who lived down the road. She was some 20 years older than he! Pa found this out and that was the cause for the beating.

His voice was heard by all: "If I ever catch you hanging around her again, you will get a beating you will never forget!"

Ma knew that Fritz would pretend he was going to bed, so when she got up to fire up the water in the wash house, she would peak in the bedroom to see if he was there. She would plead with him to give Gertrude up the next day, but she never told Pa when he was missing.

Gertrude was a nurse and worked in Atwood at the Henneberger Hospital three or four days a week. They kept meeting secretly. One afternoon when everyone was supposed to be going to milk, Fritz told Verneda to let Ma know he had to go fix the fence in the pasture and he probably would be late. Verneda told Ma. They did the milking, separated the milk, fed the hogs and did all the other farm chores. Now it was time for supper but Fritz didn't show. It now became a real concern as to why it was taking him so long. Finally, Ma sent Joe and Spuds out to find him.

They were gone two hours, only to come back to say, "He is not out there!"

That night at 11:30 PM the phone rang.

It was Fritz announcing to Ma, "I've fixed my fence! Gertrude and I got on the train in Ludell and went to Omaha, Nebraska. We got married!"

Pa went livid, grabbed the phone and yelled, "You can NOT come home!"

Fritz, of course, was not stupid. He knew Pa would be upset, so he had taken his clothes with him to the pasture and hid them in a soap weed. He and Gertrude picked up the clothes and caught a train out of Ludell the next morning to go to Kentucky. He had contacted Uncle Jake Haller and had a job to go work for him. He did not come home for many years.

Louie, Andy, Charlie and Laura On Jim's New Car

One other time, Frankie had a girlfriend and they were in the Model T making out. Pa saw him, jerked him out of the car and gave him a good wham! That girl, Millie, eventually married Frankie. Pa had rules and determination. You went to church. You did your job. You minded your mother. We all knew that you didn't disobey Pa in any way shape, or form, or the punishment would be great.

Frank and Millie

Another very scary incident occurred with a hired hand. My father decided he needed to build an elevator to store the grain. He hired a man named Ken and from all appearances he was thought to be a great hand. He liked my brother Frankie and supposedly became a very devoted friend. My brother Jim, still at home at the time, had slaughtered so many animals for other people that he saved enough money to buy a Model A Ford, a good-looking Ford at the time.

Unknown to Pa, Ken the hired hand was a little envious, so he suggested to Frankie, "Hey, we can make money off your brother."

Frankie, going along with the conversation, said, "How?"

"Well," he said, "You see the tires on that car, they are worth lots of money. If you will help me we can take those tires and sell them, then you and I can leave this place and go east where there's lots of money."

Jim and His New Car

Frankie played his game and Ken confided in him how he was going to do this. The evening was set and Frankie was supposed to take an end iron and stand by Ken as he raised the car up in the garage to remove the tires. Ken had another friend who was to sneak up behind the garage with a truck so no one would see him and they would load the tires into that truck. Ken and Frankie could then hop on and they would take off.

Frankie did a good job of going along with his plan but secretly had gone in town to the Sheriff and alerted him to what was going on. The Sheriff and three assistants parked their car down the road and sneaked up the ditch so they would be able to catch him in the act. Pa was told to go out and surprise them and the Sheriff would be right there. When Pa arrived at the garage and opened the door, Ken saw him and threw a tire iron at him! Fortunately, Pa ducked and it went over his head. Talk about the luck of a German!

The Sheriff came in and captured Ken. He was taken to the jail in Atwood, but during the night he got out and disappeared. He was never found. Frankie lived in fear for many years, as he knew Ken was a convict who had access to guns.

Pa embraced Frankie for what he had done. My father did not display affection very often, but this time he did. This assured Frankie that he was an accepted son.

After Fritz left with Gertrude to work for Uncle Jake, Threasa, who loved him dearly, contacted Uncle Jake to see if he could find her a job as a practical nurse in the hospital. Uncle Jake, fully aware of the depression, told her to come on down. He got her a job at the hospital. It was hard for Pa to see her go; they were so very close.

In 1937 and 1938, Frankie, Joe and Spuds left to find new lives as well. Time erased the family from the farm. The girls left to marry and the war took the boys. Pa broke his hip roping a steer, followed by the foreclosure of his beloved meat market. Pa went into eternity leaving behind a history of hard work and little play; tired but not forsaken. His lifetime wish to return home to Germany to see his lost family never materialized. My mother was left with overwhelming financial problems and few children left to help her. She carried on for thirty-three years beyond her husband's passing. I, Laura, know that Pa and Ma are together now. They are sharing life in eternity.

Chapter 3

THE LORD NEVER PROMISED LIFE WOULD BE EASY.
EVA MARIE-
OUR MOM, OUR PROTECTOR, OUR PROVIDER!

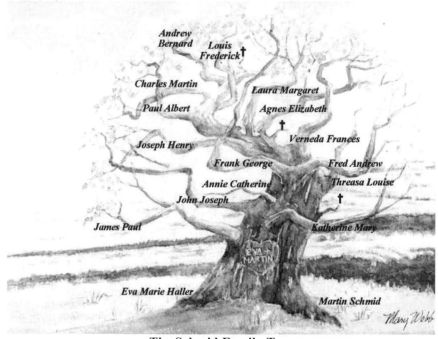

The Schmid Family Tree

Eva was a very simple woman devoted to her roll in life. She supported her husband in any way she could, including learning his trade, and enjoyed most the multitude of tasks required for raising a large family. I think she was probably five foot six or seven, staunchly built and weighed about 185 to 190 pounds most of her life. Work never slimmed her down. Discipline was her hardship! You never met a more hard-working woman (probably because she had so many children). She would always tell us to fight our own battles. I'm sure it was her lack of available time that kept her from intervening, but this was the proper way to handle most squabbles. If she knew you needed straightening out, she would tell Pa as we faced him on his return home each night. This was the way it was for us, and for many other Christian families in the mid-west at the time.

Ma In Her Work Clothes

Ma never asked you to do anything she had not done herself. She had done all the work many times over by the time she got to teaching us. She always taught us by example. She had assignments for every child and insisted that you carry them out. There was no other way to get all the work done with so many children in the house.

Amidst the importance of getting everything for her family done, she knew to do something, at least a little something, for herself. Pa gave her a battery radio and in my early years, she would take one half hour of her afternoon to sit and listen to 'Ma Perkins, Fibber McGee and Molly.' She also loved hearing the 'Grand Ole Opry.' She didn't just sit and listen, she would have mending in her hands, food to peel, or anything that needed attention. With fifteen children Ma's task list never ended! And of course, Ma loved teaching her family. So, also during her free time, she would ask Agnes and I to practice singing *Whispering Hope.* I don't know how we got the words, probably from Mrs. Meara, the organist at church. Ma taught us to sing, Agnes as soprano and I as alto. We did a nice job and were asked to sing at family get-togethers.

Ma's sisters would try to keep in touch with her at least once a week. We had a telephone system whereby the operator would connect you via switchboard. Our phone number had three rings; there were 21 homes on the same line. Any one of them could pick up the phone and listen to our conversations. So Ma and her sisters would speak German so that anyone listening who was not able to speak German could not eavesdrop on the conversation. There was another family of sisters on the same line and their ring was five rings. If any of the older girls in our house wanted to know what was going on in the neighborhood, they would listen and then report that to Mom. That was the only way we would know who was sick, or who had died, or if there was any other problem that was taking place on a daily basis. If there was a real weather problem, the operator would ring 14 times, a general alarm to all the homes on the line to pick up the phone. Whenever there was a storm, a tornado, or a fire the general alarm would come through. There were times, however, when the winter storms would knock out the lines and then you were on your own. I remember Ma laughing because she could hear the receivers going up during her phone call, and then down when they found the language being spoken was in German!

Sickness was by far Ma's greatest concern and avoiding it worked her almost to death! With so many children there were usually many of us sick each time. Because the bunkhouses were outside, illness would bring us to the main house. That meant the dining room table was folded up against the wall and the beds were put in side by side. Ma would say: "boys, girls, just get into your slot!" The nurses that came were necessary as Ma still had to do the chores; which she did with her second son, John Joseph, the only child who was never sick. For some reason John never got *one* of the diseases that the rest of us did. Nettie Koskie and Ms. Harrison, the nurses, were well known and in our house they were "conductors" of a symphony of sick children.

They would say, "Take this. Do this. Stop it!" No matter how many children were sick and making trouble, they could always keep us settled. How they were paid I do not know.

Toots and Threasa, even though ill with the diseases, still had to cook the food because Ma had too much work outside. Those of us *supposedly* sick had a good time throwing pillows and causing trouble. When we had measles, Ms. Harrison handed each of us a cup of hot water, so your measles would break out. We took our time 'drinking' it and when she wasn't looking we spilled it on the floor! Of course it would dry out and nobody ever knew what we did. Those nurses, however, were disciplinarians and you did what they ordered you to do.

Ms. Harrison, One of the Nurses

Ma had many tough years trying to battle diseases. After Annie died, the family did fair for several years. Then Spuds got Scarlet Fever. Shortly after that we all got Whooping Cough and were quarantined for weeks! We would just about get over one disease when we would get another. Measles, then Mumps! When quarantined, a big red sign was placed on the house announcing, **"ABSOLUTELY NO VISITORS, CONTAGIOUS DISEASE!"** That meant that Pa had to sleep in town, Johnnie stayed in the bunkhouse, and poor Ma had to be in a room by herself where none of us were allowed to go. She came out, however, and took care of us with the help of the nurses, and would take Johnnie's food out to him. Pa would bring groceries out and leave them at the door.

The first of a slew of diseases started in early September

1927 when Spuds got Scarlet Fever. I got it as well, but it went away quickly. Spuds was very ill, the doctor thought he might not live. It was weeks before he was better. After that we went from one disease to another and were kept home seven months out of the nine-month school year! The teacher at school would drop off the school lessons once a week, and pick up the previous week's assignments. The nurses had to supervise the exams the teacher would leave so we couldn't cheat.

Verneda was in the eighth grade that year, and took her final exam winning the highest grade in the county! She still had to go back another year, as Pa made her give up her scholarship and go back to the eighth grade twice.

Well, the day we were getting out of quarantine, they had to fumigate the house and it would take 10 hours. That meant we all had to go to the garage early in the morning and stay there all day. Ma packed up sandwiches and milk for us to eat. Ma also took her canary, a bird she loved, out to the garage even though it was quite chilly, about 40 degrees. Well, every kid in the family was higher than a kite to think we were finally free to get out of that house! Frankie and Freddie were so thrilled they started horsing around. Freddie tripped Frankie and he fell and broke his leg!

I still remember Ma today, she leaned back against an old broken down truck, the tears came down her cheek and she cried, "Oh, my God, how much can I take!?" That was the only time I ever saw Mom doubt herself.

Johnnie had to take Frankie to the hospital where he stayed for four weeks. Ma would always say, "The Lord never promised that life would be easy!" This was her rule of life as long as she lived.

One of the things I remember about Mom was that she and my sisters Toots and Threasa all had long dark hair. They would roll it up in a bun and fasten it to the back of the head with beautiful hairpins. One day a couple arrived at the house, a man and woman. They told them there was real need of hair to be sold to people. They asked them if they would consider having their hair cut, and they would buy the hair and would make for them free of charge a braided watchband with a watch. At first Mom did not want to do that, then one of the girls thought it was a good idea, so they all allowed this couple to cut their hair.

John Joseph (Johnnie)

I don't know what they paid them for it, but I do know that when Pa came home, he really flipped! He loved Ma's hair and now it was gone. He threatened to shave off his mustache because of that. But Ma said, "Don't be foolish!" So he never did cut it off. I remember the watches as being very beautiful. Ma never regretted cutting off her hair because then it was easier for her to care for. Her watch was kept in the top drawer of her bedroom bureau because she could not wear it through her daily chores. I wonder what a cow would have thought being milked with a timer!

About this time as well, medicine was hard to come by. One traveling salesman, Mr. Watkins, had a wagon that came down the road with a big wooden sign that read: *WATKINS MEDICINE*. He would pull into the driveway and come to the house. Ma made us kids stay in the house because she was always concerned about strangers. Mr. Watkins was a good man, though, and became our family's supplier of medicine including Vick's

Vapor Rub, Cod Liver Oil and Cough Syrup. We kids hated him coming because that meant we had to take cod liver oil everyday! It was supposed to make us strong and keep us well. Well, we all kept well away from it if we could.

Toots, Johnnie and Threasa

The Fuller Brush Man was another traveling salesman that knew how many brooms and mops were needed. All the bunkhouses, the milk house, the barn and chicken houses had to be swept clean on a daily basis by the crew of us kids, so you know he found a goldmine on the Butch Schmid farm.

When people came down the road, Ma was always concerned that they might be gypsies. Gypsies would pull up into the driveway and there would be five or six of them. One of them would come to the door asking for food. The others would sneak out to the chicken house and steal chickens by twisting their heads off! If any of the boys were around, Ma would yell at them to get to the chicken house. If the gypsies got caught, they would drop the chickens and hop back in their wagon. This usually was a weekly event, because times were so tough.

The Family (Except for Annie Catherine) in 1932

As the years went on, Ma got a growth on her neck that was as big as a goose egg. Dr. Henneberger, on one of his trips to the house noticed it and took her in to have it removed. It turned out to be a big goiter that when removed left an incision around the bottom of her neck about six inches long! Well later it turned out that the older girls, Toots, Threasa, and Verneda, all got goiters and had to have them removed. The doctor tested the water in the house and discovered that we needed iodine in the water and that we needed to use iodized salt. That went on for years.

Ma made sure that everyone of us kept ourselves clean, that we hung up our clothes, did our tasks as assigned and that we had a good time playing with each other when time permitted. When the older kids decided it was time to move on, around

1935-1937, my younger brothers Charlie, Andy and Louie were left with Mom to take care of the farm.

When children moved away, grandchildren came on the scene. Mom was always there to love them. She made a point with the parents that she would be there in emergencies to take care of them.

"But don't ask me to take care of them for you to go out!"

She spent her extra time making quilts from materials left over from her lifetime of providing clothes for the family. She made a quilt for every grandchild she had. She had always quilted her own quilts in the girl's bunkhouse. Her sisters would come on occasion to see her and they would all quilt together. The State of Kansas named my mother 'Quilter of the Year.' She made a quilt of the map of the United States and embroidered the state capitol in each block. It was placed on display at the Capital Building in Topeka, Kansas. Her quilt making ended when she was taken to the Good Samaritan home.

She had a Calumet Baking Powder can that had a plastic lid on it. She cut a hole in the lid and would deposit dimes that were given to her. At Christmas time she would count the dimes and divide them evenly for each grandchild. They might receive one each, two each, and the most I remember was one good year of five for each grandchild. These were to be saved by us (the parents) until each grandchild moved on from the family home. What each family did, I do not know.

A very hard time for her was what happened with my brother Frankie. He had come home from the war to find that his wife, Millie, had left Chicago with his daughter Joan, evidently to go back home to Trenton, Nebraska! She had found another man and divorced Frankie to marry him, all without his knowledge (while he fought the war). Frankie became an alcoholic, left home and never married again. Eventually a recluse, he returned home only when he needed money. One time, my brother Charlie told him he could come home but if he ever got drunk, he'd have to leave for good. Mom and Charlie went to milk one day, and when they came in to eat supper, Frankie was not around. On the kitchen cabinet top was her Calumet Baking Powder can, empty! He had found it, took all her dimes and had gone off to town to buy liquor. He heeded Charlie's warning and never came back home (until many years later).

After I left home, went off to college and married, Mom wrote me a letter, saying that it was the loneliest year of her life, as it was the first time in 41 years she never had to get a kid off to school.

My brother Joe asked her one time "Mom, what do you feel was the worst time in your life?"

Her answer, "The time I never left the farm for 17 years because I had too many babies!" Mom was always there taking care of the family, raising a garden, raising chickens to sell, handling all of life's problems.

She had a little dog, named Trixie. She loved that little dog dearly. When they took her to the rest home to live, the little dog lay outside the kitchen door and died. She never got over the fact that she had not taken it with her.

Ma had another pet, a little pig that followed her around like a dog. Pa was always joking with her about how much money he could get for that pig up at the shop. Pa was informed by Mom: that was *her* pig and he was not going to sell it. Well, one day Pa was at the sale barn and he saw Ma's pig being sold! When he went home, he accused Ma of "snookering him" by selling her pig without his knowledge. She, on the other hand, was quite upset to learn that someone had stolen her tame pig and sold it. Now her friend was gone and so was any cash value perceived by Pa. The mystery of the pig remains unsolved to this very day.

Ma also had a love for kittens; of course cats were a necessary part of a farm, as they would take care of rats and mice. She had a favorite cat, Tom, who was black and white spotted and weighed well over 30 pounds. He was always at the milk house waiting for a drink. He and the other thirty or so cats and their kittens lived in the hayloft of the barn.

During these later years at home, she still milked cows, took care of the boys and then when Johnnie and Threasa left the North Place, Charlie moved there with Verneda. Together they took care of the north farm as brother and sister until Verneda married. Then Charlie met Rita, married and started a family in the North Place. Louie was drafted into the army and had to leave home. He was stationed in Louisiana where he met Elaine Johnson, and they were married on December 24, 1945. He came back to Kansas with his new wife, but had a hard time finding a good job. They lived with Ma until Aunt Cora solved their problem by giving him a job. Aunt Cora had an empty house and asked Louie to come help with the farming. Andy was left to take care of Mom and the farm all through the war. He married Mary Jackson, and they turned the milk house into a kitchen and living area. They put in a stove, table and chairs. They loved sitting at that table and listening to the radio.

The North Place

Andy went over to the main house every morning to have coffee with Mom. Andy and Mary had three boys and a girl while living there, using the old boys' bunkhouse as their bedroom. Then Mom fell on the cesspool and broke her hip! She was taken to Atwood Hospital. Dr. Henneberger told the family she would not be able to return home, so she was put into the Good Samaritan Home, which was newly built in Atwood. This was in 1972. The entire family received a notice from Attorney Forest Brown saying the farm, all 360 acres, had to be sold! Pa had died intestate (without a will), and Ma's half of the property had a mortgage on it, owed to Forest Brown. She had borrowed money to help save the farm after Pa's death. There were 17 relatives listed for the remainder of the estate. The attorney stated that after

Ma's half paid him what was due him, there would not be enough money to take care of her in the nursing home. He then wrote each child asking that they sacrifice their share. The family had to wait for guardianship to be named for Johnnie's remaining three grandchildren. Once that took place, each member of the family signed off their share. Charlie then purchased the North Place, and Andy and Mary decided to move on with their life and moved to Colby. Then the home place was sold, for a pittance.

Truth to tell, neither Andrew nor Charlie received any extra money for having taken care of Ma and the farm for so many years. They sacrificed any return.

My brother Jim had taken charge of Mom's finances for several years. Then one day he called Verneda and told her he needed to see her. When they met, he told Verneda he was diagnosed with a serious heart condition. He told her that someone needed to take over the account. So he assigned Verneda to do it. He informed her that Ma's money was running out and she would have to apply for Welfare. That was one thing my mother always worried about. She wanted to take care of herself. The family was very concerned that the funds would be depleted in January of 1976. Well, as predicted by his diagnosis, James Paul Schmid (Jim) died of a heart attack, on September 27, 1975. Mom was never told of Jim's passing as she had already buried her husband and five children along with in-laws and grand children. She went to her eternity on January 25, 1976, six days before she was to go on welfare. We always believed the Lord heard her prayers of not having to go on welfare. Thank goodness no one ever told her that this was a possibility.

When I went off to college, she was so happy. Then I decided to get married 12 hours short of a college degree!

When I told her I was getting married, she said "Oh, and you were going to be my one kid that got a college degree."

My answer was, "Ma, don't worry, I'm just substituting for a while. I'm getting a degree: an M-R-S! And when I get to Boston, I will finish and get my real college degree."

Money problems in our early marriage years did not allow me to finish college. Have I ever regretted not finishing? The answer would have to be No. I never really needed a degree. One might now be convinced of Pa's old adage: *You can be what you want to be without that stuff!* My reward came 60 years later in life, when my daughter-in-law, Patty, tried hard to get me an honorary degree from the University of Kansas. Since the University had a rule not to give honorary degrees, they named me "A Jayhawker" with honors. It was my 60th wedding anniversary gift.

I remember as a young girl my sister Toots coming home crying and told Mom, "Can you believe I'm pregnant again?"

Mom said to her, "Stop those tears, there's time to cry when you have seven under five!" My mother saw raising seven children all under five years old as one of her greatest personal achievements. Toots had a tough life as it will be revealed as my story continues.

When Louie went off to war, Elaine and her children had no place to go. So Verneda took them into her home. Eva was the oldest child and had become very good friends with Charlie's children. Charlie and Rita lived in the North Place. Eva had spent time with them and one day Rita washed her hair with 'Rinse Away.'

Eva came over to see Grandma and Grandma said, "Eva, honey, let me comb your hair."

She started crying and said, "Oh Grammy, don't touch, my head is so sore!"

Grammy said, "Honey, come here. Let me see it."

She put her hand on Eva's head and as she did, a huge five-inch bunch of hair came off her head! Mom (Grammy) had Charlie take her to Doctor Henneberger and he told them he didn't know what was happening. He said to get her to a doctor in Hays immediately.

"She has some kind of an infection and it will get into her brain!"

When they got to Hays, Kansas, one-hundred and fifty miles east, they found that when Rita had washed her hair with 'Rinse-Away,' she failed to rinse it out. It burned through into her skull! They used some kind of medication, but it took many years for it to heal and to bring her head back to normal. She had to be taken back several times.

They tried to bring a suit against 'Rinse-Away' but they lost because the bottle specifically said: "Rinse-Away must be washed out." Eva lost all her hair and looked like a boy and the kids in school all laughed at her, and made fun of her. As the years rolled by most of her hair returned, but I do believe she still has a bald spot about two or three inches in diameter, now covered over by her good hair. Eva was my mother's only namesake, and my mother loved her dearly. Thank goodness for Grandma. If she had not discovered what was wrong with Eva's hair, it could have taken her life!

Frankie, who was dearly loved by my mother, never really was able to resume a normal life after returning from the war to find he had lost his family. No one could ever say he did not love Ma, because wherever he was he would send her a card; every birthday, every Christmas, and every Mother's Day. But he would always appeal to her for money. Understand Ma had very little. She used to save quarters, nickels and any change she could live without and had a very meager bank account. But, when Frankie got in touch, she would sell eggs and anything she could to help him out. I was still home at the time when a call came from a hospital in Oklahoma saying that Frankie was in need of an operation and they could not operate without having a $150 deposit for the surgery. Well, Ma counted all her money, asked Jim to give her some and in the end telegrammed the $150 they said they needed. Charlie, who was Mom's standby, questioned how she knew it was a real call.

She said, "Well, she told me she was a nurse calling from the hospital. So I knew it was real."

Charlie just had a feeling this was not true. So he got in his car and drove all night down to Oklahoma City to the hospital. He got there the next afternoon and went in and asked to see Frank Schmid.

The desk clerk said, "Gee, we don't have a Frank Schmid here!"

Charlie told them what had happened, and together they called another hospital. No Frank Schmid. Then he asked if there was a nurse there by the name of Mabel.

The clerk said, "Oh, she used to work here, but is not here anymore."

He called the telegraph station and they informed him that a Frank Schmid had picked up the money! Charlie tried everything to find out where he was, but all efforts failed.

Now about three weeks later, the hospital called and the girl at the desk said, "The Oklahoma paper had a big article on Frank Schmidt! Do you want to have it?"

"Of course," Mom said; now the TRUTH!

It turned out that he never needed the operation and was never even in the hospital! Mabel was his girlfriend and they went to a hotel to live it up with the money. They had a room on the third floor. They had a terrible fight and Frankie jumped out the window and got caught between the two buildings, which were less than 10 inches apart! Someone on the street heard him screaming, they called the fire department and it took them thirty minutes to get him out. The newspaper article shown below reports he was taken to Mercy Hospital, suffering from a fractured leg and other undetermined injuries. The newspaper article was in Ma's file for years. It was found by her great granddaughter, Wendi. She researched the files in Oklahoma City and found the release in "The Oklahoman." As you read on, the article reveals the story.

MAN WEDGED BETWEEN TWO WALLS IN DROP

"A fire department rescue squad worked for 30 minutes late Wednesday to dislodge Frank Schmidt, 43, packing house employee, who slipped from the third floor window of a downtown hotel into an area-way less than 10 inches wide between two buildings. Schmidt, who told police his home is in Atwood, Kan., plunged from the window and slid between the two buildings to the ground. He was taken to Mercy Hospital suffering from a fractured right leg and other undetermined injuries.

Although the victim told an incoherent story as to how he got outside the window of his room at 221 ½ N. Broadway, a companion who identified herself as Mabel Marie Fuller, 43, said he just "stepped off the window sill and disappeared!"

Schmidt was so tightly wedged between the two brick structures that firemen under the direction of John Lynn, assistant chief, had difficulty placing a dangling rope around his body in order to lift him to safety. After the victim was finally lifted to the second floor with the rope he was pulled inside another open window by police."

The newspaper misspelled Frank's last name (often done by anyone spelling the family name).

Another tragic event in Mom's life was when a telegram was received one day in the town of Atwood. It was sent to every town in the area that started with an A. It read: "Woman believed to be a resident of your town has been burned severely in an apartment house fire. We need to locate her family immediately. Her name is Threasa Louise Schmid. If her family is there, please call Detroit Receiving Hospital immediately."

The man working at the depot when the telegram came in recognized Threasa's name; he had gone to grade school with her. He immediately called her older brother Jim and asked him if she was in Detroit. Jim took the call, then called the hospital.

"She has third degree burns, she probably will not survive!"

At this time I had already married and had moved to Massachusetts. Jim knew that I was the only family member who had ever ridden on a train, and would know what to do in a big city.

Threasa on the Farm

He called me before he called Mom and told me, "You have no choice, you have to go! I cannot send Ma and Charlie there alone."

Here I was in Boston with twin babies, 30 months old with no one to take care of them. My husband was only making $50 a week at the time and we had no money. And I was three months pregnant and having a tough time with the pregnancy! I was always vomiting, and I didn't want Mom to know it. The Lord came to our rescue as my very best friend in Boston, who owned *The Haley* restaurant, cared enough for me to loan me money. I called Margaret Haley and asked her if she could loan me $100 so I could fly to Detroit.

She said, "Of course you can, and I will take care of your babies while you are gone."

Margaret and Al were my surrogate family away from home. This was a friendship very few people have ever had. We loved each other dearly. So on Sunday night December 17, 1951, around 8:00 PM I returned the call to Jim. I told him I would get the next plane out to Detroit, which was 7:00 AM on the 18th. He told me he would get Ma and Charlie to the train in McCook, Nebraska and they would arrive that afternoon as well.

That morning the sun was shining when I left Boston, but the skies turned into blizzard in the Midwest. The worst they had in years! I had a terrible time getting to Detroit; I was delayed in Columbus, Ohio, put on an Eastern Air Lines plane with only the pilot and steward aboard! All other flights had been cancelled.

Well, first thing there was a big noise and I yelled, "What's that?!"

The steward replied, "Don' t worry. One of the engines just froze out. But we still have three more."

It wasn't five minutes later when we heard another wicked noise, and again I screamed.

"Well, dear that was the heating unit freezing up, but we will be on land in about one minute so you won't freeze."

Thank God! We landed and I was absolutely scared to death. We landed about 1:30 PM. The train that Ma and Charlie were on was due in at 4:00 PM. When we finally landed, I had no idea the airport was 60 miles out of Detroit! I saw a taxi there and ran over lugging my suitcase and begged him to take me to

Detroit.

He almost flipped; "Lady, in this blizzard!?!"

I begged him because I had to get to the train station on account of my mother and brother and of course, my sister who was dying.

Bulled, but cooperative, he said, "Okay, but that's going to take some doing."

Well, the next thing I noticed was the meter was showing the cost and it was going up!

It was at $6 when I said, "Hey, how much is this going to cost me?"

He said, $26 and I nearly croaked!

Quickly I replied, "But I can't give you $26. That is all I have and I must have money to go to the hospital and to take a train to her apartment."

Well, I can't use the words here that he used but they were hot and heavy, but excusable. I had no conception that I would have to meet such a charge.

After he calmed down, he said, "Well I can't dump you here 30 miles in the middle of a snow drift. The next time you come here, don't look for charity!"

Whew! I could only give him $16 so that left me with $10. Well it took three hours. When we arrived at the train station it was 5:00 PM: only one hour late. I breathed a sigh of relief!

I ran into the train station worrying that my mother and brother couldn't find me because I was an hour late. Well, there was a big sign: *Trains from the Midwest are snowbound on the tracks in Nebraska, arrival date unknown.* Well, they didn't arrive until a day and a half later!

It was too late for me and too late for them, as my sister had died the morning before. Because I left home early on December 18th, I had not received the call that evening that Threasa had passed away the day before. Instead of waiting for Ma at the train station I went immediately to the hospital.

They told me "You are too late, she passed away yesterday morning at 9:00 AM and her body has been moved to a morgue down on Twenty Second and Main."

That meant I had to go identify her body.

There are no words to describe that experience, but I did it. It was something I would not allow my mother to do. After identifying her body, I needed to get a certificate from the priest who had given her the last Sacraments so she could be buried at the Sacred Heart Church in Atwood. I had to walk eight blocks to the parish house in that snow and cold, and pregnant, but I did. I asked for the priest and told him why I was there.

He said to me, "I didn't anoint your sister. What was your sister's name?"

"Threasa Schmid" was my answer, and he was horrified!

He replied, "She was your sister?"

"Yes."

His answer: "Dear Lord forgive me, I thought she was a black woman, she was burned that badly!"

There were no words of comfort for me, and tears rolled and I said, "Yes, I just identified her body."

He was a wonderful source of comfort for Ma and Charlie during those final hours and days in Detroit. Not one of us ever forgot his kindnesses and concern. He said a last prayer for her at the funeral home where we held a wake for her.

Because of the blizzard we were delayed in Detroit: no trains were moving. Too, we had to clean out her apartment. It was so burned it was unbelievable! It was a supposedly fireproof building, built with cement walls. The heat was so intense it melted the metal bed on which she had been lying! Even the medicine cabinet in the bathroom a good 10 feet away melted and ran down the wall. My mother could not afford an autopsy, so it was assumed that an electric light cord had started the fire. The cord ran under her bed on which she had a plastic bed spread. She had attempted to get out, but got to her front door and collapsed! Her hair was burned off as well as her right arm.

She had come home from work at 4:30 AM and asked the landlady to call her at 7:00 AM because she had promised to relieve one of the nurses at the hospital so she could go to her sister's wedding.

"I'm so tired, I'm afraid I won't hear the alarm clock."

She went on up stairs to bed.

Well, the lady across the hall arose at 5:00 AM, because she was going to work and opened her door to look down the hall through the window to see what the weather was like. Instead, when she opened her door, she heard my sister moaning! This was only a half hour after she was seen down stairs.

The lady called the landlady, "Get the fire department, Smitty's apartment is on fire!"

The landlady screamed, "Oh, my God, she was just here!"

The fire department was only across the street and they arrived at 5:10 but it was too late, she was alive but unconscious.

--

That same lady told us that Threasa was engaged to be married. We hoped her fiancé would come to the wake; if he did, he did not make himself known. Consequently we never knew whom she was going to marry. The lady told us Threasa had been given an engagement diamond, which was too big. It was taken to a jeweler in the Jeweler's Building, but she did not know the name of the jeweler. My brother Charlie and I decided we should go to the building to see if we could find the ring. Well, there were 15 floors in that building! So Charlie did the left side of the hall, and I did the right side. We walked all day, starting at 10:00 AM and now it was 4:00 PM. I finally suggested we do the last floor because they are probably closing at 5:00, so down the hall we went.

Believe it or not, the last Jeweler on my side of the hall said "Oh, Threasa," when I walked in, "I wondered when you were coming to pick up your ring!"

I looked at him and replied, "You know what, I am not Threasa. She was burned to death. I am her sister."

He was appalled and at the same time unbelieving.

I asked him the price of the repair, and he replied, "Let me give it to you as a gift in her memory."

Well, you already know I had very little money. I had gotten $10 from my mother, and was waiting for my father-in-law to telegraph me more. The ring repair was a gift never forgotten. Thank goodness, Dad Hogan sent me $200. The ring by the way, turned out to be a diamond-enclosed watch. I had never seen a watch like that before, and have never seen another like it since.

Ma said, "Laura, give it to your daughter, Margie. Because

if I remember right, Threasa was her Godmother."

I complied with Ma's wishes.

The biggest job was cleaning up the apartment. The smoke smell made me so sick and I kept vomiting, but quietly so Mom wouldn't know. I really was so sick that I said to Mom, "Why don't you go down stairs and talk with the landlady so she knows what we are doing." After Ma left I quickly called the landlady and told her my plight. She said "Don't you worry, I will keep her busy." She took Ma into her apartment and gave her food, and then suggested, "Why don't you take a nap, you have some long days ahead of you."

Ma napped and Charlie and I were able to get the Salvation Army in to take the furniture that was usable. The fire department came as well and offered their assistance taking all the burned items, even sweeping up the floors. The lady across the hall said she would mail anything to our homes that we wished to keep. The good deeds of the landlady went on, as she gave us two rooms to stay in for free until we left for home. Know that the people in Detroit will never be forgotten, even though they only knew Threasa as "Smitty" and knew she came from Kansas in a town beginning with an *A*. They never knew the town's full name, that's why that telegram was sent as it was. As you remember that repeated the reason why Pa ended up going to the Midwest; looking for an *A* town, because he never knew the full name of the town where his cousin lived. Another miracle in our lives.

After a short wake for her in Detroit, her casket was put on the train with us to go back to Atwood. In those days a person had to sit with the corpse at all times, so Charlie and I took turns. The train ride would be two days to return to Atwood. We arrived home at 7:00 AM on December 24. It was Monday, the day before Christmas. Her Mass was scheduled at 10:00 AM. Mom was tired and heart-broken, and beside herself when Threasa could not be buried because of the snow. The undertaker stored her in the home until the roads re-opened, three to four months later. Threasa Louise Schmid died on December 17, 1951 and was laid in peace beside my sister Annie and Pa. She was 40 years old when she died. She is buried way out in the country, where the skies are blue and the winds blow hard.

The Family After Threasa's Funeral
--

I finally told Mom about my expected baby on the day I left her in Atwood. I told her it was scheduled to arrive next August.

She replied, "You know, I thought your eyes showed you were pregnant! But you never said anything."

I told her, "Ma, you didn't need any more worries."

I think the timely announcement gave her new hope of finding joy again.

I returned home two days after the funeral and have always remembered my very dear friends the Haleys for not only taking care of my infant twins during the Christmas holidays, but for waiting quite a while for me to pay them back!

Well, Threasa's death was only the beginning. About this time Jim found Frankie by calling the Topeka and Santa Fe Railroad where Frankie was reportedly working.

Frankie said, "Yes, I want to come home. But I have no money."

Jim telegraphed him $200 to come home, but he never arrived. Later incidents revealed that he was living in the Bowery in

New York City and had used the money for other things (no one had any doubts about how it was used). Mom could not believe he didn't come home. She was heartbroken. In a picture taken of all her boys at her funeral, Frankie is missing. Now, one day, I got another call from Jim. Bellevue Hospital called from New York saying Frankie was in need of brain surgery. But he has no money.

Jim called me immediately: "Go to New York and see if this is true."

So my husband Dan and I took a plane and went to the hospital in New York, and with much to-do we located Frankie in a ward with 22 other indigents. He did not recognize me.

He told me, "I do not have a sister Laura, I have a sister Verneda!"

The hospital said he had a brain tumor that must be removed. Afterward he would have to be cared for in assisted living. We could only stay until the operation was completed, because once again our friends, the Haleys, had our children. Once the surgery was completed, we left to go home.

After the operation they kept him for three weeks. The hospital called and told Ma he needed to be taken back home, as he could not be left alone. The hospital would arrange to put him on the train with an accompanying nurse. Who paid for that I don't know. It was probably Jim as he was the only one in Kansas that ever had much money. Jim and Agnes got Frankie into the Good Samaritan Home, where Mom was staying.

Coming back home to Atwood, Frankie was able to see his daughter Joan. Joan and her mother, Millie, had moved to Atwood sometime before. Agnes worked at the home and was always there for Ma and Frankie. I believe somehow, Jim and Agnes were able to get some funding from the railroad to pay for his stay.

He was cared for there for six years. Frank George Schmid went on to eternity on May 26, 1970. He was 56 years old. During his stay, I worked with the railroad and was able to get them to give $300 to help pay for the funeral. He was laid to rest beside Annie on the prairie Graveyard at St. Johns.

The kids at home would take Ma out for Sunday dinner, but after an hour or so she would ask to go home. Dan and I, with kids in tow would go back to Kansas to visit her. The last time I saw my Mother, we went to the home to see her and the nurse said she was in her room. When we got to the room, it was empty.

We went back to the desk and she said, "Oh, I'm sorry the nurse put her in the recreation room."

I went into that room and there was a lady there in the wheel chair, but it didn't look like my mother.

Again, I went back to the desk, and she said, "Oh, yes! That's Eva Schmid in there."

She accompanied us back to the recreation room. Well it was my mother, but she had lost a lot of weight, had gotten very gray, and was really not able to communicate.
I went up to her and hugged her, telling her who I was.

She said, "I don't know you."

My husband Dan went up to her and shook her hands and said, "Ma, this is Dan."

She replied, "Oh! I know because I've always loved your big soft hands, how are you?"

We stayed in Kansas for weeks, visiting her everyday. She never recognized me, but would immediately talk to Dan. That was a memory in her mind from the day she met Dan for the first time.

Her comment was, "Oh, my goodness, where did you get such beautiful soft hands?"

Well of course, he was not a farmer and never had to pitch hay!

After relating this instance to my sister, Toots, she started to cry and said, "You don't need to be sad, I have visited her nearly every day since she was put there, and she always called me Threasa! You feel bad!? How do you think I feel?!"

I reassured her that we could not feel bad, because Ma was actually mourning the loss of her children, perhaps she was looking forward to meeting them in heaven. I can honestly say, my Mother cried only when things went really bad. Losing her children was almost unbearable, and whenever that happened she did cry. But she never lost her temper. When things got tough, instead of crying she would hum *The Old Rugged Cross*, a song often heard in the Midwest. That's when we knew something was *really* wrong!

The night she passed away, the nurses at the Center came to the desk and said, "Who is that singing, it's so beautiful!"

They went down the hall, it was my mother and she sang *The Old Rugged Cross*, the whole song. They clapped for her and then she died. Mom knew every verse that was written by George Bennard from Albion, Michigan. The verses reflect her life as you read them here:

"On a hill far away stood an old rugged cross,
The emblem of suff'ring and shame;
And I love that old cross where the dearest and best
For a world of lost sinners was slain.
So, I'll cherish the old rugged cross,
Till my trophies at last I lay down;
I will cling to the old rugged cross,
And exchange it some day for a crown.
Oh, that old rugged cross, so despised by the world,
Has a wondrous attraction for me;
For the dear Lamb of God left his glory above
To bear it to dark Calvary.
In that old rugged cross, stained with blood so divine,
A wondrous beauty I see,
For 'twas on that old cross Jesus suffered and died,
To pardon and sanctify me.
To the old rugged cross I will ever be true;
Its shame and reproach gladly bear;
Then He'll call me some day to my home far away,
Where His glory forever I'll share."

I was alone when I flew back home to Kansas for my mother's funeral. My children were grown and had started lives of their own. My visit would be short, as I was working for a tough boss doing his very large mailings. He was out of town when the call came that Mom had died. I had another helper and the two of us worked until 3:00 in the morning so the 3,000 letters would be placed in the mail. At 8:00 that morning, I was taken to the airport and my assistant covered the office that day. I arrived at my old home on Saturday, my mother was buried on Monday and I took the plane back on Tuesday morning, expecting to arrive home that evening by 8:00 PM.

An Early Picture of Ma

At Ma's funeral, her granddaughter, Cathy Holste sang in her memory. There were 177 immediate family members who watched the dirt being tossed into the grave, each participating with a tiny shovel tossing in a small amount of dirt. If you were able to talk or hear any of my brothers or sisters, they would always remember how hard Ma worked, how much she cared, how she survived the hard times, and how she was a good provider for the family.

One of the nicest things that happened after Ma's passing was that Marlin Schandler Funeral Home requested the Bates Casket Company to plant a tree in the front yard of the Sacred Heart Church in Atwood in memory of Mom. When I went home for another family member's funeral, we were able to see the tree. It was a large, healthy oak tree symbolizing her commitment in life.

Leaving home following my mother's burial was indeed a very difficult point in my life, as my brothers and sisters had all moved on from the prairie farm in Atwood. They were so far separated that for me to return to Kansas again would indeed be a difficult journey. There were a few sisters left, a few nieces and nephews, but it was no longer the prairie as I remember it! The new owners of the farm destroyed all the old buildings including the house. Even the five-foot water tank was gone. They replaced the house with a dugout and later added to the top. So my home now, was not among the living! I left on Tuesday morning, expecting to arrive home that evening.

Does everything happen the way you want it to? No, it doesn't. The sun was shining in Denver, a beautiful January day. I had three bags of memories my sisters had saved for me and they were loaded on the plane with me. The plane took off as scheduled and I was to land in New York late that afternoon to pick up another plane to Boston. I would arrive in Boston at 8:00 PM, Tuesday night; my husband Dan was to meet me at the airport. We were only in the air about two hours when the pilot announced that there were heavy winds in New York and we would need to fly around St. Louis for a few hours. Resuming the flight, he again announced we would not arrive on time at LaGuardia Airport. Then the stewardess came up to me and tapped me on the shoulder and asked that I come to the back of the plane. I thought something had happened at home, so I followed her with trepidation.

She took me in the back room and asked me, "How do you react in times of crisis?"

"What, do you mean?" was my reply.

"Well dear, you are seated at the exit door and we have a problem which will require a very steady hand to assist us." She continued, "Our landing gear is not working and the reason we have stayed in the air is that we had to burn off extra gasoline. What we need from you is to open the exit door when the Pilot yells, *HIT IT*. You will open the door and jump immediately onto the emergency tarmac. Can you do that?"

Dear Lord! I thought, *You bet your boots I can do that*!

I responded quickly, "You bet, I will be out quicker than you can imagine. But where will I land?"

"Mam, when the door opens the slide will immediately blow up and out. Just jump on it as fast as you can, because all the other people on this plane need to follow you. If you don't want to do that, tell me now."

My answer was again firm: "Are you crazy? I'll be out of

here like you wouldn't believe!"

"Okay." the stewardess said. "Know that we are with you all the way!"

Then the stewardess showed me how to move the door handles, had me practice, took my hand and hugged me and said, "We are all counting on you!"

"Please show no emotion as you return to your seat. You will hear the directions from the pilot. Good luck and thank you!"

In no more than five minutes, the pilot announced, "Ladies and Gentlemen, I'm sorry but you must listen carefully and follow my instructions. Unfortunately, our landing gear is not working and it will be necessary for us to make a belly landing at LaGuardia. All the emergency equipment and personnel will be there, so please do not panic. You must now bend down, put your head between your knees, and stay that way until you hear another instruction. The attendants will now place the children on the floor with pillows and they will be fine. When I call *hit it*, the people at the exit doors will open them immediately and jump onto the tarmac. Please wait in your seats until the attendant pats you on the shoulder. The children will be the first to be removed. Yes, it will be bumpy, but God willing all will go well."

Well! People started screaming, "Oh, my God."

Hardly had the words gotten out of their mouths, when we landed. *Holy Toledo*, bump, bump, bump the plane went as it belly-landed on the tarmac!

Then the pilot yelled, "Hit it!"

I did it! I opened the door and out went the ramp. Out I went along with all the other passengers! *Glory Hallelujah!* We all got off safely at 1:00 in the morning. We were greeted by the attendants watching the gate with a glass of straight whiskey and asked to sit down for a moment to relax. That was a bumpy ride down, with no tragic results and we were all screaming: "Thank God!"

They took us inside the airport to the waiting room where we waited for any announcement to tell us where to go from there. Instead, they announced that due to inclement weather, there would only be two more planes going off to Boston that night. They offered everyone a room at the hotel and breakfast so they could take morning flights. That would not work for me, as I knew my boss would have a fit. I had to try to make one of those planes! Well, there were six of us who needed to return home and here I was trying to lug three suitcases.

There were five guys there and they saw how I was struggling so they introduced themselves and helped me get down to the United Air Lines terminal for the next scheduled flight. We sat on that plane without moving for two hours.

Then the announcement came, "We cannot leave, but Trans American has a flight they believe may take off at 5:00 AM. We will get those of you to that flight if you need to try that."

Again the six of us wrangled our way three blocks to catch that flight.

And again, "Sorry, we cannot take off."

Here I was with this LUGGAGE, only $5 in my pocketbook, had no food and I needed to call home. Well, down the drain went $4 on my call home, only to find out that my husband had gone to the airport to pick me up, fell on the curb, hurt his knee and was taken to Malden Hospital. Then the luggage did me in. I fell down the escalator with the stupid luggage! They rolled down the stairway like a hundred miles an hour. They were damaged, but I gave them a kick and took them over to the corner and just let them sit. I was so exhausted, but only a little bruised from the fall, but I was so disgusted. I sat down on the floor and shed a few tears. It would be a 24-hour delay until the next flight. I think I fell asleep, hungry and concerned. Finally at 7:30 that evening, Trans American announced they would be flying into Boston. I got on that flight, waited for the plane to be gassed up, and then it finally went into the skies.

Well, now comes another announcement, "Tail winds are too strong in Boston, we will have to land in Bristol, Connecticut until the winds subside."

Dear God, will I ever get home? We did land in Boston finally at 1:30 AM.

Well, the sun does come out, when I walked down to the luggage pick up, there was my oldest son waiting for me. I had talked with customer service during the day and they agreed to let my family know about the happenings. He told me my husband was still in the hospital but could come home on Wednesday. I was exhausted, but I could finally get something to eat and sleep safely in my own bed.

The sun didn't shine long however, as when I arrived at work on Wednesday, my boss had returned home and was absolutely livid because I had not contacted him about leaving to go home for my mother's funeral.

He said, "Young woman, you did not have a right to do that!"

My reply, "Well, Sir, I had done all the work staying here until 3:00 AM, going to the post office to get the mailing out before I left. Obviously, my mother's death is not accepted by you, so you can get someone else to do all your dirty work. You never have paid me for overtime; you think I have to jump every time you holler. Well, GET ANOTHER JUMPER!" I packed up my belongings and went out the door and never saw the man again.

Without me he was forced to close his office within a month. Who cared? Not me! That boss was so cheap he docked my pay for four days work for my trip home! He went on with his life, and I went on with mine. More productive, more rewarding, and more relaxing, because then I became my own boss.

My sincere regret is that I did not finish college for my mother and that miles and finances kept us apart. But in 2006, I found an answer to my dreams. St. Patrick's Church in Stoneham was in the process of complete renovation.

Working on the committee our pastor, Father Bill Schmidt, told the committee one evening: "We need to update the memorial list, I don't see the cross for over the altar on the list."

I immediately asked him "How much would the cross cost?"

"Probably $25,000."

I replied immediately: "Please don't give that to anyone else, I want it!"

Father Bill looked at me, knowing full well that my husband had retired in 1984 on a meager retirement, and said: "Laura, how do you think you can pay for it?"

The Cross Above The Altar, For Mom

I told him I was still working in real estate, so I would set aside half of each commission for the cross until it was paid for.

His reply: "Okay."

Now when I arrived home that evening I told my husband and he looked at me and said, "Laura, where do you think we can get that kind of money?"

I replied "I will earn it in real estate."

His reply, "If you say so, if you intend to work that long."

Well, the answer came the very next day, another miracle in our lives. The mailman delivered to our door a check from an insurance company for $23,000! The credit for that check goes to our daughter-in-law, Karen, who had addressed an insurance fraud many years ago. Dan had a policy with that company. She took the policy number and sent in a claim. It was so long ago; we had forgotten all about it, and out of a clear blue sky, when we needed it most, we received the check.

If we put the check into any of our accounts, we would have had to pay income tax on it. So without any hesitation the check went straight to the St. Patrick's Church building fund. How proud I am every time I enter the church. There over the altar is a magnificent cross representing how well my mother carried her cross. I am sure our dear Lord and Savior had no doubts about giving her peace in eternity. I know she has a special house up above.

A poem from my mother's day was saved in a scrapbook, and is reprinted below. It reminds me how hard she worked and how she loved to work hard. There was no date or author listed, only "Universal Press Syndicate."

Mama's Mama

Mama's mama, on a winter's day,
Milked the cows and fed them hay,
Slopped the hogs, saddled the mule,
And got the children off to school.
Did a washing, mopped the floors,
Washed the windows and did some chores.
Cooked a dish of home-dried fruit,
Pressed her husband's Sunday suit.
Swept the parlor, made the bed,
Baked a dozen loaves of bread.
Split some wood and lugged it in,
Enough to fill the kitchen bin.
Churned the butter, baked a cake,
Then exclaimed, "For goodness sake!
The calves have got out of the pen!"
Went out and chased them in again,
Gathered the eggs and locked the stable,
Returned to the house and set the table.
Cooked a supper that was delicious,
And afterward washed all the dishes.
Fed the cat, sprinkled the clothes,
Mended a basket full of hose.
Then opened the organ and began to play,
"When You Come to the End of a Perfect Day."

Chapter 4

A BRANCH OF A DIFFERENT KIND —
NOT THE LAST, NOT THE LEAST: I, LAURA MARGARET

Life began in my memories at the age of three years old. I loved visiting my Grandma Haller and sleeping on the floor at her house. She would let me help her make cookies and we baked all day, filling a five-gallon milk can. She'd put the lid on it and whenever any kid arrived, she would invite them over, open the lid, and always allow them to eat as much as they wanted.

Grandma and Grandpa Haller

Well, baking cookies with Grandma ended when she became ill. She died shortly after; all I remember about it was her body being put into a casket in their four-room house. They took her to St. John's Church and then to a graveyard. After the service all the relatives went back to eat with Grandpa Haller and Uncle Andrew. That's how it was back then, people died quickly and the family helped you get on with your life. Aunt Tillie and her kids were there and her five-year-old Bernard and I became real friends. So attracted we were to each other, Bernard and I, that we sat on the stairs to the house and decided right then and there that we would get married!

That promise went on for years and years. That's how life and love became known to me, not only coexisting with death, but coming out of it in rebirth with all the love and efforts of family there to bridge the gap.

Bernard became a farmer and I grew up wanting something else, however our affection for each other lasted until his life ended. He married someone else and so did I, so that was that.

From the time I was a little girl I remember hating my name, *Laura,* because there was no one who ever heard of that name and I was the only one who had it. Ma would try to comfort me by telling me that I was the only child in the family that Pa named and he named me for one of their very best friends, Laura Hauptman, who had died in an accident when she was 18 years old.

"So, child, you should really love your name!" my mother prodded.

As the years rolled by I never met another Laura until I married and moved to Boston. Now I have six very dear friends with the name Laura!

I used to have my own little place at home, where I could take my doll and play house. It was a spot behind the chicken house. I made a little playhouse and put my doll in it, then one day I asked Ma for a beautiful pillow top, red and white and all embroidered. It was one of her favorites, but she told me I could use it for my doll. One day I decided it needed to be washed so I washed it, but left it rolled up. Days later, I went out to play and that pillow top was all moldy!

I knew it was ruined, and told Toots because she liked me, but she really got upset and said, "You should know better! I have to give this to Mom and she will take care of you!"

Well Ma was upset, because she did not know how to save it. That ended my times in my playhouse. Many years later, Mom referred to that red pillow top that I ruined in one of our conversations. She finally told me it was a wedding gift for her from her Grandmother! Of course that only made me feel more guilty, but I could not change what happened, so be it.

When I was five years old I walked down the road to go to Liberty School with my brother Paul (named "Spuds" by his older brothers and sisters because his head was shaped like a large potato). He was called that all his life. Spuds and I used to figure out how we could be the ones to get a ride to school, if, by chance, somebody came by with a wagon or truck. We'd fall behind the rest of the kids so we could be the first ones to meet the truck. Well the older ones would yell at us to catch up with them. So, we always had a battle on our hands. But the occasional payoff, being able to wave at them as we sped by on the back of the truck, well that was worth all the daily verbal abuse we took! We would laugh and say how smart we were and that they were too stupid to know what we were doing.

There was a railroad track we had to cross to get to the schoolhouse: the *Santa Fe* that came out of Kansas City. In the afternoons, before the train would come down the tracks a group of black men would come rolling down on a cart known as a *Hand Car*. It had large handles that they had to move up and down while riding on the cart. The wheels would then roll down the tracks and their job was to make sure there was nothing to obstruct the train as it came down the tracks after them. Spuds and I would see them on our way home from school.

We were always scared of them because we thought they never washed! Then one day Pa explained to us that they were born that way. Well, Spuds and I would run down to the tracks when we heard them coming. We decided they might be hungry so we gave them some of our food that we didn't eat for lunch. We were never allowed to throw food away, so if we gave it to the black men, we would not have to eat it for supper. Well, we had these sardine sandwiches that we didn't like. We knew they would be coming down the tracks in two days, so we hid the sandwiches in a tin can and then when they came (two days later), we put them in a bag and walked right up to the black men and gave it to them. The next day, they were waiting for us. The spoiled sardines had made them sick and they started yelling at us. Spuds and I took off running like bats out of hell! Fortunately, they could not leave their cart, so they didn't catch us. Of course, we didn't try that again.

Then a year or so later, my next oldest sister Agnes and her friend Mabel found some red berries on the side of the road. We decided to pick them for the teacher, Ms. Fisher. She loved them and put them in a vase. Well, halfway through the school day, I broke out with a rash all over my body. She sent me home with Joe. They took me to the doctor who said I had Poison Oak! It got into my mouth, into my stomach and the doctor thought I would die from it! I was kept at the hospital in Atwood for three weeks before the doctor would let me go home. Agnes and Mabel only got a little bit and they could stay in school. Of course, Ms. Fisher got rid of the berries pretty fast. Now I stay away from berries of any kind or source.

Now about this time, Joe, Spuds, Charlie and I got to play awhile after school. Agnes was always going ahead of us to be with Mabel, so I hung back with the boys.

Pa had an old broken down *Oberlin Car* stacked behind the barn. We were forbidden to play back there, because snakes had nests there. There were spiders, and the old car was rusty and a real wreck. But we could sneak there from the cornfield without anybody seeing us. We would get into that wreck and pretend we were driving. That was fun. One day, I climbed over the doors because I was tired and wanted to go up to the house. I caught my shoe on the side of the car, fell to the ground and broke my collarbone. Joe and Spuds told Ma I fell over a stock of corn in the field coming home. They knew we were in for a talking-to from Pa if they ever found out where we really were.

Another year or so later, on a Sunday, the boys were always picking on me and decided I had to play *Tug of War* with them. This meant they were the tuggers and I was the rope! Well, they were tugging at me so hard they pulled my collarbone out of place and back to the hospital I went. This time, Ma gave them a real talking-to and made them stand in the corner. Standing in the corner was a punishment we got if Pa was not available. Nobody liked that! But tradition follows one in life and as a parent, I used it on my kids. Did they like it? No way! They will tell you that was something they hated about their childhood.

This was not the end of the broken bones, however. I was less than ten years old when Joe and Spuds told me I could walk around the top edge of the big cement water tank. The walls were about a foot wide. The tank was five feet deep, twenty feet wide and thirty feet long. Because the dirt was piled up around the tank, the outside height was about four feet. They told me they'd give me a nickel to do it. So, I, Laura, tried it, and fell.

Thank God I went off to the dirt side of the tank. If I'd fallen inside, I would have drowned because I could not swim. Again I broke my arm. And again we concocted a story so Ma and Pa never knew what we were really up to.

As the youngest girl in a family of fourteen children with two older near-age brothers and three younger brothers I was always in the middle of everything. My much older sisters and brothers loved me so much; they always pampered me. Sometimes they would tease me but would always be on my side when the brothers near my age were pestering me.

Well, Pa came home from the market one night with his Model T Ford with no floor boards in front and I, Laura, was playing hide and seek with the boys. I crawled under the car and up into the front seat to hide, but fell out the bottom and broke my collarbone again! This time Ma saw what was going on. The boys got disciplined and I went back to the hospital. They should have named a room there for me.

Now in about the sixth grade, I got a real bad sore throat and was taken to Dr. Henneberger again. He removed my adenoids and my tonsils, but there were complications. He had a hard time stopping my bleeding. I was in the Atwood hospital for three weeks, because I kept coughing up blood. Then I was out of school for another two weeks when I got home, but the teacher always let me stay in the same class. I never really realized it, but Ms. Wendelin at school thought I was a very smart girl and could always catch up with the lessons I missed.

No sooner had I gotten out of the hospital, that following September Ma wanted me to learn to play the organ so she asked Mrs. Meara to teach me. She offered her a dime a time, and Mrs. Meara said "okay" and started giving me lessons. I had big hands that reached a long way, and so showed lots of promise.

She said, "Laura, if you just learn to relax you could be a tremendous player!" Relaxing is something that I, Laura, have never accomplished even in my older years.

Well, after about seven lessons, I was walking up the road to her house and fell over a rock. I tore the ligaments on my right knee and was back in the hospital for weeks. Released on crutches, I could not resume my organ classes with Mrs. Meara. So the world lost a great organist due to my clumsiness. It also got me out of milking cows for three weeks, (not that I would ever want to injure my knee like that again).

When I was in the eighth grade in school, Mr. Riedel put me into a spelling bee in town. There was a neighbor boy, Harvey

Neirmeyer in the bee as well. He and I ended up tying score with each other. In order to break the tie, the director, Mrs. Fuller, asked me to say *The Pledge of Allegiance*. Well, nerves took over and darn it; I could not remember the last line! We said that allegiance every day of the year when we started the day at school and for the life of me I couldn't spit out the last line! Well, Harvey won! I never liked him after that, because I felt she should have asked him to say the pledge as well, and she hadn't.

On April 11th, 1934 I graduated from the eighth grade (I was eleven years old). When I got home from school Pa told me I had to go back to the eighth grade, to do it twice!

I started crying and yelling and saying, "You can't make me do that! You don't know what those darn boys do to me!" I pleaded, there were nine boys and that man teacher in the school, and they all picked on me.

Pa became disturbed and said to me, "Everyone of my kids have gone to the eighth grade twice, and you are no different, you are going to do that too!"

I went in crying like crazy to my mother. I told her all the mean things those boys would do to me.

She understood and begged "Pa, please don't make her go twice."

Can't believe it, but Pa gave in (Ma could always reach Pa's soft side when she needed to).

He said "Okay, you think you are so bright, you get a job and give me half of what you make and you won't have to go to the eighth grade twice."

I was so happy. But then I wondered *what could I do? Who would hire me?* At night I would say a prayer to God to help me find a job.

Right about this time was when my older sisters married. My sister, Agnes, lived with her husband 17½ miles south of Atwood. When I asked her if she knew anyone who would hire me, she told me she had just heard that Mrs. Olson (5½ miles down the road east of her house) was looking for someone to help her cook meals for the harvesters, the seasonal help that was hired at her farm. She gave me her address and I wrote to her, asking for a job. She called me up and said she would hire me for $1.25 a week to help her. I was excited, that meant I didn't have to go back to that school.

How was the job? Well, I had to help milk the cows, feed the pigs, gather the eggs, help cook, do the dishes, clean the house, wash the windows and help do the washing! I was pretty tired at night, but she gave me a bed in an unheated porch room of her house.

Mrs. Olson had a nephew Freddie who came out to help in the harvest, he was about 16 and golly, he was good looking, and he learned to like me. One day I was gathering eggs in the chicken house and he came in at the same time, put his arms around me and kissed me! Well, Dolly (Mrs. Olson) must have seen him go into the chicken house and she came in just at the time he was kissing me. Boy, she was madder than a hornet! I thought she was going to fire me, but instead she ordered Freddie to get in the car and go back to town.

"And you won't be coming back here to work!" she warned Freddie.

She lectured me as a concerned mother would, that you don't go around kissing men, "and don't you ever do that again!" was the worst of the scolding for me. Amen to that.

I never ever got to go anywhere, except that she would allow me to go to church on Sundays. My sister Agnes and her husband Steve would come to the Olson farm to pick me up every Sunday so I could go (otherwise I was stuck there). We went to a little catholic church in an area called Tully (about two miles from the Olson farm). Tully was a little village that gave the surrounding farmers a place to go to church. Agnes and Steve would let me stay at their house on Sunday because in those days, Sunday was a holiday and you weren't allowed to work. Amen to that! Sometimes, I would just sleep all afternoon because I was so tired from working for Mrs. Olson all week.

Other times they would take me into Atwood so we could go home to see Ma and Pa. I would go home to give Pa half of my money, which was 62 cents a week. He waited for that money and would always know if I paid him the right amount. You could never in a million years cheat my Pa.

I had been working there three years when Dewey (Mr. Olson) got sick. They had a little girl, Jean, who went to school down the country road. Mrs. Olson's brother Fred (Freddie's father), who lived in Atwood, came to take Dewey to the hospital, but the only hospital was in McCook, Nebraska about 60 or 70 miles away.

He was gone about two or three weeks when Fred came and told Dolly (Mrs. Olson), "Dewey is dying, I will take you up to see him because he wants to say good-bye."

Then he turned to me and said, "You have to take care of the farm and see that Jean gets to school. I will be back someday soon."

He left with the matriarch boss I had taken direction from for so long.

Well, Fred came back about five days later telling me that Dewey was dying and that he had asked to see Jean, "so I'm leaving you here to take care of things for Dolly."

I was left all alone at 14 years of age to manage the whole farm by myself.

Off they went, it was November 3, 1937. That was a sunny autumn day, but the very next day, I heard on the radio that a big blizzard was coming.

"Get your wood into the house and be prepared!" the announcer warned.

I moved in wood so I would have heat, and put straw over the basement windows so the house would not be so cold. I got all the animals that I could into a shelter, however the cows were reluctant to move into the barn. They were in the lot, so I left them there. I put as much feed as I could into the barn and the chicken house and then closed the doors.

That next morning the Midwest was hit with the worst blizzard that anyone could remember. I woke up at 5:00 AM and could not open the kitchen door! It was pressed shut with drifted snow. I went to my bedroom window to try to get a look outside. All I could see was snow. At this point it looked like the whole house was buried in snow.

I decided I would use a kitchen window to escape. I would push it open, use the shovel to dig a hole in the drift, melt the snow on the stove, make the water hot and pour it back into the hole to make a tunnel. It took six hours and I had to crawl out, and crawl back in bringing the snow to melt for the next try. Finally, I got to the end of the drift only to find out, if I had of gone to the window next to it, I would have gotten out in half the time.

It was 30 degrees below zero! The snow was everywhere. I don't remember how long it took me to shovel to the barn and the water tank. When I got to the barn I found that the cattle had gone in, but one old cow "Mollie" hadn't made it, and was lying on the ground outside shaking and shivering like crazy.

I tried to get her up, but she was too weak. So, I thought, *I'll start the tractor and tie a rope around her and pull her into the barn.* Wouldn't you know it; the tractor wouldn't start. So I took a bunch of newspapers and started the papers with a match and put them under the carburetor of the tractor, knowing that it had probably frozen.

That move should have caught the tractor on fire, but God was with me that day and to my surprise the fire under the carburetor worked and the tractor rumbled to a cold, sputtering start. *Hurray!* Why, the tractor didn't catch fire, I don't know. Man, I couldn't believe it.

I was absolutely freezing even though I had layers of jackets on. I took the rope and tied it around Mollie's legs as that is all I could do, and pulled her into the barn. I covered her with straw and went back to the house to bring her warm water thinking that would save her. I did that every three hours even during the night, but she lived only two days and then froze to death. I did everything I knew and she hung on for so long, but eventually she died.

Water was another big problem. They had a cow tank but it was frozen over (no surprise). I had to take an ax and chop the ice. It was frozen over a foot deep and I had to use my hands to pull out the chunks because they were too heavy for the shovel. My hands were freezing and I started to cry! My tears froze on my cheeks. And I continued... I, Laura, survived.

Will I ever forget those days? No way! The telephone lines were down, there was no electricity, and all I had was a battery-powered radio. The days went on, five weeks alone on the farm and every day was a terrible day for me. My only consolation was looking at the Montgomery Ward Catalog at night and dreaming a dream. *If I am here all by myself all these days and knowing all I have to do, I know Dolly will give me maybe $5 a week. That means because I have been here five weeks I will make twenty-five dollars. I have to give Pa $12.50, that leaves me with $12.50. So I could buy a new pair of shoes for $1.49, and a magnificent, rose-colored bed spread for $4.49. Then I will still have money left over.* That dream of having the money to buy something I wanted was all that I could do to escape the reality of those tough times.

After all this time, nobody knew whether I was dead or alive. My sister Agnes convinced her husband Steve to shovel down the road to the next neighbor. He did that and got other neighbors to help. They shoveled 5½ miles to get to the Olson's farm, and found me alive. That meant, thank goodness, that Dolly could now come home.

Dewey had died and was buried and she and Jean had been at Fred's house in town because the roads were not yet open. By that time, the phone lines were back and Dolly was told the road could be traveled. Steve arrived at the farm with the first shoveling crew, and told me that Dolly was coming home. I was so excited that *oh, boy! I will get what I want from the catalog and Pa will be surprised!*

Dolly arrived home, walked into the kitchen door, looked at me and said, "Well, how was it while I was gone?"

I started to cry and said, "Well, I nearly froze to death taking care of the animals but old Mollie died!"

She looked at me and said, "What did you say? Old Mollie died?"

I shook my head and said, "Yes, I did everything to save her, but she just died."

She turned to me and replied, "Well, young lady, I know you think you should be paid more money, because you were here alone, but old Mollie was worth at least $60 and you just cost me that."

My heart broke. She went on, "I am a widow now, so all I can give you is your regular money, $1.25 a week."

There is no description worthy of my heartbreak. I just turned and ran into the bedroom and shut the door. I immediately decided, *I'm getting out of here!* So, I took a gunny sack, put in all my clothes except two pairs of long underwear, two jackets, two pair of socks and my boots, which I put on. I tied a scarf around my face and covered my head with a stocking cap. I left her a note that I couldn't stay any longer, crawled out the bedroom window and walked 5½ miles to my sister's. It was 22 degrees below zero! I nearly froze to death, no question. But I made it to her house by 4:00 AM.

You should have heard my sister screaming! "You crazy brat! You could have frozen to death and died! Pa will have a fit, now how are you going to give him money?"

My answer, "How can I give him anything? It cost me $6.25 because she never even paid me the money I was supposed to get." I said, "Just leave me alone and shut up!"

I went to Mass on Sunday. Mrs. Pancake (a neighbor) had told me she would like for me to come work for her when I left the Olsons, so I looked to her for work. Well God was good to me, Mrs. Pancake was in church that day and she hired me on the spot to wash her walls for $3.00 a week. This was more than twice what I was getting at Dolly Olson's! After finishing her whole house in three weeks, other neighbors started calling me to do the same thing, for the same price.

In the fall of that year, my sister Toots was having her fourth child. She and her husband Walt had started crop sharing for the Steele family out in Beardsley, Kansas, about eight miles out of town. Jerry and Joseph, her two sons, were four and five years old then. Walt was working in the fields and Toots needed me to take care of the boys and baby Betty who was two, so I went out to Beardsley to help her out.

Well, all was going well until one day I went out in the yard to hang clothes and it was getting dark. I had to light the coal oil lamp on the table for light. When I reached down to pull clothes out of the basket, I looked up and gasped "Oh, My God! There's a fire in the house!"

I ran in, the boys had knocked over the lamp on the kitchen table and the tablecloth had caught fire! I grabbed a rug off the floor and threw it on top. The Lord came to my rescue as it smothered out the fire! I still can't believe that I knew you had to smother a coal oil fire. I could have thrown water on it and that would not have extinguished an oil fire.

Toots had been in to the hospital to have her baby, and would be coming home in a day or so when, low and behold, the boys got sick with the measles!

The doctor told Toots, "You can't go home with that baby girl!"

So it was up to me to stay at her house and tend to the children. I was stuck out there in the country for a good six weeks. You see, my sister Toots was living on peanuts. She couldn't pay me anything but love. When she finally got home I could now go back to making some money.

I knew that a Mrs. Knutson wanted me to work for her, so after I got home, I called her and she hired me immediately. She had a little girl, and while I was working for her she had another baby. Even though I was 15, my Mother and Father had never talked to us about the facts of life, so I was amazed as to where that baby came from. My sister Agnes kindly explained the facts of life to a very confused Laura.

Mrs. Knutson was a great employer; she liked what I did and always complemented a job well-done. She was sympathetic to the plight of a hard worker and knew that I had not been given any time to myself. So one Saturday she asked me if I would like to go into Atwood with her while she did her shopping. I loved that opportunity and went into Bellamy's Drug Store to have an ice cream soda. This was *the day that changed my life!* I was scheduled to move on from the Knutson's, so a new job was in order.

There was a girl there, making ice cream sodas, I asked her if that was hard to do and she quickly replied, "No! You want my job? You can have it!"

Well, I was thrilled and she told me to see Mr. Bellamy in the back room. I went back and asked him if I could work for him.
Of course, the first thing he asked was, "Can you make sodas?"

"No, I don't know how, but I can sure learn!"

"Okay. If you want the job, you can have it."

"How much?" I asked.

"I'll give you $5 a week."

Oh boy! I thought, that was more than I'd ever made before. But then I remembered that when I worked on a farm I had a place to sleep. Where would I sleep if I worked in town?

So, I said to Mr. Bellamy, "The only thing is, I have a problem, I have no place to sleep."

"Oh, no problem!" he said. "Mrs. Beamgard around the corner has rooms to rent for $9 a month."

So, off I went to see Mrs. Beamgard. On the way, I got to analyzing what that would do to my money. If I earned $5 a week x 4 weeks a month, I would get $20 each month. I had to give $10 to my father, and give $9 to Mrs. Beamgard, that meant that I would only have $1 left!

Okay I thought, *I know what I will do.* (I had a plan.) So I rang the doorbell at Mrs. Beamgard's house and she came to the door. I told her who I was, but she already knew as her family bought all their meat from my father. She asked me what I was there for and I told her I needed a room to live in as I was going to work for Mr. Bellamy. She replied that yes, I could have a room for $9 a month.

Then, I said, "Tell you what. If you will let me stay here for free, I will wash your dishes every night, do all your ironing, and clean your whole house every Saturday."

Mrs. Beamgard looked at me and seemed delighted. She hesitated a moment, then said "Okay. You can move in."

Also at this time, the Sacred Heart Church did not have anyone to clean it, so I asked Father Hubert if he would pay me 25 cents to do so every week. He hired me. I had to do this in my spare time as I was expected to be at either Bellamy's Drug Store or at Mrs. Beamgard's during the week and on Saturdays. Sometimes I would get up real early on Sunday morning to go down and get it cleaned before Mass.

I had to walk about nine blocks and would have to dust all the pews as well, so that took me about an hour and a half. But I did it when I had time.

I worked at the drug store every day. Not only did I make the sodas, but I also ran the cash register, cleaned the store and took the telephone calls including prescription orders. Many times I not only opened the store in the morning, but closed it at night as well. Then in about five months Mr. Graves, who operated a dry goods store across the street, came into Bellamy's and asked me if I would like to come work for *him*.

"How much?" I asked.

"Well, I'll pay you $7.50 a week."

"Okay! When do I start?"

"Give your notice to Mr. Bellamy so he can find someone else and then you can start working for me."

Well, I had made friends with another girl who lived at Mrs. Beamgard's. Her name was Clara. I went home that night and talked Clara into going to work for Mr. Bellamy. I also talked her into starting the next day.

I trained Clara in less than a week. So I started work for Mr. Graves ("Bike," as he was known by his first name) the next Monday. He liked me personally because of my work ethics. I arranged all the dry goods, dusted, swept the floor, opened and closed the store as I had at Bellamy's.

In addition to working his store, he and his wife hired me to baby-sit their two boys. Boy! That was an education of a lifetime. Those two little devils would not mind me. They would jump up and down on the bed and get into all sorts of trouble. One time Danny fell off the bed and broke his arm! I had to tell Bike and his wife what happened and I thought, *Oh Man! They are going to fire me, for sure.*

They must have known their boys more than I gave them credit for. Instead of being upset with me, they got nervous thinking that I was going to quit. They were only paying me 25 cents a night to baby-sit so they raised it to 50 cents a night. (Sometimes two or three times a week – that meant an extra $1.50 in my pay every week!) What they didn't know was that I never intended to quit; I was happy with the 25 cents; but now even happier with a raise. I decided not to tell Pa that I worked baby-sitting, so that gave me a little extra cash for myself, which of course I loved.

After a year there, Glen Williams, a grocery store owner came over. He was a friend of Bike Graves and he told me he had asked Bike if he would be mad if he hired me to sell groceries.

Bike said "No. If she wants to go, that's okay."

So when Glen asked me to work for him, again I asked "How much?"

"I'll give you $10 a week and you can still baby-sit the Graves boys at night."

Now after I was there one year, I turned 18. When I would go home at night I would ponder about what lay ahead for me. I decided, *I've got to go to high school, this is NOT the kind of life I want!* I was making money but it wasn't enough. I was still poor, and wanted more from life. I knew that as long as I could do Mrs. Beamguard's housework, I could continue living there; I certainly wouldn't be living in Pa's house if I went to high school. (She got so used to me doing the work there, she cried when I eventually graduated high school and went on to college.)

So when I got off work on Saturday, I went home to tell Pa.

I knew that telling Pa that I was going to high school would be very hard. The words that came from Pa were something I will never forget.

"Are you crazy? YOU CAN BE WHAT YOU WANT TO BE! NO KID OF MINE IS EVER GOING TO HIGH SCHOOL!"

I stayed calm and said, "Pa, I don't want to be poor like the rest of my family! I want to *be* somebody and that means I've got to go to school!"

He slapped me across my face!

This was the first and only time he'd ever hit me, but he slapped me across my face with his hand and yelled "NO KID OF MINE HAS EVER GONE TO HIGH SCHOOL AND YOU ARE NOT EITHER!"

I moved back away so he could not hit me again and I said to him: "Pa, I am eighteen years of age. That means I can make up my own life. You can't stop me! I am going to school."

"Young lady," he replied, "You go to high school and you can never come home again!"

My answer was firm: "If that is what you want, I am giving that to you!"

I went in and told Ma, "Pa will not let me do what I want to do. I want to go to school and he told me I can't come home again. I'm going now, but I promise to see you in church on Sundays."

Poor Ma, she hugged me (one of the few times anyone ever hugged me) and told me, "Honey, work hard and do well."

I walked out without looking at Pa and went back to town.

Now came Monday, so I went up to the high school to see Mr. Nicholson the Principal.

When I told him I wanted to sign up to go to school, he looked at me and asked, "How old are you?"

I told him I was 18.

"How long have you been out of school?"

I replied, "Since I was eleven years old, seven years!"

He looked at me and said, "You can't make it; you've been out of school too long."

My reply: "I don't think you can keep me from going to school!"

He looked me in the eye and said, "Well, I think you are right. You seem to be very determined so don't tell the other students how old you are, because you don't look 18."

"Fine, when do I start?"

He said, "Well, you know what I think you should do, try to make it in three years. I'll have the teachers give you an extra class a year, and if you study, you should be able to do that."

"Okay. I'll try that. When do I start?"

"I'll see you Monday morning, you've got some work to do as you have already missed three weeks of school."

"No, problem, I'll be here!"

Now, I had to tell Glen Williams at the grocery store that I couldn't work at all during the school day, but I could come after school and work till 8:00 at night; and I could still work on Saturdays. Naturally, I was afraid he might not like that and if he didn't, then what would I do?

Well, the Lord acts in funny ways, he threw his arms around me and said, "You know what Laura? That's the best thing you can ever do. If you need any help I have some sisters who will help you and you can come and work as long as you want."

Oh Man! Now I could pay my own way to school (you had to pay an entrance fee and buy your own books), and I could still give my father some money.

The good news did not heal my wounds, but school began again for me and it was wonderful to pursue the education I wanted. And I worked. And boy, did I work! It seems my determination paid off: everyone that knew of my situation wanted to help.

The principal said: "When you have study hall, if you need to make some money, you can help the secretary with filing and anything she needs help with."

Even the banker down town when I would make a deposit of 50 cents or so, he would say, "Would you like to wash dishes for my wife?"

So, I took yet another job washing dishes, 25 cents a night.

The Lord did my homework I think, because I never had time to do it. But I was determined and smart, and had a bit of an age (and maturity) advantage, and so got mostly A's.

What kind of reaction did I get from my older brothers and sisters? Well, Toots said she was so glad for me. She wished she had tried that. Verneda wished me well, and told me I was lucky (she had wanted to go to high school also).

My sister Agnes had a less sympathetic attitude. She told me all I wanted to do was to become "high toned." "Why do you need to change?"

My oldest brothers had left home a number of years earlier, but the next oldest were now headed off to World War II. My brother Frankie had come home for a visit before he went off to war, and he bet me 50 cents that I would not even stay in school one year. I took the challenge. I won, but I don't know if Frankie ever recognized it, as I never got my 50 cents.

High school turned out to be both challenging and fun. The other kids liked me so I became a cheerleader, I got elected to be a class officer, was selected to be in the chorus, then was chosen for several parts in plays put on by the school. Later I was elected as editor of *The Annual*, a yearly school publication.

Laura and Class in Atwood High School
(Laura, editor of *The Annual*, is front, center)

Billy Henderson, a sophomore took a liking to me, so he would always help me when I had little time to do what I was supposed to do. After I left school, he went on his way and I went on mine. That didn't mean that I didn't have other guys. Wayne Gatlin (another of Mrs. Olson's nephews) started taking me out when I came home. The only thing he ever took me to was roller-skating. I was not good at that, so he gave up.

While I was still in school Glen Williams' sister Martha and I became really good friends because she worked in the grocery store as well. Well she had an eye on a boy named Vincent and he had a brother Danny who liked me. One day they decided that we would all go swimming. Well, I thought I could fake that out (they didn't need to know I didn't know how to swim) so we went to Lake Atwood, a man-made lake built by the C.C.C. (Civilian Conservation Corpse). Swimming was allowed in one spot on the lake so off we went. I thought we would just walk out and I'd fake swimming because the water wouldn't be that deep.

Martha and Vincent

Danny

What I didn't know was that the other three were great swimmers and the first thing they said was, "Okay, let's get on the diving board and we'll dive down."

Don't think for one minute I was not going to do what *they* wanted to do, so up I went. Vince dove in first, then Danny, then Martha. Bravely I jumped in, and when I hit that water I couldn't do a thing. I went down, down, down! Then I realized I would drown!

I came up the first time yelling, "I'm drowning!"

They thought I was joking.

The second time louder: "I'm drowning!"

They still thought I was kidding.

The third time I screamed louder and was crying "Help me, Help me!"

Danny then realized this was no joke. He yelled at Vince, "She is drowning, we've got to save her."

They dove in and I was so frightened that I grabbed them and nearly drowned them as they were trying to save me. Again the Lord was with me and we got out okay.

Well, I got a lecture you wouldn't believe from kids my own age. They made me get in the car and go with them to the priest's house. Father Walter was there and they told him the story.

He gave me a lecture as well, then gave me a blessing and told me: "Don't ever do that again!"

Of course, I never did.

The Girls of the Pep Club, Atwood High School
(Laura is Head Cheerleader, Front, Center)

My father's worst enemy, Mrs. Ratcliff played the piano and organ, and taught so many students that she had little time to do her housework. Well, she hired me to come on Saturdays and paid me $1 a time to do it for her. Also, Father Walter, who had taken Father Hubert's place, hired me to clean the church once a week at anytime I wished, so I earned another 25 cents for doing that. Mr. Yager, president of the bank also hired me, to do ironing and housework for Mrs. Yager. They would pay me 50 cents. These people got special attention because that was a lot of money back then. And I was trying to make enough money to go to college. By now I was beginning the third and final year at high school and my bank account was up to $7.45. I had to pay $1.15 income tax that year.

The school year started in August because farmers needed their children for farm work early in the spring. I started, but in the first week of September my mother called me and said, "Laura, I need your help. Pa is very sick with cancer and I can't take care of him by myself. Please come home and help me."

"Ma, how can I come home? Pa told me I could never come back."

"Oh child, just come home and tell him you are sorry."

"Ma, I can't tell Pa I'm sorry, because I'm not. I am going to finish high school. I'll come home because I do love Pa, but I cannot say I'm sorry because I'm not."

I told Mr. Nicholson that I had to leave school to go home to help my mother because Pa was dying.

Mr. Nicholson said, "I understand, but let's get your teachers to give you lessons and you do your homework at home. You will have to come in once a week to take an exam in each course, then I will give you credit for being in school."

Crying, I thanked him, and I went home to assist Ma.

When I walked into Pa's bedroom, he rose up in bed and said, "You came home to tell me you're sorry."

"No, Pa, I came home because I love you. I am going to finish school."

He laid back in bed and that subject never came up again. He was not able to digest any food; he kept vomiting. Dr. Henneberger told Ma to try giving him beer, knowing full well that Pa never drank. Pa made beer for his hired hands, but never drank it himself. Ma would give him a small glass and they found that it did not make him vomit. The amounts were increased during the weeks ahead. He lost so much weight. He had weighed around 230 pounds, but after one year of being sick he was now down to less than 140 pounds. At this stage he suffered severely with pain and Dr. Henneberger told Ma he would have to be hospitalized.

He was taken to the Atwood hospital and Ma and I took turns staying with him. He passed away on October 25, 1943, at the age of 72. It was exactly twenty-one years after his daughter Annie Catherine had died in his arms. She had passed into eternity on Thursday, October

25, 1922, at about 9 PM; Pa joined her on a Thursday night at about 9 PM.

The doctor had personally called my sister Threasa earlier that day, because he knew of the great affection between them. She got on a train but didn't arrive until after he had passed away. Because World War II was in full blast, the five boys overseas never received notice that their father had died. Any bad news was always censored.

Threasa was very distraught that she missed getting home in time to see Pa. He would not have known she was there as he had been in a coma before he passed away.

She said to me, "Laura, you will finish school, won't you? If only I had been allowed to go, I would be a registered nurse, not a practical nurse. You know I don't make much money, but I will back you up all the way." Threasa was a dear, devoted sister and always encouraged me not to look backwards.

After Pa died, I went back to school to pick up the pieces. The teachers were great, and the year rolled by. Then it was nearing graduation time and Mr. Nicholson counseled me about what lie ahead. I told him I wanted to go to college.

He said, "You know, I'm retiring at the end of this year and will be going to New York to live. Maybe I could get you into Bryn Marr, a women's college, but you know they won't like a country girl. They are uppity up! There is also Fordham University, but it is so expensive. Well, let's keep trying to find a place where you can afford to go. If you went to a school in New York you could live with us for free, but of course, you would have to be able to work, and I doubt you could earn enough money to stay in college."

Shortly after that talk, I got a call from him telling me to come in as he had news for me. The news was outstanding.

"Laura, you did such a grand job all these years, you have a solid A average and now you are Valedictorian! That means you can go to the University of Kansas free of charge. They will even give you room and board."

Oh, my God! I was absolutely flabbergasted and elated. Quickly I called Mom and told her the good news. Ma was so happy she cried. Then I told everybody else in town. Wow, was I feeling lucky that day.

Then a fatal day arrived. Less than a week later, Mr. Nicholson called me again and said he needed to talk with me.

I asked him: "What's it about?"

He answered: "I can't tell you over the phone, we need to talk in person."

Principal Nicholson

"I'm coming right now," I replied, so I left work and up to the school I went.

The expression on his face was indescribable, so I knew something was wrong. He put his arms around me and told me to take a chair.

"Laura, I have really bad news for you, and I am beside myself because I can't do anything to solve the problem."

"What is the problem?" I asked.

He took my hand and he said, "You cannot be Valedictorian because you have only been in school three years. The rules say to qualify for the scholarship at the University you have to attend the same school for four years. I'm so sorry."

The tears started rolling and I said, "But, you are the one who talked me into going through school in three years."

"Yes, I know that I did, but I never knew the school committee would not allow you to win. I did everything, I begged, I pleaded. I called Forest Brown, the attorney, and he said, "A rule is a rule! If they change it for her, they would have to do it for others.""

I thought, *Well, now what do I do?*

I left the school and on the way down the hill with tears flowing all the way, I thought: *Mr. Yager, the banker, likes me, so I will go tell him what has happened and maybe the bank will loan me enough money to go without the Valedictorian scholarship.*

When I arrived at the bank, Mr. Yager was there and he saw that I was crying.

Affectionately, because he and his wife really did like me, he said "Laura come sit down, what I can do to help you?"

"You'll never believe this, Mr. Yager, but the school committee won't let me have the scholarship to go to the University. Now how can I go? Do you think I could borrow $70 so I could go down there and find a job and get into college? I really need $5 for the train ticket, $60 for the tuition, and then I would have $5 left to find someplace to live."

It was something unbelievable again, to have a friend there to help me in my time of need. He came up, put his arms around me and said, "Laura, the whole town knows how hard you have had to work to put yourself through high school. Mrs. Yager and I want you to be able to go on to college. We will personally loan you $500 interest free and when you get out of college, you can pay us back."

Well, completely overwhelmed by his generosity, my tears dried up quickly and then I threw my arms around him and said, "Thank you, Thank you!"

I immediately called Mom and told her that now I could still go on to college and again she broke down and cried. She again used the words she used all her lifetime, "The Lord never promised life would be easy! Laura, honey, I know you can do it. You have made me so happy!"

Now it was graduation time. My work friend, Martha, and Margaret Williams, Glen's sister, and their mother knew I did not have enough money to go to the prom because I needed a long dress. They went to Bike Graves, the dry goods store owner, and ordered for me a beautiful long pink gown. I believe he let them buy it at cost. Billy

Henderson took me to the prom. He put up with my lousy dancing, I was always too tense to relax.

Graduation took place. They gave Valedictorian to June Beamgard. The hurt remained for many years as every time we met, I felt that tinge of *Why Me?*

Laura Graduates High School (age 21)

Graduation took place in May so that meant I could work for the summer at the Farm Bureau doing secretarial work, still work at Williams' Grocery at night, clean Mrs. Beamgard's house and clean the church. I was able to save about $20 so that meant along with the money from Mr. Yager I would be able to have money to live until I found a job at school.

The end of August arrived and now I'm on a train for the first time ever. I arrived in Lawrence, Kansas with enough money to buy a hat. Ms. Frisbie, one of my teachers told me that you must wear a hat when you are being interviewed for a job. It was a neat hat with a wide brim and it was red. I went up to the college and told them I needed a job and they sent me to an interview with a Mr. Keeler, who ran the Lecture Course Bureau for the University. I walked into his office and what do you think he said?

He said, "Look Miss Schmid, would you just take that hat off! I want to see *you*, not that thing."

All I could think of was, *Darn it, it cost me $1.75.* But I took it off. That hat remained with me for over 40 years.

The Lord acts in funny ways, Mr. Keeler didn't even ask many questions, just "When do you want to start?"

I said "Tomorrow."

"Okay. Show up here at 9:00 AM and you can go to work."

Laura, on her 21st Birthday

I always believed Mr. Nicholson had gotten in touch with the college and told them my plight as it happened so quickly. He must have also told him how hard I had worked to get through high school and how nearly everyone in town had hired me. Then Mr. Keeler told me to go see Ms. Habein, the Dean of Women. She would have a place for me to live. That I did, and again, I was treated so graciously! She put me in Harmon Coop for six months. All I had to do to pay my room and board was to share in the work by either washing the dishes, scrubbing the floors, or cooking for a week at a time.

There were twenty-four girls at Harmon Coop and we really became great friends. Only once in a while would one of us get upset, because the one before her did not clean up as they should have. I was working six hours a day, and had signed up to start classes. As time went on, I learned to apply for scholarships and I really think the college management felt sorry for how hard I had to work, so I would receive about $100 to $150 a year in scholarship money.

At the beginning of the first summer session I signed up for *Social Science Survey* with a Mr. Hilden Gibson teaching the class. I always scheduled a class during the noon hour and went without lunch, that way I did not lose hours on the job. Class went well the first week or two, then one day we went to a new chapter in the book and it was titled *Evolution*. I really didn't know what that was all about until Mr. Gibson started teaching it.

He told us, "You were nothing but a cell on the side of a water body, and the movement of the water caused you to develop into a cell which became a frog and from there on you developed into a person."

It might have been my hunger, but somehow I didn't like what he was saying so I held up my hand and said, "Mr. Gibson, you forgot to say that God intervened and gave us life."

Holy Toledo! Mr. Gibson went haywire. He started screaming at me and then announced, "Oh, students, we have this little Western Kansas Catholic in our group, and she's no different than the people who believed in their God and raised him up on a mountain side and adored this crazy image."

Naturally, I objected and said, "You don't understand, we may have been a cell, and evolved, but then God gave us life. Evolution is a theory, it is not a fact."

Mr. Gibson jumped up on the desk and said, "Miss Schmid, get out of my class and don't you ever come back!"

What could I do but leave. Now I went back to the office and of course, I was really upset and the first thing I did was to go to Mr. Keeler and cry because I had paid for that course and now he threw me out.

Well, Mr. Keeler said, "Laura, don't be upset, call Dean Lawson, he is the Dean of the college, and is a Methodist minister, and ask for an appointment."

I was quite concerned because I was a freshman and he would think I was crazy.

Mr. Keeler said, "Laura do it. His secretary will make the appointment. Just make sure you keep it!" Then he added, "He has a big office and when she lets you in, it will be a long walk up to his desk. Just be friendly and say *hello*."

"Oh, all right."

Mr. Keeler and Laura

I called and the secretary made the appointment for the next day. Man was I scared. When I got to the office she immediately announced my arrival and across the floor I went. After the initial greeting, the Dean said, "And what can I do for you?"

Mr. Keeler had told me what to say: "Dean, do you believe in God?"

His answer was: "Of course I do, young lady, why do you ask me that question?"

Immediately I explained to him what had happened in class and that I had paid for that class and Mr. Gibson said I couldn't go back. The Dean picked up a pencil and wrote a note, signed it and handed it to me.

Then he said, "If you have any further problems, please call me immediately."

I looked at the note. It very clearly said, *Miss Schmid has full returning rights.*

"Just take this note and return to class tomorrow."

Holy Cow! I was so happy but of course, very nervous.

Arriving the next day on time to go into the class, three students were waiting for me on the stairs; two young men and a young girl. They said they were so upset by what happened they went down to the local priest and asked him about evolution.

"So, if he starts on you today, we will stand up for you. Come on in and we'll sit together."

Well, when I went in the door, Mr. Gibson saw me and you have never seen or heard anything like what he yelled and screamed at me.

"Get out of here! You are not welcome!"

I handed him the note and he almost fainted! He started screaming, jumped up on the desk again and said, "This idiot has gotten me in trouble. Class dismissed. Go home now!"

The very next day, he calmly announced, "Due to this disruptive Catholic, we can no longer discuss evolution, we will move on to the next chapter."

Well, again the Lord acts in funny ways. I got desperately ill, had an appendicitis attack and had to go home for the operation, because I could not afford surgery at the University. I knew Dr. Henneberger would do it for me for free. The train ride home cost me $5. The surgery at the University was going to cost me $75! I had only been in class three weeks out of the six-week session.

I returned after two weeks and now it was time for the final exams. I went to Mr. Keeler and said, "What am I going to do? I have no idea what they covered while I was away. I'll fail the exam."

"Laura, just go over, take the exam, and stop worrying. I assure you, Gibson will not fail you because he knows he would lose his job if he did."

On his encouragement I took the test. I answered about a third of the questions, that's all. The grade card came and I got a D. That meant I did not fail, and got the credit for the course. Years later, Mr. Gibson and I had another encounter. This will be revealed later.

A memorable experience developed after that with the three students who decided to come to my rescue. One of them, a minority student named Vernie, was so impressed with Father Flanagan that he joined the catholic church. Within a year he went into the Benedictine Seminary and became a catholic priest. The other two, a boy and a girl, became friends after the incident and married each other before I left school. We four enjoyed each other so much at college. Vernie, the Seminarian, played the organ at my wedding, which was held at the church where Father Flanagan was assigned. Father Flanagan probably never realized it, but he was responsible for Vernie's conversion. Father Flanagan was one of the officiating clergy at my wedding.

About this time, I wanted to write home to my mother and I did not know where the post office was. One of my friends told me it was in Strong Hall in the basement, so off I went to find it. I needed to buy a three-cent stamp to send the letter home. I got to the hall and was wandering all over the basement to find the office. I saw a stairs so I went up it to the top floor and there was an open door and I walked in.

Holy Murder! Here in front of me was a whole group of Navy Men reclining in leisure attire. I am not sure who was more embarrassed, they or I. After a lot of to-do, I tried to explain to them what I was doing.

Then one of them took me by the arm and said, "You need to get out of here and I'll help you find what you are looking for."

He took me back down the stairs to the other end of the hall and guided me up another stairs. Then he left me. Well the Post Office wasn't there either! I went back downstairs and another student showed me where it was, in the basement. The story didn't end there as someone reported that incident to the college newspaper, The University Daily Kansan, and I, Laura Schmid, became a headline story about the wrong way of getting acquainted with one's campus. The report was headlined: "To Live and Learn!" It was known on the campus (but not by me) that the Navy had taken over the top floor of Strong Hall to give the sailors returning from the war a place to sleep and live. "They were enjoying their privacy until Laura unexpectedly walked in." There was no denying that they were in leisure attire. There were more than a few red faces.

How did University life go after that? Well, I was able to advance in Mr. Keeler's office and became his official secretary. I had a tremendous memory and I knew the names and locations of nearly every school principal in the five states where we provided lectures. I even became so proficient I could finagle Mr. Keeler's signature and he himself didn't know whether he did it, or I did it.

My only problem arose, however, that in order to keep that job I had to pass a Civil Service Test given in Topeka, Kansas. Well, I tried three times and failed all three. I would be so nervous I couldn't type fast enough! Mr. Keeler decided that he would hire a civil service examiner to come to his office without me knowing it and he would dictate a letter to me while they were with him. He did just that, and you know what? I passed with flying colors, typing not 30 words a minute (the requirement) but 55!

Now the only other requirement was that I take a blood test. I did that but low and behold they called and said that I had Syphilis and needed treatment! I had no idea what they were talking about, so I went to Mr. Keeler crying, and asked him what Syphilis was.

He asked me "Did you ever have relations with a man?"

"Oh, my God, No! I wouldn't do that!"

So, he sent me back for another test. Again, the Lord came to my rescue. They had the tests mixed up the first time, and this time I came out clean as a whistle. Whew!

In order to make money, I babysat for people. Mr. and Mrs. Keeler, known to everyone as Guy and Ora Mae, did not have children. One day Guy told me that a couple down on Lawrence Street had a baby girl, which they were giving up for adoption. Guy and Ora Mae would adopt her, so he asked me to deliver a check to them for $500 and they would give me the baby. I brought her back to him and Ora Mae who were waiting at the office. From that day forward, I was the babysitter for baby Barbara. She was a cute little girl and I took care of her all the time I was in college.

Many, many years later, after college, Barbara made contact with each me. She had never been told she was adopted, and somehow she had found out.

She asked me straight out if she had been adopted.

I had to answer honestly, "To my knowledge, yes, but Marcella, the office manager at the time, would be able to tell you more."

I received a letter later, telling me she was sorry to have gotten together with me, that the truth hurt so bad. I replied and apologized, and to my knowledge she is somewhere in the Midwest. Her parents, my friends and mentors, have passed on.

I had to work so many hours that I appealed to Dean Habein to let me live in a place where I didn't have to do housework. She helped me with a scholarship and I lived one year in Scholarship Hall. The last year I was able to get into Corbin Hall and that was a great place. The housemother was phenomenal. She helped me so much. She allowed me to serve the early breakfast so the cost of living there was reduced.

Then I got accepted into Theta Phi Alpha, a catholic girls' sorority. We used to join the events of Phi Kappa Theta, the men's fraternal group. Friendships of a lifetime developed.

At this time however, I had to take six to eight hours of classes a day so my work hours had to be cut. This particular semester I went down to the Farmer's Bank to see if I could borrow $60 for the semester's tuition.

The bank president asked me, "How do you think you can pay for this?"

I told him, "I promise to pay you 50 cents a week and every time I get extra money, I will bring it in." That worked (that's all you had to do to get a loan back then).

Well, my determination, and long hours allowed me to accomplish my goal and I paid it back in only six weeks.

Not long after that, the bank president who had helped me get the loan retired. His son, returning from the war, was given the temporary position of President of the bank. Another semester arrived and I didn't have enough money to pay the fee, so I confidently returned for another loan. Well, that was an experience! That son, one who I cannot forget, was unbelievable!

He answered my plea with: "Ms. Schmid, we don't run a charity here. Get out, don't waste my time!"

Again I returned, tears flowing rapidly, to Mr. Keeler.

I told him what happened and he said to me, "Laura, you know, I will loan that money to you, but I know that guy. His wife and my wife are best of friends. He has ambitions, so you can be sure that guy will one day run for President of the United States. Well, I'm sure he won't get your vote."

Truth to tell, that did happen, and HE DID NOT GET MY VOTE, nor did he get enough votes to even stay in the race. Should I rejoice?

No matter how hard I worked, I always needed money to stay in school, but I guess I impressed the college enough that I would end up getting a hundred dollars and maybe a little more each year in scholarships. They were always kind to me and that was my salvation. The first year I received $100, the second year $125, and the third year $150. If I hadn't received those funds, I certainly would have had to drop out of school.

Laura, College Years

I'm not sure as to how I was always in the middle of school elections, but I ended up being elected as an officer, Treasurer, Secretary and even Class President! Father Towle was the first to ask me to start a catholic club on the college campus. That I did, and in the first year we gained 200 members! The club grew and became a very important part of campus life.

Mr. Buehler, who was my public speech instructor, got me involved in the public speaking contests. I managed to win one, and then I was to speak in the final selection for the speaker of the year.

My speech was titled Onward Kansas. Maybe it was luck for me in a hidden way, but the day of the contest I awoke with a 104-degree fever! Mother Brown called an ambulance and I was taken to the hospital where I was retained for three days at a cost of $1 a day. I had to have an X-ray that cost me another dollar. It turned out to be pneumonia, but I recovered and was back to work in two weeks. I never got to present my Onward Kansas speech. Orville Roberts, my competitor, won the title (only because I didn't compete)!

Later that year, I was elected the first woman president of the Newman Club, a club for students at the local catholic church in Lawrence, Kansas. The membership grew and we had a magnificent group. We were very active on the campus, participating in nearly every activity. Any activity that any other group wanted us for, we participated. The number of members kept growing.

Now the war ended and the soldiers who had been in college returned. One of them, a short guy, quite interested in the Newman Club, was elected president following my term. Well, he needed to know what was going on with the club, so he asked me to go out for coffee. That was the beginning of a change in my life. The boy was William Hogan (actually his name was Daniel William Hogan but he grew up believing his first name was Bill, so everyone knew him as Bill or William.) He eventually became my husband.

That is how I met him, by passing the presidency at the Newman Club. Through those early years his name became a challenge since someone always knew him as Bill, but his war friends knew him as Dan. The challenge was resolved when I started calling him Hogan, because that identified him under every circumstance and I didn't have to worry about confusing other people that were present.

I had some great professors in the studies I was taking. One of the more outstanding ones was a Mr. Blocker who taught accounting. He seemed to sense how tired I was, but also noticed that I was always on top when it came to giving him the right answers. I loved bookkeeping and could do that quite easily, getting A's most of the time. He suggested I become a C.P.A. when I finished college. His wish did not come true. His wish did not come true because my fiancé insisted that I could finish college in Massachusetts after we were married. Money prohibited that undertaking when I married and I moved on.

One of my worst classes was Algebra and I just could not fathom spending my time learning all those equations! My poor performance made it pretty obvious I had to study harder, but time was not at my disposal. Fortunately, one of my first cousins from Midwest Kansas, Leroy, was taking the same class with same teacher, the day before me. He knew my plight so every night he would come by to help me solve the next day's problems. If it were not for him, I would have flunked for sure! Leroy became a big cheese with Blue Cross and Blue Shield and moved on with his life from there. He and my brother Joe were in World War II together and were both at the Anzio Beachhead. He now lives in Chicago, Illinois and each year we renew our relationship and catch up on each other's accomplishments.

Then I enrolled in Price and Distribution, and that professor knew it was a tough subject for me.

After taking a couple of tests, he called me in and said, "Ms. Schmid, I really don't want to flunk you in this class. You are such a nice person, I think that what you should do is resign from the class. Your record will not show any grade, you will just have to find other credits."

I thanked him and took his advice. He seemed so relieved and we remained friends for as long as I was at the University.

Along about this time, I met Dick Conroy, a very handsome six-foot junior who took a liking to me and would take me to movies, or dances if I asked him or made the first move.

After a while I would go visit the store where he worked and he would say, "Are you going to the dance with me?"

"I guess so, if you want to take me," was my reply.

Now Hogan was different. He would call me to go to coffee down on Louisiana Street. We would go and have a quiet chat. Then he learned I loved beer, so he and his friends would take us in their car out to the Tepee Café. The Tepee was on a country road outside of Lawrence so it would take us a little while to get there. Long work hours and long school hours had not changed for me and as soon as I would get into the car I would fall asleep, and they would have to wake me up to go into the café.

There were months at a time where I only had work and school and not much else.

During this time I had a roommate Mary Ellen who said, "You need to stop working so hard, you have to have a life! My boyfriend, Jerry, has a friend that he will bring along for a blind date and you can come with us. Okay?"

"Well, okay I'll go."

Was that a good move? Not really.

This friend was a good-looking guy. He did the driving.

When we started to move I asked, "Where are we going?"

The answer was: "For a ride."

What did that mean? A five or six mile ride out into the country only meant one thing in those days. Jerry and my roommate were making out like bandits in the back seat and I got very nervous about that! Then what does this guy do, but pulls on to a country road and parks the car and immediately moves over to me. He started to clutch me and put his arms around me.

NO WAY WAS I GOING TO ALLOW THAT! I said to him, "Please don't touch me."

He replied, "Hey gal, why do you think we came for a ride, the least you can do is let me kiss you."

It only took me seconds to grab the door and jump out of the car. I started to run back to the main road, but it was pitch dark.

He backed up the car and caught up with me and yelled, "Come on get in here."

I resisted and said, "The only way I will get back in that car is if Mary Ellen and I can sit in the back seat and you and Jerry get in the front seat, and you take me home!"

Mary Ellen reluctantly said, "Okay, we will go back to the Coop."

I got out of the car at the Coop and Mary Ellen and Jerry and his friend went on their way.

The next morning Mary Ellen, unhappy with me, told me outright "YOU ARE GOING TO END UP BEING AN OLD MAID!"

"Maybe, but why should you care?" I replied.

Mary Ellen and I remained friends but only went out together on specified occasions. She ended up marrying Jerry and they moved to Missouri. They were married only a year when Mary Ellen contacted Polio and she died.

About that time, I was going home and decided I would like to see her; I did not know she had died. When I got to Kansas City, I called and called. Finally Jerry answered.

When I told him this was Laura he said, "Oh, Laura, I should have written you, Mary Ellen passed away on Christmas."

Traveling through Missouri years later, we stopped to visit her grave.

--

Now after a few more dates with Hogan, my friend Dick Conroy got a little jealous and one day I was walking to class and he caught up with me and bluntly said, "Laura, you are too beautiful to be running around with that guy. You are tall and he is at least three inches shorter than you! And you should be wearing heels, not running around in those stupid flat shoes because they won't make you shorter. I love you the way you are."

Then I told him, "Well time will tell and it will."

I ended up marrying Hogan. Dick did not come to our wedding.

My dates were just dates and were few and far between, so I always thought I would end up being an 'old maid.' Guess I had to work so hard, I didn't really have time to worry about that. Over those years I had plenty of boyfriends, I just didn't have time to get in deep with any of them.

I met another fellow, known as Digger O-Dell, who was tall and handsome and he lived in Atchison, Kansas. We were dating pretty regularly, and had planned to get together one Friday evening. Well, my friend Jerry called and said that Digger could not come on Friday night so he and Mary Ellen would drive me up to see him.

I asked Jerry and Mary Ellen, "What happened that Digger couldn't come?"

They replied, "He will tell you why."

Digger was in an accounting class with me and I had never asked him what he planned to do after college. Well, it was a beautiful sunny night and we drove the 45 miles up to where he lived.

Laura, in Her Early Twenties

We pulled into the driveway and out came Digger saying, "Jerry come quick, I'm running short of time!"

Jerry jumped out of the car and ran into the house. It was a two-bedroom ranch and looked nice on the outside.

I asked Mary Ellen what was going on and she said, "You'll have to wait and see."

In about ten minutes, Digger came out and apologized, "I'm so sorry, but I didn't want to tell you that I am an undertaker, and there was a big accident last night. Two young couples were killed and I have them here. One of the families is coming to view their son's body by 7:00 PM, then we can go on our way."

Holy Moses! What he was telling me was that he had those bodies in his home! Talk about a surprise. I was in a full shock.

Digger said, "Come on in. When the family arrives you can go in the back bedroom and they won't know you are there."

Mary Ellen said, "Come on Laura, it won't hurt us to go in."

Unhappily, I went with them. In the front door… oh, my God! A body was in a coffin in the living room! Out in the kitchen, another body covered over with a sheet lay on a stretcher. And in the first bedroom, two more bodies!

I looked at Digger and said, "FORGET THIS! I'm out of here!"

Jerry and Mary Ellen looked at me and said, "Hey you, we just drove up here for you, now you want to leave?"

"You bet your boots! No way can I live with this!"

Digger looked at me and said, "Laura, I never thought you couldn't live with this."

My answer was curt, "Sorry. But you should have told me before and this wouldn't have happened."

It was then I realized why they called him Digger O'Dell. His real name was Daniel O'Dell. Guess you might say Digger buried himself! I only saw him once more in class and of course, that was not a happy occasion. I could tell Jerry and Mary Ellen were unhappy with me as we went straight home (no food that night) and from then on they were very careful about where we went. Their tough luck! Next time they won't pull such a stunt! Digger may have just been waiting until I asked about his future to tell me; Jerry and Mary Ellen were responsible for the whole 'deception trip.' Jerry drove in from another road so I wouldn't see the sign O'Dell Funeral Home at the end of Digger's driveway. That romance ended in a grave!

Now the University decided to build a campanile in memory of the soldiers who died in World War II and it would be built on the top of the hill overlooking the KU campus. Orville Roberts, my competitor and friend in the Forensic League, who had won the contest because I had gotten ill, asked me to help him raise funds.

War Monument That Laura and Orville Roberts Helped Fund

So the two of us went to work. We gave speeches on the radio appealing for funds, we showed up for meetings all over town giving our appeal: "that we must not forget those who gave their lives in the war!" And we truly did well; the campanile was paid for in full. In return Mr. Buehler gave us a beautiful framed photo that still hangs on my wall today. The reality of all those soldiers losing their lives in World War II will be in our memories forever. The monument stands as a testament of climbing to the skies.

Well, Hogan and I became pretty steady about seeing each other and he was in his senior year. He came to Corbin Hall for dates and on this October night he asked me to be his wife! After a few days consideration and speaking to Mother Brown, I accepted his offer.

Laura and Hogan

Mother Brown said to me, "Laura he is shorter than you and he is already semi-bald, so you know what he is going to look like in his old age."

What she didn't say was how bald one really does get.

But looks didn't matter to me and I was in love with Hogan! Come February we decided that we would marry after his graduation. We planned it to take place on my mother and father's anniversary, October 13th.

Now Hogan needed one more class to get his degree and he told me he had signed up for Political Science.

"And who is teaching that class?" I asked.

"Oh, a guy by the name of Hilden Gibson."

"Holy Cow!" I said, "No way, you can't go to his class!"

Of course he asked, "Why Not?"

I told him the story about being thrown out of his class because I questioned his theory on evolution. And, I told him, "If he ever finds out you are marrying Laura Schmid, you will flunk his course. He hates me!"

After thinking a little, Hogan said, "Well, he won't know that we are getting married, so I will just sign up because I need the credits."

He did, but we always walked to class together. Wouldn't you know it, we were walking to class one day and who is coming down the other side of the street but Hilden!

"Hogan!" I said. "Get across the street before he sees you with me, he will flunk you if he sees us together."

Naturally, Hogan accommodated my suggestion and he crossed the street. Then he spoke to Hilden! Hilden apparently didn't see me as I turned in to Fanueil Hall quickly to duck out of the way. Their words were limited, just the usual good morning, and how are you?

Did he pass the course? Yes. I think he got a B and he only needed the credit. Hilden died a few years later. I always wondered what it was like for him to meet God for the first time; his philosophy was that There is no God! He certainly could have used him when he was confronted by a Western Kansas Catholic!

Hogan's father wanted him to come home to Boston after graduation as his father was a widower with three sons. One of them had gone to the military academy at West Point and moved away. His younger brother Paul never had much direction and lived day to day, doing various jobs around town. Hogan was needed at home by his father.

Hogan had promised his father that he would return after college, and there was no way he was going to break that promise. He told me I could finish college in Boston, but we didn't know then that I wouldn't be able to afford it. That meant I would have to leave my home and family in Kansas. We had to change our wedding day to June so his father would come to the wedding and at the same time attend Dan's graduation.

Laura Engaged

Changing the date meant that I would be leaving home after the wedding. We would be going to Boston together.

When I approached Mr. Keeler, my boss of three years, he said, "Laura, you can't leave until you train another person to replace you. You have to stay until September so I can get re-organized!" He was really surprised by this and quite upset. "Why don't you and Bill stay here in Kansas and I will get you a job down in Leoville as the head of the Lecture Office there? I will pay you $4,000 a year. Bill can teach in Wichita only 15 miles east and he would earn about $3,000. That would be a great beginning in your married life."

I begged Hogan to accept his offer, but Hogan just could not disappoint his father. He decided he needed to go back and get a job and stay with his father until I could come; maybe I could come in September after training a replacement. We did not know that salaries differed so. Hogan went back east and got a job in

Mansfield, Massachusetts for $1920 a year, a sum quite a bit less than what he would have earned in Wichita, Kansas.

Well, who paid for the wedding? I had to work harder than ever trying to save money for our big day. Hogan was in school, so was not working.

My friend Winifred had gotten engaged as well, so we decided to go to Topeka to buy our wedding dresses. We went by train with her announcing she wanted a sheer looking gown, and I wanted a satin one. We looked all day. She ended up buying a satin one, and I bought a sheer one for $20. That meant I had to give them five dollars down and then send them a minimum of $1.50 a week.

Money was hard to come by so I made my own veil using the sewing machine at Corbin Hall. Then my bridesmaids, three of them, had me make their dresses. I stayed up many nights until 4:00 AM to finish the dresses in time.

During the ensuing months, my dear friend the Dean of Women, Dean Habein, showed concern. Knowing how hard I had to work and that money was a real problem, she really cared for me and was concerned as to how this wedding was going to happen. So secretly she arranged with the biggest women's store in Kansas City, Harfields, to bring out four different dresses so I would have a going away outfit. She had them bring hats, dresses, shoes, jewelry, under clothing, hose, purses and luggage to her apartment. Then she invited my housemother, Mother Brown, the bridesmaids, Mrs. Keeler and myself over for lunch.

You have no idea how overwhelmed I was when they came out with all this stuff for me! They even removed the prices so that would have no influence on my choices. I got everything from top to bottom and as you know, again the tears flowed. I was so taken by her affection and kindness. In later years she came to Boston and became President of Wheelock College. We saw her after she married, and we were able to be present at her funeral.

At this time I was enrolled in a Home Decoration class and was going there during the noon hour. My friend, roommate, and maid of honor, Marie, also took the class at the same time. Lucky for me, as my eyes would close during class from my heavy work schedule and I would sleep. Ms. McAuley saw what was happening and would deliberately ask me a question. Marie would always sit beside me, and would quickly give me the answer. Ms. McAuley could never figure out how I could recite the correct answer right out of a dead sleep!

In one class she gave us an assignment, due in three weeks. We were to furnish and decorate a four-room apartment for $800 or less.

The only thing in the apartment would be a stove, "So you don't have to buy that!" she said. "I want you to go to the furniture stores, catalogs, whatever source you like, and bring me an itemized list of what you intend to buy. It must not exceed $800."

Oh, Man! When was I going to have time to go shopping? So I took a catalog and cut out pictures and put on my own prices. In total I ended up with $800.50. Ms. McAuley never questioned the report and gave me an A. Then I got my report card and she gave me a D for the course!

I went to her and asked her, "How come I got a D? I got A's on all my quizzes and on my report I got an A."

Her terse reply: "Ms. Schmid I don't understand you. You slept through all my classes, and I am not going to let you have a different grade. Even though you may have earned it."

My reply: "Don't worry, I didn't need that grade anyway. I am getting married and that grade won't do anything. All I needed was the credit!"

She stayed friendly with me, but it was obvious she was still wondering how it happened that I slept through all her classes but still did so well. She attended our wedding as we remained friends.

My roommate and friend, Marie, was my Maid of Honor. We are still friends and why wouldn't we be? She married an attorney and moved to California. We were able to visit her once, and an annual letter keeps us in touch.

Now the weeks were flying by and the wedding was getting close. I wrote my family and begged them to come to Lawrence as I could not afford to go home to Atwood. My sister Threasa said she would come from Detroit to help me cook the food as Mother Brown told me I could use Corbin Hall for the reception. That we did. Money was so scarce I could not afford to buy flowers, but spring had sprung and there were beautiful roses blooming on the fence around the football stadium and the fields were blooming with white daisies. There was no sign that said do not pick, so I talked my bridesmaids into going down and picking the roses off the fence and the daisies out of the fields, and the lilies blooming on the road side; that way I could make the bridal bouquets myself. They got enough to do the bouquets and decorate the church! The St. John Evangelist Church was over-flowing with flowers and everyone loved them. Father Towle, Father Weisenberg and Father Jones were celebrants at the mass. Many of our college friends participated in the mass in one way or another and, my friend from Hilden Gibson's class, Vernie, the Seminarian came to play the organ.

My brother Charlie, my mother, and Toots came from home. I had asked to have Toots' four year-old daughter, my godchild Berniece, as my flower girl so they brought her as well. Also my brother Paul and his wife Shirley came with their son, four year old Dennis, who was our ring-bearer. Threasa came from Detroit. Bill's father came from Boston. All this made June 14, 1947 a very special day!

Little Dennis was bored, so he lay down on the steps of the sanctuary and went to sleep. Later we were looking for him to take pictures. He had gone out to the car and found Bill's father's prayer book. We asked him to come out so we could take a picture.

His answer was loud and clear: "Leave me alone, or I'll tear up that old man's cook book!"

His mom and dad finally convinced him to come out for pictures.

Money was still a big problem so for our honeymoon, Paul and Shirley drove us to Kansas City to stay one night at the Hotel Muhlebach. Bill's father was staying there that night as well. We walked into the ballroom to be greeted with The Anniversary Waltz, our favorite song even today.

Dancing is not one of my accomplishments. Hogan manages to tolerate it, or works around my stiffness.

On Sunday we had to return to Lawrence on the bus because Dan was graduating the next day (the real reason Dad Hogan had come). Dan's graduation took place, Dad Hogan left,

Dan then had to finish one course in July and at that time he returned to Massachusetts to await my release from Mr. Keeler.

Finally in September I was able to take a four-day ride from Kansas City to Boston on the train. My college friends took me to the station, handed me flowers, and wished a new life for me!! I was 12 hours short of a college degree, but gave it all up to get married! That was the way back then, and I am still today, A NON GRADUATE.

Saying good-bye to the prairie, my family, college friends, and a wonderful employer managed to occupy my thoughts as the train blew its whistle and took off roaring east. Four days alone on that train, thinking of all that had taken place, and trying to predict what lie ahead left me almost sleepless as I awaited my arrival in the east. I truly had no idea that our salaries would be so much less and that due to that circumstance, to finish college would be almost impossible.

Arriving in Boston was so exciting! Missing a few initials behind my name was not a concern for me then. The sight of the huge buildings, the number of people, and now starting a new life with the man I had chosen to marry kept me from shedding any tears. It is now 62 years later, and five children, 13 grandchildren and three great-grandchildren; life leaves me with no regrets. I did a lot of things in those early years, had a lot of fun, and learned a lot. I, Laura, have always remembered that through it all, there was never a promise that life would be easy. Now I hope for A FEW MORE YEARS AND NO MORE TEARS!

Chapter 5

A REMAINING BRANCH REMEMBERS

This is 2010 and my brother Joe is my one remaining family member. He has outlived all my other siblings reaching 91 years of age. Joe agreed to share many of his growing years with me. He was more near in age to my older siblings, and so can remember lots of the "hard years" a little better than I. He recorded many of those times so that I could use them in this book. Many of the events are printed as he reiterated them to me. He never went beyond the eighth grade, but was one of the most successful of the family not only in fame, accomplishments, and overcoming hardships, but in honesty, dedication and fortitude as well.

Joseph Henry was born to butcher-farmer parents in Atwood, Kansas on March 22, 1918. He had eight siblings. The branches of the Kansas tree grew, after Joe came Agnes Elizabeth and Paul Albert. After Annie Catherine died in 1922, I, Laura Margaret, came into being with Charles Martin, Louis Frederick and Andrew Bernard following behind. This is Joe's story.

The experiences of Joseph Henry Schmid:
Our Pa, Martin Schmid, was like Ma, he could do anything that needed to be done with his hands. Pa had strong, German hands and a stout build, accentuated by his long mustache. Pa taught us to slaughter animals by demonstrating with the skill of those hands. But that wasn't all: he showed us all the barn building, well digging and field plowing himself. He always had a way to do things that he thought was right! He could hitch up two horses to a wagon quicker than anybody.

Pa bought a couple of ponies from a guy named Madison who lived up town. Their names were Don and Bill. Pa bought them so the boys could serve mass on weekdays, something the boys of the church were encouraged to do. Pa would put the saddles on the ponies and sometimes I would watch him. He had a little cart that could be pulled by one of the ponies, but I never saw him hitch that up. I only saw him hitch up the big two-horse wagon up at the farm.

No one ever showed me how to do it or told me anything. But one day I wanted to take a ride in the one-pony cart, so I decided that I could do it myself!

There was a shaft on each side on the front of the cart and so I backed Don the pony up in there. There was a strap that went over the top of his back from one side to the other and you fastened it in the loops so the shafts wouldn't fall down. There was another strap that went under the stomach to keep the shafts at the same height all the time. That much I knew from watching Pa; but nobody showed me how. I didn't hook up the strap over the pony's back, I just hooked up the one that went under his belly. Next I got up on the cart and cracked the reins to go. We took off, but the shafts kept hitting Don and then they fell down on the ground, hitting him on his feet. Well, old Don got loose, took off and ran away. He ran clear back up to his old home up town, which was about three miles away. I had to get one of my brothers to help me and then we had to go up town to get him. It was quite an experience for a little kid like me to try to do something that I didn't know a thing about. But that taught me a lesson and after that I learned how to do it right.

Travel was most often via horse and wagon. Pa would get up at 4:00 AM, and get the horses hitched up to the big farm wagon. He'd leave about 4:30 to go get livestock for us to slaughter. He drove all over the place buying pigs, goats, cattle, whatever he could get at a good price, to be back at the farm by 6 or 7 so we could harvest the meat before school.

He'd do all the heavy work of tying up and killing the animal, and hoisting the body up on the rope-and-pulley for us to slaughter. He was eleven years senior to Ma, but was still killing and hoisting large steer in his sixties.

Sometime in the early 1920's, the family was growing and so Pa bought a second-hand Model T, and used the car to go into town. That was known as a touring car. Of all the things that Pa was good at, driving and taking proper care of a car was NOT one of them! On the farm it took a beating. The goats ate off the roof, the floorboards fell out, the exhaust pipe got disconnected; but all the kids loved it! Pa would take us up town in the car with a two-wheel trailer tied behind it. In the trailer Pa would have whatever he needed for the next two or three days at the market: beef, hog, milk, vegetables, and always eggs, which were most important for his customers. They were loaded into the trailer in a bucket, and whenever the model T would hit a bump, some of the eggs would break. When we got to town, Pa would take the broken eggs, punch a larger hole in one end and suck out the raw egg! He ate them like dessert! We would all grunt, "ugh" and he got a big kick out of that.

Pa was not a driver. He always had a tough time and never did learn how to drive a car with a gearshift. That's why we never had anything but a Model T. He would pull the trailer up town (more than 3 miles) and pull into a lot beside the butcher shop. Then he would try to back up. He never did learn how to back up properly, but he wouldn't listen to us kids. He did what he wanted to. He just always turned the front wheels on the car the wrong direction every time. He'd back up until the trailer stopped, usually hitting something.

Then we would reassure him, "We will empty the trailer and pull it back."

That worked because he would get frustrated and would not admit he created the problem. He used to run into the ditch once in a while, but he would never tell us what happened. The guys down at the garage would tell us that our dad was in today. They had to put another wishbone on the car. A wishbone was a piece of iron that would go from one side of the front wheel back to the end of the engine to a ball joint there. It fastened on both sides, then onto the other front wheel. (New cars haven't had them for years and years.) The trouble was, that thing would bend easily. Pa would get it fixed but would never tell us kids about running into the ditch or whatever he did.

One of Frankie and my jobs was to grind corn so the cattle could eat it better. That way they would not bloat up and die. We had an old Case Tractor from 1919 and it could not be used in the field because it wouldn't go fast enough. So Pa modified it for grinding the corn, and immobilized and anchored it. Pa told us to run it, so we kids would have a hay-day playing that we were driving it.

In the late 1920's rain was scarce, crops failed, there was no food for people or animals and the dust storms were beginning to come. They lasted for years and will always be remembered by those of us that survived. No rain was a huge problem because the animals needed food and it only came from the ground.

While the farm was still producing there were big piles of corn and stacks of hay from the alfalfa fields. Farmers would come in the middle of the night and steal grain to feed their starving cattle, as long as they could get away with it. To help solve the problem, Pa decided to hire a guy by the name of Majors to build an elevator for the grain. He also built a cement tank because we didn't have enough storage for water. They built us a big old tank out of concrete and they put up some forms for this thing five feet deep, twenty feet wide and thirty feet long. We had this windmill by the elevator and Pa put the Model T Ford there to pump the water. We had a pump jack and we'd fasten that up to the windmill when the wind didn't blow. We had to pump water this way almost all the time because at this time Pa had four to five *hundred* head of cattle that had to have water. After a while we learned to have fun in that tank! In the summer we boys would jump in there naked. We didn't have swimsuits and nobody had money to buy them. That's the way we took a bath until it got so cold we couldn't jump in there anymore. But even in the summer the water was always cold as we had to keep the pump pumping all the time.

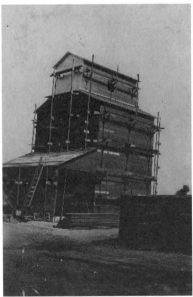

Building the Elevator and Water Tank, 1928

The neat thing about this tank was that we could put watermelons in a big sack and tie it shut with a rope, lower it down in the tank and the watermelons would get cold. That made them great for eating. The other thing we did without Pa and Ma knowing was that we also put beer in there to cool it off. We little guys would swipe the beer once in a while. Of course we couldn't drink that much, but we loved doing it.

When Pa had Majors build an elevator, that was quite a chore. He had to have a place to store grains for the cattle so the people couldn't steal it from the mounds. It had to be built really strong because the grain was so heavy it would bust the sides out. Those workmen knew how to do that. One of the guys out there working was using a measuring tape, left it on the ground and one of the goats went up there and started eating the measuring tape! It was a fifty-foot tape made out of cloth. When the guy saw the goat eating it he started pulling on that tape so he could scare the goat and get him to stop eating it. He was pulling on that tape just as easy as he could getting it out a little at a time, but after a bit the goat took off. He kept running behind him holding onto the tape, but eventually the goat won the race and he lost the tape. He tried to charge Pa for the tape. He didn't win out.

Jim and Johnnie Building the Garage

About 1929, the butcher shop and the farm kind of slowed down. It was due to the hard times, the depression and the bad weather. It was getting real dry and of course all of us kids would get the chicken pox, mumps, measles, whooping cough, and when one kid got well, another would get it. In those days, every time you were sick you would get quarantined and you could not go any place and no one could come see you. One time Spuds got Scarlet Fever. That was a bad disease. Only two of us got it at first. Spuds got it first and then my younger sister, Laura. I remember being in the bedroom and poor Spuds had it pretty bad. He was trying to climb up the walls, he was so out of his head! When the rest of us got sick the doctor figured out that we had to get vaccinated. We had to have three shots, each a week apart. After three weeks those shots felt like they would kill you. You were so scared of getting those shots it was pitiful. Poor Mom had to calm us down quite a bit at each shot.

About this time the dust storms arrived. They went on for years! People just up and abandoned the land. Some took off to California I understand. The drought was unmistakable and even as a child I remember we could see the mounting black clouds forming in the sky between 9:30 and 11:00 AM. People would see it getting dark and they would have to turn on their car lights if they were on the road. They could see the storm rolling in and they knew they had to get somewhere fast. We kids would really get scared if we were outside because we would not be able to find the house! There were lots of rabbits in those days (they were part of our food). They were so smart, they sensed the storm coming and they would run ahead of the storm to get away. Unfortunately many of them were caught up in the wind and dust and did not make it. You would find their dead bodies everywhere. There was nothing they could do or that humans could do to escape...NOTHING!

We'd hang wet bed sheets over the windows and tape the doors shut, but the dust came in 1,2,3, even 4 inches in a day. Everything inside and out was covered. When you went to bed at night, the dust had gotten in between the bed sheets. We had to sleep with washcloths over our mouths and noses.

On one of these days, my brothers Freddie and Frankie had to take a couple of wagonloads of hogs up to the Sale Barn; there was no food for them so they had to be sold. They left early but the dust storms hit before they got home. You couldn't see anything! They had this wonderful team of big black horses, 'Dan' and 'Chubb.' They were coming back to the North Place (an addition of land and a house two miles north of our home) and the horses seemed to know which way to go. On their way the team stopped. You couldn't see your hand in front of your face there was so much dust, so Fred and

Frank followed the wagon around to the horses' heads. The poor things had gotten off the road and couldn't see anything and they ended up on the edge of the creek and ran into the trees there. It was almost pitch dark from the dust, though it was mid-day. Frank and Fred had to pull the horses with one hand and follow the barbed wire fence with the other hand to lead them back home.

We worked in the fields starting at an early age. When I was eleven I was told to work the field because times were bad and Dad needed more help than ever to produce on dry land. He sent me out to cut sunflowers. I had to use a big old hoe that was made out of cast iron. It was real heavy. I had to use that hoe to try to chop out those big sunflowers by hand. It took a big hoe to do that. An ordinary hoe just wasn't heavy enough to cut out those sunflowers, which were taller than me. This is how Pa raised his boys, strong and productive from an early age.

At this time we had cows in a corral and those poor cows would go down and lay in this hole in the creek to keep cool in the water. The water was now gone, however, and the poor cows would lie in the hole for days. Every day we would take a team of horses down to pull them out of the hole because they were too weak to even get up. We would throw a lasso around their necks and pull them out. But things got worse by the day. We would pull them out dead. They got dust pneumonia, they had only thistles and maybe a tiny bit of straw to eat. They either choked to death or died of starvation.

Thistles are weeds, but they were food as well; if they were left to grow they became full of stickers. While crops would not grow, thistles would grow without moisture; they liked dry land. They could be cut when green, so Pa hired Art Frick and a neighbor, Gusty Blackmore, to help me stack the thistles and any remaining straw. Gusty was the best hay stacker in this part of the country. We'd go out there and mow the thistles to feed the cattle and the rest we would stack for future use. The trouble was that the wind would blow the dust into the stacks so bad that the cows and horses were eating dirt. Consequently we lost a lot of cattle from dust pneumonia. If you opened their stomachs, you would find inches of mud, how could they live? We tried hard to keep the faith.

I remember trying to work the dry field. I spent one full month of May planting corn in the dust. We usually started planting corn around the 10th of May and it would take a couple of weeks. We'd plant this corn with a tool called a one-row lister. The lister had four holes, but because of the corn shortage I only used three.

Things got so bad we had nothing to feed the animals. We even fed them Cane (which we weren't supposed to do). Cane was a pithy stem that when dried was used for many things (but not fed to cattle). If they ate too much they would die of indigestion.

After 1934 it started to get a little bit better but I still had to cut the thistles because they would collect the dust and become big mounds of dirt in the fields. I couldn't sit on the disk to plow them under because if I hit one of those mounds, I would fly up in front of the plow and get run over and hurt real bad. The fences were on the side of the road and those thistles would blow across the side of the road, catch in the barbs of the fence, and fill up with dirt. Then there would just be a big ridge over the fence. If there were any cattle around, over the top they would walk and they would get away. This is how bad the dust storms were. The cattle would get mixed up with the neighbor's cattle. Unless your cattle recognized you, you could not know who was their rightful owner.

Also at this time our pigs got cholera. That's a disease hogs got and ours got it bad. There was no way you could stop it. You would just have to let it run its course. My brother Johnnie, still home at the time, helped me get the old iron wheels off the headers and we made a corral where the hogs were and every day we would drag those dead hogs on top and set them on fire. Every day we would drag more and more of them and the ones from the day before would still be burning. Some hogs died every day and we would put them on top, as they would keep burning because they were fat and fat burned very well, like kerosene. Pa could not buy any new hogs until they all died off. Finally we got to start buying young ones off and on again, but we had to vaccinate them for cholera every time for many years. To this day, I think they still vaccinate hogs for cholera.

At this same time, my dad still had the butcher shop up town and hard times really came. My dad was good-hearted and he would charge anybody only what they had to pay, even the bums that came around and there were quite a few of them. They were mostly good guys; hunting for a job they had a hard time finding. Dad sold lunch meat and when it got down to a hunk, he would put it aside in the show case and when one of those guys came in begging for something to eat, he gave it to them along with a nickel box of crackers or something like that. That's what crackers sold for in those days and working people would buy lunchmeat and crackers for their lunch.

There were gypsies everywhere and they would come into the shop with aprons. They would steal food by putting it in the apron and pretending they had their clothes in the aprons so you wouldn't see. They stole vegetables, eggs, and other food off the shelves. My dad would give away the shirt off his back. My sister, Toots knew Pa was too kind, so she would desperately try to get the beggars out before they saw Pa. They weren't dumb, however, they would just go outside and wait until they saw Pa, then in they came again. That worked for them.

Even our Doc Henneberger, the richest guy in town, would come into Dad's shop and get his food. Doc lived in the hospital he operated, so Dad would not charge him because if anything went wrong to anybody in the family, we always had to go see Doc Henneberger. For some reason or another most of my brothers and sisters had appendicitis and Doc could take them out with his eyes practically closed. He'd make a little bitty cut there. He was good at that as well as delivering all of Ma and Pa's babies. He was well to do, which probably had a lot to do with being able to eat all he wanted for free. Pa's meat was out of this world. He knew how to feed the cattle gathered for slaughtering.

My next to the littlest brother, Louie, broke his arm once. I think he fell out of a tree or something. Doc set that arm, but he was not good at broken bones. Anyway he fixed that arm, but when he took off the cast, little Louie couldn't straighten it, so he made him carry a bucket of sand around almost all the time. That worked. I have to say, Doc was treated so well, he lived off Pa and never paid a dime for his food. But then Pa got all his family's medical problems solved for free so it was a mutually beneficial relationship.

The doc and his wife Frances used to play Fox Horses quite a bit in Kansas City. They used to do what they called 'The Board of Trade.' I never knew what that was or what they did. Once in a while they made money, but usually they left broke, so they would have to stay home for a while until they got some money to go try again.

Doc was around when most of my siblings and Ma and Dad had gone into eternity.

In fact, when Mom passed away Doc Henneberger announced, "If anyone should have died of hard work, Eva Schmid should have died 50 years ago. She was the hardest worker I have ever known."

The Hay Rake

Spuds and I were always in the field mowing hay and then having to stack it. One day the wind was blowing like crazy and Spuds was knocked down by it into the damn hay rake. The rake was rolling around with Spuds in it! Lucky for him the rake tripped up because it was too full and he was dumped out on the ground. The horses got scared and ran away over to the fence. We were able to catch them. After that however, we decided to put the raked hay into rows and made aisles between them. We had to do that by hand. Pa objected. He always wanted to do things like they did in Germany. We convinced him that times had changed. People had better ideas. He never really liked our decision, but he went along with it. After we had the rows we would go get the wagon and pitch the hay up into the wagon. We'd have one guy on the wagon and the rest of us would stay in the field and throw it up to fill the wagon. We could do two wagons if we had enough hired hands. When we had two wagons full, we would go over to make the haystack.

Pa would always hire Gusty Blackmore because he knew how hay had to be stored. He would start at the bottom and stack up about three feet high, then he would start widening that stack out to make the stack bigger. Then he would have us walk on top to stamp all the hay down so that it would settle more on the outside, that way it would shed rainwater. If it was not stacked properly, the hay would get moldy and it would all be lost. The stacks had to be eight feet high, and if they were not stacked properly, they would fall over. We could see when they were going to fall over, so we would have to take fence posts and prop them up.

So Much Hay

Another time, Art and I cut the top out of the windmill and put it up higher so we could let the water spray out a little bit and had it go into a 50 gallon barrel. The barrel would be filled with water and because the sun was so hot in the summer time, it would get warm. That meant at night we could turn on the spray and wash under it. That was the way we showered.

Frankie and I were very close, two brothers that had to work hard even though we were young. Frankie had access to the old Model T and he had a hang up on a girl named Millie Flood who lived in Trenton, Nebraska. That town was about 30 or 40 miles away, so it would take a long time for him to come home when he went there. Most of the time he wouldn't get home until daylight the next day. The problem was that when he would be coming home, the old ford would get hot because the water would boil out of the radiator or the radiator leaked, then he would run it into the ditch. He didn't care, so he would take a nap until the car cooled off, then he would drive some more. Even if there was a farmhouse along the way, he never bothered to stop to fill the car with water. He would just keep on driving and that's why he never got home until morning most of the time.

Consequently, when I would go out to stack hay, I might be out there all by myself because he was not home yet. Pa would be upset when Frankie wasn't there, because one person couldn't do this alone. When that happened Pa would have to go up town and find three guys and bring them down to catch up on the farm work that had been missed. Of course, those guys never had to work hard all day long for weeks on-end, so they couldn't keep up with us. By noon they would be played out! Pa knew this so he would come back out and bring three more guys and take the first three back to town. None of those guys could ever hang in like Frankie, Gusty and I. We worked all day every day, except Sunday. Pa raised us to work hard.

There was a young kid that was the son of old man Wolfe, a guy I took violin lessons from, that would come out to help. His name was Waldo, but he would get played out too, and it would make him boiling mad because he couldn't keep up with Frankie and I.

He'd say, "I am going to prove to you that I can work all day!"

Each day thereafter he would try to work 15 minutes longer than the day before. Well, he finally made it all day without getting played out and he was happy as a lark.

Dogs would come out from town and chase our cattle and hogs, so we would have to shoot them or they would kill the animals. They would get into packs and one night Freddie went out and saw a little bitty bulldog following the pack. That little dog didn't know what was going on, so Fritz thought he would have some fun. Fritz shot a few of the dogs, but didn't shoot him. The little bulldog got scared and ran back to town with the other ones that got away.

One night there was a dog chasing the hogs. Those dogs would rip those hogs up badly and many times we would lose good hogs to the dogs. They wouldn't eat them; they would just bite and kill them. That night I had my Model A. Lee, a hired hand staying with us that night drove it and I sat out on the front fender firing shots at these darn dogs in the alfalfa field. We took after this one dog and were chasing him like crazy. I kept shooting but he kept running. Well, he ran into the crick and of course we couldn't drive in there so that was the end of that chase and we left. About three weeks later I was down at the crick and there was the old dog, dead. I must have wounded him.

"Hey, I got him!" I said, but I kept that info on the QT because it turned out he was owned by Old Heavy Warner, the owner of the restaurant in Ludell. He had been a heavy weight champion boxer, and if he ever found out where his dog was, he would have worked me over good.

We had two dogs, Shep and Fido. I would take them for a walk down to the crick where the cattle used to go to get water. Fish would gather around, the dogs would run into the water but could never catch anything. The dogs stirred up the mud. Then the catfish would come to the top of the muddy water and I could scoop them up by hand. That meant we would have fish for supper!

I have to tell you another story, it was kinda dirty what we did. There was a little short Mexican guy up town. They called him 'Shorty.' He shined shoes in the pool house to make money. The problem is, we were farmers and wore work shoes. Nobody would ever spend money to shine them, but we did have a 'go out' pair, so once in a while we would get *them* shined. Of course, Shorty could not make a living from that kind of income. So Pa, knowing he could pick him up to work, would bring him out to work with the other guys he'd find.

Frankie and I loved to be ornery at times. Sometimes we would pull some pretty rough tricks on these guys. Most of them wore hats to keep the sun off their heads, so Frankie and I bought Limburger cheese (a real stinky cheese). The smell was unbelievable. It was so potent you could smell it all the way down the block. We would cut the rind off the cheese and then when they were resting we would stick it in their hat behind the rim. Or we would sneak it in when Toots, Tressie and Mom had to cook for these guys and would bring the food out to the field. One day when they were eating in the shade of a tree that was there, we slipped a rind of that cheese in Shorty's hat. The next day Shorty came back and he was down pitching up the hay and you could smell it clear up on the wagon. He kept grinning and wouldn't say nuthin'. He wasn't a big talker anyway. The next day he came back still smelling! Finally we asked him what he was grinning about.

He said, "Well you know the other day I went home and you know what I smelled like? I can't say for sure that you know, but I took my pants down, took a bath and I looked around still trying to figure out that smell. I changed my clothes again and on the way here, I finally looked in my hat and found out what you guys did. Ha! Ha! I fooled you too."

Frankie was always asking to borrow my car, and one day Pa called me up and said, "I need you up at the butcher shop today."

He used me for that a lot because I was really young to be working in the fields. I was about to leave in my car for the shop when Frankie stopped me. Frankie had been working in the field that day and he wanted to go over to Trenton to see Millie. He asked me to switch cars with him so he could take my car to Millie's. He claimed his old car wouldn't make it over and back. I didn't want to let him have it because I knew what he had done with my car before. He begged and begged so finally I gave in, because I knew his dumb Model T wouldn't make it.

I had just gotten my Model A overhauled. They had bored out the cylinder walls, put in new rings, new bearings, ground the valves and did everything to bring it up to par. It nearly killed me because it cost $34 to get it done (of course today it would be about $2000). When you had this done, you were supposed to drive no more than 30 miles an hour until you had gone 500 miles. I had only a few hundred on it, and I should have known better than to let Frankie have it. But I did, and I drove his car to Pa's shop that day. Evidently, Frankie drove it wide open all the way over and all the way back. When he got back that night and stopped out front, the car was hotter than Hades and steaming like crazy. He had ruined the engine! He was so mad! He claimed the car was no good.

Well I knew the mechanic at the garage, he was a really good guy so he rebored the cylinders and found out that the new pistons had gotten so hot they melted in the cylinders! So he had to replace everything again. After that the car was just no good, it was using a lot of oil and just wouldn't work right.

I'll tell you the story of when I had to sell my little spotted pigs. Threasa was living with me at the North Place and we had 60 or 70 white hogs that were under our care. One old sow had nine little pigs, some spotted, some white. Well the sow got what they called milk fever and she died. So Threasa and I took the little pigs up to the milk house. We would have to get up every couple of hours during the night to feed them with a bottle. We had to do that for quite a few days and then it eased off because we taught them how to drink milk that we poured in a pan. Then one Sunday we went to church and when we came home our little pigs were gone. We said something to Ma and she told us that Jim had come over and Pa gave them to him. Well, you talk about being mad, both Threasa and I were madder than hatters. We had the little spotted ones in another pen because they were growing bigger. We got the pigs back from Jim before he sold them.

I told Ma, "You tell Pa to leave our spotted pigs alone! They are mine!"
After that I took special care of them giving them milk and grain, all they could eat. Thank goodness these pigs got to weigh about 90 pounds, usually you kept them until they weighed 180 pounds, but I was afraid Pa would take them. So one Wednesday, Sale Day at the Sale Barn, I took them up and sold them for $70. That's where I got the money to buy a new car.

I got Ed Rippe to go with me and we went over to McCook and I drove that old Model A as it was in pretty bad shape. We looked around over there and we finally decided to buy a '31 Pontiac. It looked pretty good and it wasn't too bad a car. I think I paid $250 for it. I forget how much they allowed me for the old Model A. That $250 was partly from the money I got for my pigs, plus I had a little bit more saved up and my sister Threasa gave me some. Threasa was always very good to me. I don't think I ever paid her back. The Pontiac turned out to be a pretty good car, and it was sure a lot better than driving those older models.

About this time the depression was taking place. The government started the C.C.C. (Civilian Conservation Corpse) camp for young guys, 18 to 21 years old. They couldn't get a job so they were sent out to build barracks with mixed up mud and straw and made what they called dobby bricks. They would lay the bricks and build the barracks and they did a pretty good job. Those guys were kept under guard and were disciplined pretty hard. They would let them run around with the local girls a bit, but kept them away from local guys because the guys would get jealous of them fooling around with the girls.

One of those guys was a pretty good fighter and they used to have boxing matches with each other. They nicknamed him Spider. I think he was a pretty good boxer. I never did try to box him.

We were still stacking alfalfa at this time. There would usually be about four crops a summer. The first crop always grew a little taller than the others. After you mowed it, it would have to dry a little, but if it dried too much you would lose all the leaves and then you would only have stems. The leaves were the part of the hay that the cattle would eat. I would try to use Bess and Bute to mow this hay. I trusted those horses pretty well and I got along fine with them. Once in a while I would stop and go into the house to get a drink of water or something to eat. I would go off and not unhitch the tugs. I would just let them stand there until I got back. Well, one day I stayed in a little longer than I was supposed to and pretty soon I heard the mower going and I looked out and saw Bess and Bute out there just cutting that hay by themselves, walking around the patch as always but this time without a driver! They were doing just as well as if I were driving them.

When we would get to the haystack to stack the hay, the grasshoppers were really thick at this time. They would congregate around the haystack and when the horses would come nearby they would fly up in droves off the ground; little bitty ones, and big green ones, sometimes two inches long. These were the things we had to fight, but had no weapons to use. Grasshopper invasions happened many years during this trying time. They would devour everything growing on the earth. You have to know grasshoppers were weird bugs, long legs, long and big bodies; ugly to say the least. They did not bite, but we didn't like them. The horses didn't like them either.

Water is essential for field workers. The modern guys today can run around with insulated jugs and thermos to keep what they want to drink cool. Well, we only had a big glass jug that we had to wrap gunnysacks around. We'd wet the gunnysack and fill the jug with water, and then take some nails and pin the edges of the gunnysack together, wrapping the jug. The gunnysack was then kept wet to keep the water cool. That way, the water would stay cool for maybe two or three hours. Then we'd have to go to the pump and refill it and rewet it.

We had to drink a lot of water or we would have died of thirst, it was so hot in that sun. Some days we had to quit working because it would be 120 to 130 degrees in the shade! That meant we took a two or three hour break, but it didn't seem like much of a break in that awful heat.

After a few years there were a lot better ways of putting up hay. There came a machine that had wooden stakes, called gongs about six feet long, about a foot apart, and the whole thing would be about eight feet wide, it was called a 'hay buck.' We could take that thing and drive it under the rows of hay that we had raked up. You'd put a horse on one side, and another on the other side, and we would sit in the seat behind the horses. Then we would force the horses to drive the gongs under the rows and the hay buck would then pick up the hay. You pulled a lever and it would take it up a foot or two off the ground. We would then drive over to the haystack and raise it up to the top and dump it off. It was sort of an early forklift, driven by horses. It meant we only needed guys to separate the hay and spread it over the stack. We didn't need guys to pitch the hay. Separating and spreading was a hard job too, but the hay buck sped up the whole hay stacking process and we didn't have to do it all by hand.

Back then we had to pump our own water, but we figured out how to connect Dad's old Model T to the pump and when the wind didn't blow we would start up the car to run the pump to fill up the tank. Then that old engine finally wore out. Louie and I were out there playing and Louie was cranking and playing and he got his little finger caught in the gear. I was turning the wheel and didn't know it. The wheel went all the way around. That crushed the end of his little finger, but he never said anything to anybody about it. One time, later on when we were in school, the teacher noticed him picking on that little finger quite a bit. She went over and looked at it. It was dead on the end and Louie had just picked the fingernail off of it! Finally the end just rotted off about an inch and a half. It was hard to believe that he never got an infection. It was very sore, I am sure. He spent the rest of his life with a short finger. As well, one day Pa was grinding hamburger, stuck his finger in the grinder when it stopped working. Yes, he lost a finger, never to get it back.

About this time, the W.P.A. (Work Projects Administration) was started for married men to build roads. They would work at least two weeks out of the month, stay on the road and stand around, lean on the shovel, do anything like that and they were paid $15 a month. You were supposed to live on that, but naturally they couldn't so they would come in to Pa and run up a tab for food. They could never pay their bill. I remember Dad hired Frank Chester, Otto Clepimeyer, and Bill Barren to cut firewood for us to burn in the wintertime. Right over by the school there was a crick (these days they would call it a creek) near the corner field and there were old cottonwood trees that grew real big, along with a few willow trees. We could not farm that part of the land as it was near the crick; the crick would just dry up and leave a hole. We used to play in it during recess. The guys would finally get a wagonload of wood cut and I would go over there with the team of horses and the wagon and we'd throw it on and I would take it home. After two weeks they would start cutting again. They didn't work very hard. They would just sit there by the fire that they made by burning up the little twigs and the little pieces of wood. For their work, Dad would give them a dollar credit on their bill. When wood would be short Pa would send them into the pasture to pick up the cow manure chips that had dried in the sun. They were used to heat the house when wood was scarce. When we had to start the fire in the school for the teacher, we even used cow chips there as well. There was no cost for that heat.

We worked all during the week and also on Saturday, but we could pass the time the way we wanted on Sunday. We did not work on Sunday as Pa and Ma would not allow that, so we would go up town and of course there was nothing to do there. We would sit on the sidewalk and watch the girls go by, maybe one or two. Frankie couldn't drive that Model T worth a damn and there was what we called a parkway, a two-lane divided road with a center meridian.

We would sit with the car about five blocks down the parkway at the bottom of the hill. There was a schoolhouse built at the top of the hill, they called it a high school (foreign to us since we were not allowed past the eighth grade). There were two or three friends of ours, the Frick boys and Lyle Most, that lived up town and they would meet us there. They loved riding in that Model T up the hill. Frankie was a daredevil, so he would drive that old T up the hill as fast as he could, and take that u-turn at the top with just the right speed. He could get it up on two wheels and then come right down the hill again. The schoolboys could never get enough of that ride! To my knowledge Frankie never overturned that car.

Of course, Frankie liked being Frankie. One day he had a horse in the corral and he was trying to get him to come through the gate, but the horse wouldn't go. He got mad at the horse and believe it or not, he punched him on the side of the head and knocked him flat on the ground. That's how hard he could hit. At that time he was using two of our greatest horses, Dan and Chubb, they weighed about 1650 pounds each. My gray horses were not as big so Dan and Chubb would pull all the heavy loads of hay.

This particular season Pa bought hay from a guy named Obert, west of Atwood. Frankie was sent to pick up the hay, which he would do and then drive down into Atwood to stop at Shorty and Otis's place. They were big guys, and good friends because we would go see them a lot. Frankie would stay there for hours and hours, and poor old Dan and Chubb would get tired of standing there, so they would just take off and go back home with no driver! It was three miles and those two horses would just stay on the side of the road and make their way back to the farm without Frankie. Once, they were in the middle of the road and had to turn to avoid a car. The rack tipped over and they were stuck until Frankie came by to help them. After that they always stayed very near the side to stay clear of the cars. They did this all on their own, and from then on would go all the way home with no driver at the wheel. I wonder what people thought when they saw them coming down the road with no driver.

Frankie liked to show off as well, so he would let them go down the street a ways and then yell at them to come back. If the street was not wide enough to turn around, Dan and Chubb would actually back up all the way. You wondered how they knew what to do, but there was a thing on the rack called a reach, it would run from the front wheels to the back, and I believe when the wheels hit that reach, the horses knew enough to try to straighten out and then proceed with their journey. Frankie would brag, showing them off. Horses became your friend if you treated them right. Dan and Chubb respected Frankie, but never liked him much.

Now when we would go up town, I had a good set of boxing gloves and I would bring them. They were pretty big gloves, about 14 ounces I think. They were more or less to play with, but I would throw them in the back seat of the car and that's where they stayed when we would drive into town. There were a couple of guys that worked in the filling station that Joe Youngblood owned. I can't remember their names but they would be in the beer joint longer than necessary and they would put on the gloves to see if they could whip me. Old Frankie would fight them off to save me and he wouldn't box around like the other guys. He didn't play around and stuff, he went in for blood and he'd try to hit you just as hard as he could. He was way too much for those bar hounds to handle, and knocked several of them out cold on several occasions.

Then he and Spuds boxed a little bit. Spuds was younger than he and once, he knocked poor Spuds out cold. But when I would box him, I would just get out of his way a little bit and I would watch his eyes and he would come at me for the kill. Then I would just step to one side and duck real low and he would swing that right hand over the top of me. While he was vulnerable, I would hit him over the heart just as hard as I could. That would knock him back because I knocked the breath out of him, and then he couldn't do anything till he caught his breath. He never learned how not to fight that way. You had to know that to ever let him hit you with his right hand, that would mean the end of you. You would definitely see stars. So I always used that trick and it always fooled him.

Art Frick, Mike Folke and I became good friends so we would go off to a dance, play ball and stuff like that. Well, one night we went to a dance in Goodland, Kansas about 80 miles away. That was a long way to drive in those days with an old car, but we used to stay until 1:00 AM anyway. They would start about 9:00 or 10:00 at night. This night I was driving home in my '31 Pontiac.

I was tired and I said to those guys, "Stay awake cuz I'm sleepy."

Mike was sitting up front with me and Art was in the back seat. Art lay down in the back seat and was sleeping away. The roads were made of gravel. They would pile extra gravel to make a ridge on the side of the road, so you would not get into the ditch. Those ridges were about 15 inches high or so. Well, I was going along and I fell asleep. I drove over the ridge half way with two wheels over the side. That woke me up, so I tried to back out of the ridge, and it worked! I'll be darned, I actually didn't roll the car over. We should have known you couldn't work hard all day, then party all night *and* drive 80 miles home!

Not all people were honest. We had a neighbor who also had cattle. He would go down the side of the road where a fence indicated our land. He would take three or four rows of the barbed wire fence surrounding our land off the posts, so his cattle could walk into our fields and eat our feed. One day my friend Lyle, my brother Johnnie and I were riding in the car and saw the neighbor's bull calf in our field.

Johnnie yelled, "Let's get him!"

They jumped over the top of the car before it even stopped, and jumped over the top of me. Lyle knocked the calf down and sat on him. Well, Johnnie, my brother, decided he'd fix the neighbor so he castrated the bull calf.

By the time I got out of the car Johnnie said, "Come on guys, we gotta get out of here."

A long time later that neighbor discovered the calf was no longer a bull, but he couldn't figure out how it had gotten castrated. He had been keeping him for milk cows and now he was no good. Johnnie loved to castrate anything he saw. He would catch rabbits and castrate them. He also would castrate the neighbor's dogs if he caught them in our place. We would then tie tin cans on their tails and turn them loose. Other dogs would hear them and chase them like crazy. After that they never came back to our land!

Johnnie stayed on the farm for a while, and then started dating Nina Lintner. Her father had four brothers who had received their father's land and so they were pretty much the richer farmers in the area. Well Johnnie courted Nina for a year or so and everybody thought he would marry her, then all of a sudden he walked away about 1931. Nina then took a shine to Johnnie's older brother Jim. Time seemed to prove that Johnnie wanted a family and that was not

Nina's cup of tea. In March of 1932 Johnnie married Olive Hatch and they had a baby that year. They lived in the North Place. Unfortunately Olive was not a housekeeper, or a farmer's wife. One day she just took off, left Johnnie and took baby Evelyn to California. My sister Threasa, who used to go clean up Olive's mess, washing her dishes and cleaning up the house, decided to move in with Johnnie.

In September of 1932, Nina and Jim married. Jim worked in the butcher shop until he got ill, then he and Nina went to Colorado and after their return lived in downtown Atwood for a short time. He then built a new house north of Atwood with Nina. Years later, when Johnnie would return home on a visit, Nina was the first person to go see him. That made the family think she only married Jim to make Johnnie jealous.

Just about this time, my brother Fritz started sneaking off to see the neighbor girl, Gertrude who lived with her brother Shorty. Their farm was only a quarter of a mile north of home. She worked for the doctor when he had something to do, cooked for Shorty and obviously courted Fritz who was 20 years younger. Shorty was real tight with money, like we all were because of the economy. He lived like everybody else in those days, on eggs, potatoes and a few vegetables.

After Olive left, I moved to the North Place with Johnnie and Threasa. I had a pony at home and let my brother Spuds take him. His name was Tony. I had gotten tired of him and I wanted the bigger horse that Johnnie had, that he called Babe. That was a full-grown Bay horse. Well, poor old Tony got sick and he kept getting worse so we made a pen for him in our barn and put him there. He would just try to walk around but would run into the petitions, skinned his head real bad and shortly after, he died. We never could figure out what was wrong with him.

Pa had hired Art Frick; his family lived up town. Art would stay at our house for several weeks to help me out. In those days you would usually hire a veterinarian to castrate your livestock, but we Schmid boys loved to do that. So, when we had 50 or 60 pigs we would castrate them and save the testicles for "mountain oysters." That's what you called bull's balls that were preserved in a tasty recipe. We would have two-thirds of a five-gallon bucket full. I would have to clean them which was quite a job as you had to peel them, wash them out the best you could, then soak them in a bucket with a lot of salt water for several days. Then you would change the water, add a little less salt, and soak them for another day or two. Then the water would be drained. We would sneak them up town and hide them in Pa's cooler until we had a party. Once in a while, however, Pa would find them and sell them out from under us. When he didn't find them, we would invite our friends over, fry them and have them with beer.

At the party there would be the Kastens, the Newhearts, and Rose Nelson that we kind of ran around with down in Ludell when we had the dances. Well, I had to cook the dang things 'cause I was the only one who knew how. You'd take a bunch of crackers and mash them up, then mix the crumbs with eggs and roll the oysters in that. If they were big enough, you would stuff them, but you really had to keep them the size of the end of your finger. After they were covered you threw them in hot frying fat. We used lard in those days and they were darn good when finished. I could brag because I was one of the few who knew how to cook them. They were so darn good we would have a hell of a good time drinking beer and eating them. Of course you could only have that party when you got more pigs.

One day, my brother Fritz and his wife Gertrude came over.

So I said to Art, "Let's all go to town and buy ice and make ice cream and drink beer."

You have to know beer and ice cream really didn't mix. Our beer was in these large stone jars so we sent Fritz and Gertrude to town to get the ice. While they were gone we took bottles, brown and a lighter color and filled the brown ones with beer, the lighter ones with water. Then when they returned we made the ice cream. It came out great! We gave Fritz and Gertrude the beer in the brown bottles while we drank water out of the lighter ones. They got sicker than dogs and started vomiting like crazy. What they didn't know was that Art and I had the water, and were not drinking beer. They couldn't figure out why we didn't get sick! Art and I had a ball eating the rest of the ice cream.

Then there was the outhouse near the windmill. We didn't have paper so we used red and white corncobs kept in a bucket to wipe ourselves. We would use the red cobs first and then use the white ones, so we knew when we were clean. Then we'd drop them down the hole. Those cobs filled the hole pretty quickly; before long we had to dig another hole and move the outhouse because it was full and smelly!

My sister Threasa had gotten sweet on Mike Folke, a friend of mine. He was a neat guy and we got along great. He started dating Threasa and they were about to become engaged. This night, however, he was going home and evidently fell asleep at the wheel, the car went off the highway on a hill, he flew into the canyon, and was found dead at the wheel. I know Threasa never got over losing him.

Agnes and Joe (back row) at Verneda and Ed's Wedding

Verneda eventually married Ed Rippe and moved away. Fritz's marriage was never accepted by the family because of Gertrude's age, so he wrote Uncle Jake in Louisville, Kentucky and Uncle Jake got him a job. Fritz and Gertrude moved there. Fritz got a job with A & P, a grocery chain and worked there most of his life. Threasa then got tired of the farm and decided to join Fritz in Kentucky. After Verneda married Ed Rippe, I stayed with them for a while, but then wanted a better life so I decided to move to Denver around 1939. Thereafter Charlie took over the North Place, later married and lived there until he died.

My life changed dramatically as World War II came into being and I was drafted. That story is related with the story of my other four brothers who were destined to take the same route. Those stories are told in a later chapter.

After coming home years after the war, I visited an old farmer by the name of Pete. He was one of the richest farmers in the area, but he was tighter than you can imagine with his money.

He started talking about the war and he said, "I know you won't like what I'm saying, but why are they paying those God Damn soldiers money? They got their food to live on. Why should we have to pay income tax just to pay them, for what?"

In those days, we soldiers were getting just $21 a month! Down the way they raised it to $30 and by the end of the war they paid us $50. Of course, what Pete said didn't set well with me, but I didn't talk back to him. About five years later I returned home and ran into his son-in-law. He told me poor old Pete had been in an old-folks home for about four years. Everybody felt so sorry for him.

My reply was, "Well, if he felt us soldiers in the war got paid *so well*, why didn't he go fight the Germans and the Japs like the rest of us? They would have just as soon shot his 'you-know-what,' as they did mine then *I* could have stayed home! Then I could be rich like him, instead of being unable to have a good life."

Of course, the son-in-law could not reply, only shook my hand and wished me well. Unfortunately many of the citizens had Pete's attitude. But the war ended and we are still paying income taxes.

Chapter 6

THE RAVAGES OF WAR

World War II changed the Schmid Family in many ways. Seven sons were of drafting age, however Jim and Johnnie were too old to be inducted because they would have gone over the age limit by the time they were trained. Jim went on to his own farm with his wife Nina. Johnnie went on to California. Frank and Fred, fraternal twin brothers, having moved before the war to different areas of the country were in the age limit and would have been drafted. Frank, living in Chicago with his wife Mildred, volunteered into the Navy and in 1944 was sent to the Solomon Islands. Later, he was assigned for some time as a Petty Officer on a ship guarding Munda, Island in Alaska. He was wounded in action with a leg injury and came home in 1945.

Fred (also known as Fritz) was living in Louisville, Kentucky. He too wanted to join the Navy and so he did and became a parachutist stationed out of Florida. There he was put on a supply ship and sent to service those in the water who needed food. He and Frank had not been in contact with each other for six years. This particular day Fritz's ship was servicing the ship at Munda, Island. The one receiving the food was Frank. The one sending the food up the ramp was Fred.

Frank said to Fred (without realizing it was his brother): "Where are you from?"

Fred's reply, "Well, I actually live in Louisville, Kentucky, but I was formerly from Kansas."

The words were hardly out of his mouth when Frank ran down the ramp, "Oh, my God! Fritz!"

Fritz replied, "Oh, my God! Frankie!"

The captain of the ship, after being informed of this meeting, allowed Fritz and Frankie to have two hours together alone. Then the ship went on its way. They never saw each other in the war again. Shortly after that Frankie was injured and was sent back home.

Joseph, who had left home to make a new life in Denver, was drafted into the Army. If you asked or referred to anything about the war or the Government, Joe would quickly reply "WE DON'T GO THERE!"

To this day in 2009, he won't talk about the war or the results of it. But I, Laura, have not forgotten. Because the war was in full swing shortly after I left for college, and I was 21 years of age, the full account of World War II having to do with Joe, I well remember!

Joseph Henry

He was drafted and sent to Fort Warren in Wyoming. He was to be there for six weeks of training. After being there for only two weeks he received a notice that he was being transferred to Fort Meade in Maryland. He knew that to be a step along the way to being shipped out to active duty overseas.

He immediately complained, "You can't send me overseas, I've only been here two weeks."

"You shut up you liar, you've been here long enough and you are going, like it or not!"

Well, it happened. He arrived at Fort Meade and was only there a few days when he was transferred to Camp Kilmer, New Jersey. He complained again that they had not trained him.

"You are a liar! You are being shipped out!"

From there he was sent to South Africa where he was shot in the arm. From South Africa he was sent to heal in North Africa. He was there until he was re-assigned. While in North Africa he wrote a letter home to the family. It is re-printed here to reiterate his experience during his recuperation period.

"Dearest Mother, Dad, Bros. and Sister:
    Well just dropping you a few lines as I can write you. I'm living in North Africa and am somewhere in the beautiful hills. There are many things to see here that are different than in our States. I have visited Algeria, Spain, Morocco, Rock of Gibraltar, Oran, Bizerte. But time marches on and so have we these past few months over a land in many ways in North Africa and in the other place we are now in. History has really been made more ways than one. Roads are rough at times and the paths very dangerous as battles are here and there. It all depends on the conditions. North Africa is a land of bare hills, where people made their homes when Christ was here.
    There are still such places remaining to visit as where Daniel and the lions were kept, the ancient and crumbly Roman churches and the old and very dirty Arab. He is as human as we are. His woman is a most sacred one. She wears a cape of white with only one eyehole to see through. If you enter their homes, you remove your shoes. Their transportation is the old camel or the stubborn donkey. Their chief products are grapes. Their food consists mostly of vegetables mixed all in one bowl. They gather in one room where you find chickens and their old family dogs.
    The most beautiful thing I saw here was the old cathedral at Carthage, North Africa. That was worth the sight. It leaves memories never to be forgotten. It is a city of very few people, and is over three thousand years old. Bizerte was completely destroyed by aircraft bombing, and not one home was left untouched. It has a population of one thousand, but today there are about two hundred at the most.
    So folks, these are some of the experiences I have been through in North Africa. Perhaps I had better close this, but hope to hear from you soon. Wishing you all the best of luck and good health and may God bless you all.

Your son,
Joe."

Some time later Joe was promoted to Sargeant and was then sent over to Sicily, Italy at the Anzio Beachhead, known as one of the worst battles of World War II. This particular day his company (some 180 to 200 men) were in full battle.

A call came to Joe: "Get the company in the trenches, they are throwing hand grenades."

Joe yelled "Get down in the trenches, hand grenades are coming from everywhere!"

Unfortunately, the soldier next to Joe didn't jump down, so Joe jumped over and pushed him into the trench. The result was that Joe was hit in the back with a hand grenade! They took him to the hospital and they operated to remove the shrapnel. Joe was in such terrific pain that he screamed and screamed. They finally put him on a ship and sent him back to Fort Meade in Maryland. When he arrived there, they found that at the Anzio, they had sewn a needle in his spine. A re-operation caused him paralysis and the doctors informed him that he would never walk again. They sent him to FitzSimmons Hospital in Denver, Colorado where he was further diagnosed. They found he had serious bowel disruption, serious scar tissue and that he would probably never walk again. After nine months in the hospital, they released him to go home. Even at this time Joe was not receiving benefits from the Government. They ignored his pleas. Hospitalization was necessary nearly every two weeks because of his damaged bowels.

His wife Lottie, who was working in a factory, was making the only income in the family. In desperation she bought Joe some material to make stuffed animals. He fixed their sewing machine so he could lie on the floor and pump it by hand making some beautiful stuffed animals, little sheep and other animals. Lottie would sell as many as possible at the factory, then would mail the extras to me to sell to the students at college for a pittance, $2 or $3 a piece. I was able to sell them all. The little sheep were especially adorable as she was able to find real sheep's wool for him to use in making them. Those little animals sold to everyone I showed them to. He then started tooling leather pocketbooks, and they were more profitable ($8 to $11) so I sold them as well. All this bothered me a lot. Then one day, I was talking with Mr. Keeler, my boss, about his plight.

He said to me, "Laura, there is something seriously wrong with this situation. In Kansas City, Missouri there are two doctors who were head of the European Medical Theatre in the war. Why don't you go over to see either Dr. Dixon or Dr. Dively?"

With this knowledge I got an appointment with Dr. Dixon, went over to see him, told him Joe's story and he said, "You get your brother here, I will gladly look at him and see what we can do. Bring him as quickly as possible."

I called Lottie, and she arranged to take a leave so she could accompany him on the train to Kansas City. I met her there in about three weeks. Her finances were in poor shape so even though I had little to give, I gave her a little help. Dr. Dixon, knowing their plight, offered her a job at the Bellevue Hospital where he was working, and where Joe underwent the operation.

After some long serious tests, he told Joe, "Joe, I'm not sure I can help you, but if you wish, I will re-operate and see if I can remove the scar tissue so you will walk again. This is not a promise that it will work, but I will promise to do all I can to help you."

Joe replied quickly, "God, I have to have help, do it as quickly as you can."

Dr. Dixon replied, "You will need to be in a cast from the tip of your neck to the tip of your toes for a minimum of 11 months."

Lottie, said "What can I do? We are not getting any compensation."

The doctor reassured her that he would make sure she got good pay while she worked there so that she could be with Joe. I made a promise to go over each weekend for a visit, which I did. It was a long haul waiting for the answer. Eleven months down the road, Lottie and I got together and waited for the cast to be removed. The results? Not good! Joe could not move.

The doctor was so distraught, he said, "I'll arrange for you Lottie, to get your old job back in Denver and I will pay for your transportation back home. I promise you, however, the story doesn't end here. I will keep in touch with your sister Laura. I will let her know my findings. Understand you owe me no money. The hospital bill has been taken care of."

Sadly, Joe, Lottie and I went on our way, Joe back to tooling, Lottie back to work, and I, Laura back to college. About six months later, Dr. Dixon called Mr. Keeler's office and asked that I come to Kansas City to meet with him. I returned his call and made an appointment to see him that Saturday because I did not have classes or office work on Saturday. The events of our meeting were earth shaking. He told me that he had taken six months off and had gone to Washington D.C. to the army headquarters to find out what took place; why Joe was sent off to war without the proper training. He also wanted to know why it was that he was not receiving compensation. He had gone through all the files and uncovered the truth.

At Fort Warren in Wyoming there was a Sargeant who had the same name, believe it or not, Joseph Henry Schmidt. Note that this man had a "t" on the end of his last name. Dr. Dixon found that Joe had gone to war on Schmidt's dog tag. How did this occur? He found that when Joe was asleep one night, Schmidt, who was scheduled to go overseas, went in to Joe's room, took Joe's dog tag and left his. The result was that Joseph Schmid was not registered as having been in the war, he was there under Schmidt's name. Because of this, Schmidt got Joe's compensation while *he* stayed at home! Dr. Dixon then did all the necessary work to get Joe his rightful compensation. He had Joe's personal history from his hospital records. President Roosevelt was notified and Joe was not only put on the payroll, but Mom Schmid received a very special award for her five sons in the service. It was at this time that the five Sullivan brothers who had all volunteered in the Navy were on the same ship when it had been bombed and they all died together.

After Dr. Dixon uncovered the truth and sent it to President Roosevelt, the President personally called my mother to apologize and to tell her, "You will receive a very special gift."

The gift was a large plaque citing the Schmid contribution to World War II. The results of Dr. Dixon's contact with President Roosevelt obtained for Joe a long overdue check. The amount I believe was $1500 (a lot of money in those days). He also obtained for him permanent disability pay. Whatever happened to the other Schmidt, I am not sure, but Joe was awarded a Purple Heart. It was a wonderful Christmas for me as I took off to Denver to greet Joe with his check and the great news. The other miracle that happened was that shortly before Dr. Dixon had solved this problem, Lottie became pregnant.

She was so disturbed she called Ma Schmid and said, "Ma, I'm pregnant, how can I have this baby as we have very little money to live on? I have to stay working."

Ma quickly replied, "Lottie, that's wonderful. You just go ahead and have the baby, bring it out to me and I'll raise it."

Lottie was so relieved when she got home she told Joe.

"Holy Cow! NO way can you take that baby home to Ma. Just have the baby, put it on the bed beside me, I can feed it the bottle and change the diaper. My mother has raised too many babies already."

Lottie reluctantly said okay. Baby Joseph was born and Joe took care of him. As you know, however, babies grow and start squirming and moving. Joe learned to roll himself off onto the floor and then tie a rope around the baby's waist so he could not get away from him. During the hours spent with baby Joseph, Joe watched the baby crawling and moving. He mimicked the movement and very slowly regained some of his own movement. Today baby Joseph could be credited with the rehabilitation of his father. Next, Joe found himself getting up on a chair. Joe asked Lottie to bring home some crutches. And yes, he started to walk! He tied young Joseph to his waist and went outside for walks and saw builders building new houses. Spending time watching the builders, Joe was inspired and desired to learn the trade.

Wanting to be somebody and to overcome his tremendous handicap, he asked Lottie to go to the library and bring him home books on how to construct houses. He studied hard. This happened right before the check came from Dr. Dixon. A true gift from God, when the check came, he and Lottie found a lot of land that he could purchase for a very small amount ($200). He purchased the land, dreaming of building his own home. Paul, his next younger brother, by this time had come home from the war. Joe paid $200 for the foundation to be poured. YES, he actually was able to construct most of that new home himself. He walked with crutches but could crawl up a ladder to frame-in the home. Other carpenters knowing his condition helped when they could. He lived in this beautiful home until 2007 when he finally had to go to assisted living. He had sixty-two years of marriage with Lottie, and had two more children, Marilyn and James. Lottie passed away June 29, 2002.

After he received compensation from the government, he became a contractor and put his children not only through high school, but through college as well. He knew how to save money. He worked hard, accomplished an incredible amount of home constructions, and ended up being one of the 'better-to-do' in Colorado.

I asked Joe in recent years, "What was your biggest disappointment in life?"

"Laura, the fact that I never got to go to high school, I never learned how to spell."

His three children are a tribute to his accomplishment. Today, he still has a determination to live on as well as he can, as long as he can. Health problems however, have changed his way of life. He receives physical therapy, uses a wheel chair, and has a mind of steel. To live on is a goal; to live independently is no longer possible. He had to leave his beautiful lawn, his flower garden, which he accomplished by doing the work in a wheelchair and on the ground on his stomach. He was taken to the hospital and then to assisted living. Returning home is no longer possible. He wonders what his home looks like today. Perhaps he will be able to view it from the heavenly skies.

The information on Paul, the younger brother, that I'm using from here until the end of this chapter is the result of an interview many years later obtained by his daughter-in-law, Charlotte, a teacher who wanted information on World War II to use in her classroom. The contents of these conversations are reported here.

Paul (known as Spuds), the next younger brother left home in 1941. He went to Colorado and worked with a contractor to do lathing for new homes. Later that year he left to go to California. In 1942, at 19 years of age and facing being drafted into World War II, he joined the Navy and was sent to Faragut, Idaho. In Paul's words he recounted that his first company was called Company #1 and that it was formed to do things for the other recruits who were joining. This meant his company didn't have to do basic training right away. He worked in the Post Office and was sending all the other recruits clothes from their loved ones, or mail to the families back home. Paul had married Shirley Jones in April of 1942. Shirley went to California to live with him until he went to Faragut. Then she returned to Denver to live with her folks. After being in Faragut, he was assigned to go to school in Norman, Oklahoma. They sent him there to be trained three months to become an aircraft sheet metal smith. In April of 1943, he was shipped to California to the No. 2 Naval Air Station in San Diego where he remained for two or three months. They were so crowded at the Naval Air Station, there was no room for a group of the guys sent there to sleep. They put 1½-inch thick mattresses under the airplanes in the hangar, and that is where they slept. During the day they rolled the mattresses into sea bags. Paul remembers some nights it was so cold with only two blankets that they almost froze, even though it was the end of May, early June.

One day Paul was working on planes, patching and repairing, when he got an order from the Chief Building Officer that they were sending him out for special duty. He was handed a piece of paper to get on the aircraft carrier down at the dock. There were a total of ten men doing this who had no idea where they were headed. Paul was chosen to go because the guy ahead of him on the list had a day off. Consequently, he was assigned to take his place. At that time, none of them knew where they were going. The aircraft carrier was loaded with planes and when they were out in the middle of the sea, they learned they were headed out to Australia. The reason for them going was that they needed to increase the forces there.

On the way there, the Japanese tried shooting torpedoes at them! The carrier, however, had several battleships, cruisers and destroyers protecting it. The Japanese were trying to sink every craft they could! Fortunately, the craft arrived safely in Brisbane, Australia. After arriving in Brisbane, they were transferred to Perth Fleet Airways, at which 300 men were stationed. This was a Sea Plane Base PBY (sea rescue planes and night bombers). They were all painted black so they could fly night raids against the Japanese ships. The job for the ten men was to repair these PBY planes.

In 1944 the S. Naval Carriers sank several Japanese Carriers. After staying in Perth approximately one year, they were shipped to the Los Nigras Islands, close to the Philippines. Paul was assigned to the Navy Repair Base to work again as he had in Perth. Heavily damaged planes and some crash-landed planes were brought in for repair. On the island they lived in Quonset huts for about six months. There was no communication with anybody; news was very scarce for fear enemy spies would intercept any news of the war. The Japanese suicide bombers (kamikazes) were a serious threat to the U.S. Carriers in the Philippines. One day, February 15, 1945, news from the mainland came. President Roosevelt revealed that the war had gone so well that anyone who had put in a certain amount of time could be recycled and sent back to the United States. Paul was sent to North Island off the coast of San Diego, California. "Thank God, I was homeward bound," said a relieved Paul.

In Paul's own words, the story continues:

North Island was so close to the border of the U.S. that a bridge connected us to the mainland. Upon arrival there, I received news from my wife, Shirley that my father had died in October of 1943. My baby son, Dennis was now 16 months old and I had never seen him. On May 7, 1945, Germany officially surrendered to the Allies, but World War II continued as the Japanese were fierce enemies of the United States Allies, who were now joined by Russia. By this time, FDR was the first president to ever be elected for a third term, but unfortunately he died before the completion of that term and before the war ended. Truman took over and at that time I was an Aeration Metal Smith 1st Class. We were fighting to end the world war and had not heard much about the change in presidency. The Naval Air Station at this time put up a big sign that said, *War costs millions and millions of dollars, but it's a darn sight cheaper to win than it is to lose.*

The next six months saw a lot of service men being recycled and were being sent back from overseas. Some had been there for three or four years and it was a thrill to see someone I had served with or someone I knew from the states. The biggest memory of my life was when the news came that the Americans had dropped a bomb on Hiroshima and that it had done the kind of damage no one believed possible. Very few believed a bomb could be that destructive. The Japanese refused to surrender, and then, Oh My God, a second big bomb hit Nagasaki and within two days the Japanese surrendered. The Japanese were warned that if they refused to surrender, the U.S. would wipe out the city of Tokyo with bombs that would clean them out! They surrendered and you have never seen so much confetti and noise as the people of San Diego celebrated. Later, an agreement was signed onboard the battleship "Missouri" by General MacArthur.

People were now concerned with what lie ahead for them. So many did not have a job to return to. While the war was in progress, there were no new automobiles manufactured, tires were rationed, you could not buy a refrigerator and you had to have food stamps to buy the two pounds of meat allowed per family per week. There were no canned goods; everything came in jars because the metal was needed in the aircraft factories. Hope arrived, as it became a promise that jobs would be available in factories; automobiles, refrigerators, cans and other things would have to be replenished. It also meant that it would be possible to build a home.

Now came the news that I was being sent to a unit where officials waited to give me a thorough physical examination, to get final pay ($20 a month) and then I could go get a train ticket to go home!

"Oh Yeah!" I cried.

The Navy made the arrangements for all service men to get their tickets on the Island. I stood in line from 6:00 in the morning until 9:00 that night.

When I finally got to the front of the line, I was greeted with, "Oh, I am so sorry, we don't have a ticket for you. You'll have to get it down at the train station tomorrow."

Sure, that train station was OVERPACKED with service men trying to get home.

When I got there, I stood in line like the Navy told me, and again I was in that line for a whole day.

A guy looked at me and said, "You have to get on that train?"

My answer: "Yes, I have to get on that train."

Just then another sailor came up and said, "I'm going ahead of you, I went up to the head of the line, and they told me that I only have a minute to catch that train!"

I told that sailor, "NO WAY! I am going on that train first, you are not going ahead of me!"

He yelled, "You're what?"

I yelled, "You heard me, you are after me, I am going ahead of you."

The train started pulling out, I ran and jumped on the platform, got into the door. All I had on my mind was getting home to my wife and my baby son who were staying with my wife's folks in Denver. WHOOPIE! I got on that train!

Shirley said she found a three-room apartment, and the guy I used to work for in lathing called and said, "I want you. We need to build small houses for the soldiers coming home."

Yes, that was the beginning of my new life learning to build. Proceeding in the construction business, I became my own boss, helping other people, building new homes and taking care of my family. The war was over! I AM HOME!

I took the time on my return home to learn about what had happened to my family. Who had gone to war? Where were they? How did they make out? And what had taken place at home? How was my mother doing? Who was taking care of her? And what happened to Pa's market? Then I was told all the things that took place in my absence. Louie, the youngest of my brothers was drafted into the army and sent to Italy in the Infantry. He had gotten shot in the hand the first day he was in battle. He received a Silver Star and a Purple Heart. I know that he was sent back to the U.S. to a camp, I believe in Louisiana. While there he met Elaine Johnson and they married. Then he and Elaine returned home to Kansas.

World War II had very strict regulations. Any letter written to soldier or family was strictly censored. Any news of weather, family, good or bad was blacked out. It was impossible to read. They were very concerned that the enemy would pick up any weather news and therefore they could identify where the soldiers were stationed. That meant that the soldiers had no news of family about illnesses, deaths, or births. Coming home was traumatic for all. I do know that when Louie returned home to western Kansas life became an insurmountable problem for him. My sister, Laura, has not forgotten the passing years in his life. She can tell you what she remembers. From that time, I went on with my own life, and Louie went on with his.

Laura continues the story:

I, Laura, being far from home, only partially learned about things happening with my family. Louie had not left home before the war, and had been helping on the farm, leaving him with no background for a better life. When he returned from the war, Aunt Cora had a two-bedroom ranch up in Benkelman, Nebraska. She told him he could come work for her taking care of her farm. That he did for about nine years, but during this time the memories of war and his financial hardships beckoned him to drink. At first it wasn't too bad. But time took its toll and he became an alcoholic.

Mom got him into Alcoholics Anonymous, which was headed by Knute McDougal. Louie liked him a lot, and would attend the AA meetings every week. As long as he attended the meetings, he stayed away from drinking. People are not always considerate, however. Louie had stayed sober for many years when the family was invited to a cousin's wedding. The guys at the wedding thought they were being funny and offered him a wine soaked cigar. Yes, Louie smoked it and that night he gave up his sobriety.

The next years became increasingly worse. He gave up helping Aunt Cora and moved to Denver trying to get away from his drinking friends. He got a job in a car shop, fought his addiction, but just couldn't conquer the problem. He and his wife separated leaving her with the four children. He moved on to Arizona. Then Ma Schmid passed away in January 1976. Louie came home for the funeral and was to return back to the church afterward for lunch. He did not come back; no one knew what happened to him.

Louis Frederick, After Ma's Funeral

My sister Agnes worked in a small restaurant on the highway in Atwood. Then on October 1, 1977, a year and a half later, Louie walked into the restaurant.

Agnes, asked him, "Why didn't you come back to the church after Ma's burial? We were all looking for you!"

His answer, "Sis, you know my problem, I have never overcome it. I'm here today because I came back to see Knute McDougal. I know he can help me."

Poor Agnes said she felt like crying because she had to tell Louie that Knute McDougal passed away two weeks earlier.

Louie looked at her and said, "Well, Sis, your brother just died!"

He walked out of the restaurant, went back to Arizona and on October 5, 1977, the news came that Louis Schmid had been found dead of a self-inflicted gun shot wound. He was 51 years old. His body was returned and buried at Saint John's Graveyard next to his brother, Frankie, his sister, Annie, and his mother and father Martin and Eva Schmid. World War II had taken its toll. He left behind his ex-wife and four children along with many brothers and sisters.

The war was over and the results of that war affected the whole family and the whole world. The remaining Schmid family moved on with their lives in many different states, in many different ways. The story does not end here. The remaining family was always glad that Ma had gone home before any more tragedies took place.

Chapter 7

GONE BUT MEMORIES REMAIN

James Paul, the first and foremost in a large family, lived his role well all through life. Whether his dreams came true or not, his goals achieved or failed, that was less important to him as was his countless deeds of love and concern. If Jim ever had second thoughts, no one knew. He always stood firm in his decisions. We all knew him as a quiet, stable, honest, dedicated, good-looking older brother who spent his life thinking of family. He learned the meat market business from Pa, and could slaughter a cow in minutes. He knew every part of any animal he slaughtered and took care of every detail that came his way. Did he ever argue? I doubt that!

James Paul (Jim)

My first memory of him was taking me with him to the pasture to feed the cattle and to keep me out of trouble. He would harness up Bill, the pony, and place me on a special saddle for children. He would hop on the back and up the hill to the pasture we would go. From there we could see all the cattle. The pasture was partially fenced off so the cows that were used to produce milk were on one side, and the cattle that were destined to be slaughtered were on the other side. He would check to see if there was water in the tank and if the bench used for feeding grain to the cattle had enough corn for the day or week. I loved that ride on the pony with Jim.

This was also my first introduction to that huge tree where there supposedly were three graves. Did Jim know who was buried there? I don't know, he never told me. That tree was so old the trunk took five to six adults and three children holding hands to go around it. After the home was sold, a twister tore it into pieces and the branches lie on the ground. My mother always told us not to disturb the graves. None of my brothers or sisters ever talked about the graves, but I honestly believe my three stillborn sisters were buried there.

The Prairie Tree, After the Twister

I was probably five years old when Jim brought home a car, a beautiful Model A Ford. All of his siblings loved him for that. He saved money that he made working to buy the car. I believe that car cost about $600 and my sisters Threasa, Toots, and brother Johnnie helped him pay for it. In return they got to go with him to the dances in Ludell, and to go out on dates in his company.

Once he got a car, he used to go deer hunting up in Wyoming. How proud he was to return home with a deer or two tied over the roof of the car. They would let it lie for nearly a week before it was skinned. They called it curing, and did it so the wild taste of the meat would lessen. Why it didn't spoil, I don't know. Nearly everyone loved the meat. Mom would cook it and it would last most of the winter. He did the hunting every year if he could come up with the money to take a partner with him. Deer stew was a daily staple as long as the meat lasted.

In September of 1932 he married Nina Lintner, a good-looking woman who had dated his younger brother Johnnie for a while. But Johnnie walked away, and Nina turned to Jim. During those years, Jim had contacted dust pneumonia, and nearly died! He survived through many months of hard breathing. The doctor advised him to go to Manitou Springs, near Colorado Springs, Colorado to see if the mountain air would clear up his lungs. He and Nina were there several years. Then they returned and took an apartment in Atwood.

Toots and the younger brothers had taken over the market with Pa. So Jim and Nina decided to move on to a new life. Nina, having come from a well-to-do family was given land by her father, Monty. With Monty's help, they were then able to build a good-looking three-bedroom home.

Nina never liked children, so they never had any. Their visits to home were limited because a large family with its confusion was more than Nina liked. Jim, however, loved going home, and when he was out working in the field, he would sneak away during the day and go home to help out Ma and Charlie. Charlie had nine children and was having a hard financial struggle. Jim would slip him money and slip some to Mom as well.

Whenever any of the family went to visit them, Nina would come to the kitchen door and tell the kids to stay in the car. Only then, and after having removed their shoes at the door, would she allow the adults to come in to visit. One time, when Dan and I went home to Atwood to visit Mom, we were actually invited to supper (we had three year old twins at the time). To my knowledge we were one of the few families allowed into her home. But the children had to just sit and not move.

My husband Dan complimented Nina for the great fried chicken, and Jim busted out laughing telling Dan, "I guess you have never eaten wild rabbit. That is what you just ate. I killed two of them this morning."

Dan never forgot that night and whenever he ate any fried meat again, he would first ask, "What kind of meat is this?"

Other times when we would visit Jim and Nina, Jim would take the children down to the barn to show them his sheep and baby calves and little pigs, keeping them occupied until we came out to leave. He would take them up in the hayloft and sit and talk and play with them to keep them out of the house.

For some reason, however, my brother Paul could come out from Denver with his daughter, Lorrie, and two sons. They were always welcomed, always invited, always loved as long as Nina lived. Lorrie was her favorite and Lorrie loved her as well. To my knowledge, none of Charlie's kids were ever allowed in the house.

When I was working for other families cleaning houses, Nina hired me to wash her walls and even let me sleep in an upstairs bedroom. I remember her paying me $3 for working two weeks for her. You have to know, I was darn careful about not leaving any stains, spilling any water, and making sure it was done right. I always got along well with her, but always felt badly that Jim was so isolated from the family he loved. She was always nice to me and I could go visit alone or with Dan.

Nina was a very active member of the Eastern Star Church, a Methodist association and would not allow Jim to go to his church. However Jim did not accompany Nina and her sister Mary when they attended Methodist services. When a brother or sister were married, or passed away, Jim would show up at the wedding or funeral; as well he would if any of his acquaintances passed away.

When Jim was aware that he was suffering from congestive heart failure the doctor told him he would only live a week or so, and placed him in the Atwood Hospital. Verneda went in to see him daily.

One particular day he was really not feeling very well at all when he turned to Verneda and said, "Sis, I have a favor to ask of you."

Verneda said, "Sure, what can I do?"

"Well, Sis, you know that I am a Catholic, and that I want to die as one. Would you call Father Flavin and ask him if he would give me the Last Sacraments?"

Verneda, replied, "The trouble is, Jim, what if Nina is here when he comes, you know she won't let you see him."

James Paul (Jim)

He replied, "What I thought you could do is tell her you would like to take her out to eat, there's money in that drawer, and I'm sure she will go. Then the nurse can let Father Flavin in. Just be sure to tell Father Flavin what we are doing."

Verneda complied with his wishes, took Nina out to the restaurant and when she came back with Nina, Jim remarked, "Well I guess it's time for me to go. Think I'll just fall asleep."

He passed away that night, September 7, 1975. He had just turned 70 years of age the month before. Whether or not Nina ever had an inkling that he went back to the church that night, no one ever knew.

He was buried through the Methodist church, but Father Flavin said, "Don't worry the Lord has his soul."

He passed away five months before Ma died. The family, knowing what a dear son he was, decided that no one should tell Ma he had passed away. I am sure she went her way not knowing he was waiting for her.

--

   Katherine Mary, the oldest of the girls, was nicknamed at an
early age as 'Toots.' She lived all her life answering to that name.
Like Jim she too was a very loyal, dedicated daughter who
throughout the years always felt a little under-rewarded for all her
efforts toward the family. She and Threasa got along great, but a
problem began when Toots and Verneda were in their dating years.

Katherine Mary (Toots)

   Toots had a handsome guy known as Darrel who came from
eastern Kansas who dated her for quite a long time. He was always
bringing her jewelry and it seemed that he was going to marry her.
How it happened, I am not sure, but somehow or other Toots
discovered that Darrel was married to another woman! Darrel had
never told her one thing about it. When she learned this news, Ma
said she was so upset. She was shocked to think that she had trusted
him and loved him. Ma advised her to give him back all the stuff he

gave her and never see him again. When Toots confronted him, he said he was divorced. But he wasn't! That ended that romance. He told her to keep the jewelry, and that she would always be sorry that *he* walked away.

Now Edwin Rippe was a neighbor boy, born and raised in a very religious Lutheran Family. After Darrel, Toots dated Edwin and the two seemed to be getting serious. Then one day he announced to her that he really liked her sister, Verneda, better, and that he wanted to date her. That was the end of Toots' second romance. That was the beginning of a sibling rivalry that lasted their entire life. Verneda ended up marrying Ed.

Then Fred and Frankie had a friend Walt Conant that Toots liked. He was the same age as Frankie and Freddie, born on their birthday. That meant that Toots was eight years older. Pa was not happy with Toots being older than Walt and Mom discouraged her. But they ended up marrying anyway, on October 12, 1937. From the very beginning life was tough for Toots and Walt. I don't think she ever had an extra dime in her pocket. When she married Walt they moved to Lucas, Kansas where Walt got a job running a filling station and auto repair shop. He was not a good mechanic and the station failed, so they returned to Atwood.

At that time a family in Beardsley was looking for a 'Share-Crop-Farmer' and Toots and Walt were still looking for a home, so they moved to Beardsley. The family started growing and they had two sons and a daughter. Then one day a woman named Esther who owned a dobby house, half underground, on a piece of land in the back of Pa's North Place, hired Walt to do her farm work. They could live in the dobby house. Because the house was half underground it was dark and damp inside and had only two rooms. Not too many years along the way, Esther decided to move into town and had Walt and Toots move into the big house. It was an old style Colonial with two attic bedrooms and one bedroom on the first floor. It had an enclosed porch, which many years later was turned into a bath area by putting in a tub and a stool. They kept the outside water closet for farm hands. Living in the big house was much better than living in the dobby house. The family grew: four girls and three boys. Remember that this was a crop-sharing agreement and when times were good, it paid off, when times were bad, not so good.

About this time, I had graduated from high school and went on to college. My sister, Toots, always regretting that she never got to go to high school, wanted to make sure all her children would go on to school. Joseph, Toots and Walt's second son wanted to follow in my footsteps so he went to the Atwood High School, and as the years went along the other children followed. Joseph decided to put himself through college and ended up in Denver, Colorado after graduation. For a while he lived with his Uncle Joseph Henry (my older brother Joe) and his wife Lottie and helped them in their new home. He got a good job with Martin Missile Company as a Good Will Agent and ended up renting a house with two more fellows he met at work. Joseph would often be sent to Boston on a good-will tour and when he came he always called his Aunt Laura and her husband, Uncle Bill. We introduced him to submarine sandwiches, which he loved.

Atwood Community High School

So, when he was in town, the phone would ring and the first thing we would hear was "How about a submarine sandwich for supper?"

We loved seeing him and looked forward to his visits.

Then one time in November of 1965, the day before Thanksgiving the phone rang, "Any submarine sandwiches today?"

When he came over he was quite distraught. He had read a few months earlier that a plane had gone down from high winds in New York and everyone on it was killed. He was engaged to be married on December 12, 1965. He had a very serious discussion with me stating that he had a premonition that he was going to die tragically.

"You know, Aunt Laura, Knute Rockney went down in a plane and when his body was recovered he had his hand in his pocket holding a rosary. I've decided that I will always carry my rosary and now that I am flying a lot, I keep my hand on the rosary as well."

I listened and tried to relieve his fears, but he continued, "Aunt Laura, you know my mother never had a dime for anything she wanted, so I decided before I get married, I will buy her a dining room table and chairs, so she could have everyone sit at the table at one time. I ordered it to be delivered before Christmas this year. I want you to know if something happens to me, I did that for her, and as well, I changed my life insurance policy over to Mom And Dad. That means that they can have a decent end to their life."

Then, I said "But Joker (his nickname), what about your new wife, what will she say when she finds out you turned over your insurance to your parents?"

"Don't worry, Aunt Laura, once we are married, I will buy another policy and will put her on it."

Joker left that night to fly back to be with his parents for Thanksgiving dinner the next day. He had left his car there and would be driving back to Denver from Atwood. When he left his parents on Friday, he kissed his mother good-bye.

His Mom said, "Joker, please drive carefully!"

"Don't worry Mom, just know if anything ever happens to me, I've taken care of you and Dad."

He drove away, the last time to ever see his family. On Saturday morning, his bride-to-be was having a wedding dress fitting, and he and his partner, Dale, had decided to go skiing. They flipped coins to see who was going to drive.

Dale said, "Heads up I drive, tails you drive."

Dale won the bet and drove. They got into Dale's car and had gone only one block when a car coming down the other street that was supposed to stop at a stop sign went through it at 70 miles an hour, and hit Dale's car on the passenger side! Joker flew 60 feet into the air, down to the street. He was injured very badly and was taken to the hospital. He passed away at 8:00 PM that evening, December 5, 1965. He was only 26 years old! The only ones at his side when he died were Uncle Joe and Aunt Lottie. His mother and dad had to drive to Denver from Atwood, 240 miles, as there was no train or air connection from Atwood to Denver. They arrived one hour too late.

The driver of the other car was drunk. Dale managed to live, but was hospitalized for months with a broken back and hip. He often returned to Joe and Lottie to grieve his loss, wishing he had lost the coin toss. He passed away about 15 years later. Whether or not Joker had his hand on his rosary, I never heard. I do know that the priest was called and he received the final prayers, and went into eternity before his parents got to Denver to see him. The doctors would not allow them to view him after he had passed away.

--

Five years later, in 1970, another tragedy struck. Jerry the oldest son of Toots and Walt, having returned from the army, obtained a job with the State Highway Department in Atwood. The night of November 1, 1970 he went to Trenton, Nebraska to see a girl he was dating. He did not come home that night and he was supposed to go to work at 5:00 AM the next morning. The highway department called, but Toots and Walt had no way of knowing where he was. They went off to Mass at the Sacred Heart Church in Atwood as it was "All Souls Day", November 2, 1970. During the consecration, Marlin Schandler, the Atwood undertaker came into Mass and tapped them on the shoulder asking them to come out. They instantly knew the worst had happened. Evidently Jerry, driving Joker's old car, must have fallen asleep at the wheel. His foot must have gone heavy on the gas pedal; the car went off the highway hitting the hill across the ditch! They found him dead on the hill, the car demolished. It was a time of grieving for us in Boston as well, as Cardinal Cushing died on the same day. I was working at the parish house at St Raphael's Parish in Medford for Auxiliary Bishop Daniel A. Cronin when I received the news of Jerry's death. It was devastating to not only Toots and Walt, but to our entire family.

Jerry Conant Killed In One-Car Accident Monday Morning

CRASH SCENE—Above is shown the Conant car. The photo was taken early Monday morning. Highway 25, looking north, is at top of photo. The car left the road between the bridge and the highway patrol car, shown in top right corner. The motor of the car is visible at left of the picture.

The community was shocked and saddened Monday to learn of an auto accident which took the life of Jared "Jerry" Conant, 32, son of Mr. and Mrs. Walter Conant. The accident took place on Highway 25, nine miles north of Atwood, just north of the Rudy Vap farm home. It is surmised the accident took place shortly after 2 a.m., as that is when the watch that Jerry was wearing, had stopped.

Jerry was traveling south on the highway, and apparently went to sleep, leaving the road on the east side, and the auto plunged into a rather deep ravine. The car was totally demolished, and Conant was killed instantly. (see picture)

The accident was not discovered until early Monday morning.

The highway patrol and county sheriff's office investigated the accident.

Jerry was a very popular and friendly young man, and was employed by the Kansas State Highway Department, headquartered in Atwood. The community extends sincere sympathy to the Conant family.

Services for Mr. Conant are to be held Thursday morning, Nov. 5, 10:00 a.m. from the Sacred Heart Church, Atwood, with Fr. Valerian Brungardt, O.F.M.Cap. officiating. Interment is in Mount Calvary cemetery.

A couple of years later, Toots' husband Walt went through a two-year battle with encephalitis brought on by a mosquito bite. He survived that, then contracted cancer and went home to eternity on February 28, 1978. He was 64 years old. Esther deeded her part of the farm to Toots and Walt before he died. This meant Toots could remain on the farm. Her younger brother Charlie would come to help her. Another family, who lived one half mile down the road, also became great neighbors and would help as well. Later that year, in 1978, she sold her share to her daughter Evelyn, and moved into an apartment in Atwood. Toots remained there until the family recognized she could no longer live alone. They were able to place her in a home in Hays, Kansas, where she could be near her daughter Berneice, who would visit her everyday, and would take her home for a visit when she was feeling okay. Berneice and her family were always with her in the home and would take care of all her needs.

During her stay in the home, her oldest daughter Elizabeth (Betty) passed away from cancer, on November 26, 1992. She was two days short of her 52nd birthday. Her body was cremated so her remaining sisters and brother arranged for a Memorial Mass at the home so their mother could be there. The children decided, however, that she never really understood what the Memorial Mass was all about. She passed away on April 5, 1993, probably never knowing Betty had gone on before her. I honestly believe, however, that she mourned herself to death having lost her sons, husband, and if she realized it, her daughter. Toots was a second mother to me during my childhood years. She was 87 when she went on to eternity. She was buried on my birthday, April 9. She always said, "I was really your mother, I raised you."

--

When Toots was alive, and I would go home to Atwood for a visit, I would buy a 'Toni' home permanent and would go to Toots' house and do her hair. She loved that! She was a hard working mother and would always insist that we go for a goose or duck supper. My kids loved the geese running around the yard. Then one day, the gander didn't like interruption and he chased the kids away. They remember that day!

Dear baby sister Laura -

I hope & prayed by time this letter arrives you have reached home safe & sound, may God be with you always for I love you dearly.

I ask God to give me strength to let you go with out my tears, but my heart was breaking and even when Curt & Cathy arrived I kept from crying - I did shed many tears later.

Laura I know you do not remember but to me I loved you as if you were my child. You were born in Apr in June I had operation for appendicitis was in hospital 15 days & no heavy work for one year.

You were a good baby, poor mom did milking cooking cleaning & all other work besides hoeing all the garden. after your bath she put you in the buggy, put diapers & bottles where I could change you without taking out of buggy, heat & give you the bottle, if you fussed which was seldom did, I shook the buggy, and you were a pretty baby.

I'm so happy you get come home while Bushy was feeling so well - It is hard for me to talk to people asking questions if Rita will stay. I do say, I never ask."

By the way "Thanks" for putting in permanent t'was 10:30 before top was dry, I haven't combed completely out, as put on a net & it looks nice. Cathy will come either Tues or Wed - I will wash & she will set it for me.

I will close now but did want you to know why I did not break down. Keys in place. Please had a wonderful Dec 25 with your family.

Love Toots

Toots was an excellent cook, and always had plenty of cookies for the kids. I capitalized on her recipes; her chocolate chip cookies, her snickerdoodles, her homemade noodles, her canned dill pickles and her sauerkraut are still a part of my cookery habits today.

Without a doubt she loved me beyond measure. Unfortunately scarce money would not allow me to go home for her funeral, but know that her memory lingers more often than anyone can imagine. My birthday cannot pass without a prayer for her peace in heaven above.

Toots' Son Jerry and Verneda's Son Bobby

I remember well how funny it was that Toots and Verneda had gotten married only months apart, and both gave birth to a son on the same day the following July. The Rippes were true Germans so Edwin, Verneda's husband had a large framed body with dark hair. Walt (Toot's husband) came from Nebraska and had a more common stature. Verneda named her son Robert, and he was known as Bobby. He weighed about nine pounds at birth and had dark hair. Toots named her son Gerald, he was known as Jerry and was seven pounds at birth but his ears were large. One day, Toots overhead Pa saying to Ma that Bobby was so cute, but Jerry had big ears. I've always lived by believing *it's not what is said, but how it's heard.* That statement rang in Toots' ears all her life and she would cry because Pa felt Jerry was ugly. That pain lingered on even as years rolled by and when both sisters again had baby girls a few months apart, Verneda's dark haired, Carolyn overshadowed Toots' blonde little Evelyn. The girls grew up knowing who was recognized as the favorite.

Verneda would say, "I don't know why Toots feels that way!"

I would tell them, "Try to know that neither Pa or Ma had any less love for either of them!"

They were not brought up to know that affection can be shown in many ways. The girls grew up knowing who was who.

John Joseph (Johnnie)

When my brother John Joseph was born on October 17, 1907, Pa welcomed him happily because he needed sons to help him along the way. Well, John became Johnnie and he was a pre-destined, bright kid who was born as a lively, energetic, intelligent little guy. Ma said he was walking at six months of age, and even then would take apart a toy, put it back together again and throw it away! He learned to help his older brother Jim with butchering at a very early age and knew exactly what went where, how it went, and then went on his way. Johnnie could do just about anything he wanted. He loved fixing broken down cars, tractors, and machinery of any kind. He decided he would rather fix things than become a farmer. So he got a job fixing John Deer Tractors. He liked it at first but quickly got bored. He went to work for International Harvester fixing combines, and grew bored with that as well. Then he decided he would go west.

About this time the war was beginning. He was on the draft list, but was at the end of the age limit so they didn't take him. He went to Northrup Aviation to ask for a job. The manager told him you need to go to school to learn about aircraft.

"I can't hire you until you take a six month course."

Johnnie looked at him and said: "Six month course! Are you crazy? I can fix an airplane with my eyes shut!"

The manager thought he was an egotistical smart aleck and thought he would show him up.

So he said, "Okay, you think you know so much! Go into this room and I will give you the test. If you pass it, you can have the top job. If you don't, you are out the door! It will take you about six hours to do the test so get yourself a drink of water before you start."

Well, Johnnie didn't blink an eye. He returned with the test in just three hours.

The manager laughed and said, "Ha, you aren't as smart as you think you are, are you?"

Johnnie's reply, "Well you grade my test and then we'll know."

He took the test from Johnnie's hand and saw that he had finished it, and said, "How did you do that?"

Johnnie's reply: "With a pencil, how else."

Johnnie sat down to wait for the manager to correct his test, and when he came out he said, "Man, I owe you a real apology. You got the highest grade that has ever been given on that test! Show up tomorrow and you can take over being the manager here."

He was there only a few months when he was named Vice President of Northrup Aviation. How long did Johnnie stay? About five years, he got bored again and decided to open his own repair shop for the jeeps that were coming back from the war in need of fixing. He had a son Jack who was in his teens at the time so he got him involved in the repairs as well. Then he found he wasn't feeling too well but kept putting off going to the doctor. On one particular day, he decided he had better go to the hospital as he was having serious chest pains.

The doctor examined him and gave him a grave analysis, "John, you have a very serious heart condition, you can drop dead any minute! I can't do anything for you."

Johnnie left the hospital, got into his truck and drove down the street to find a church. He found a rectory, went up to the door of the rectory and asked to see a priest.

When the priest came in Johnnie told him that he was born and raised a Catholic, received all the Sacraments, but had married a second time out of the church and had not been going to Mass for 10 to 15 years.

The priest told him "If your first wife is alive, I can't help you."

Johnnie told him she had died many years ago, "But my second wife was a non-catholic and was divorced!"

The priest told him, "You must leave her or I can't forgive you."

Johnnie said, "Father, I have been married to her for 35 years, I cannot leave her, and I don't think the Lord will condemn me for that!"

The priest replied, "Well, John, you do have faith and the Lord just heard your magnificent Act of Contrition. I will give you provisional absolution."

That he did! The priest blessed Johnnie right in the rectory.

Johnnie walked out of the door, got into his truck, went to turn on the key, and he died in front of the rectory. Johnnie died on May 24, 1963, he was still so young, 55 years, 7 months and 7 days. He had so much to give, an unbelievable mind in a complicated world. The priest went to the funeral home and blessed his body a second time.

His wife thanked the priest saying to him, "Father, he was a true Catholic, he had a kind of faith that I have never seen. He just never got around to going back to church. Thank you for blessing him."

His wife Opal lived on until November 24,1992. She lived to be 90 and she never forgot the man who worked so diligently for the world giving his natural born intelligence to make it a better place. Johnnie proved his father's rule of life, *You can be what you want to be without going to High School!* (Johnnie never went to high school).

--

Threasa Louise

My sister, Threasa Louise was a beloved daughter to Pa and Ma. She was there to help them, give them money when she could and help raise the younger siblings. She could drive a tractor, do housework, cook, and yes, would even help skin the animals. She, Johnnie, Fred, Frank, and Joe were pretty much buddies during their growing years. Dan and I used to stop to visit her in Detroit when we would take our young family to visit my original home in Kansas. She came to Kansas to help me at our wedding and later we asked her to be the godmother of our daughter, Margaret Anne. The girls were too young to remember her, but the year she died she had purchased one of the first sets of walking dolls and had mailed them to the girls for that Christmas. They loved those dolls until they gave way to breaking down. The family remembers them as we took a home movie of them walking, the Christmas following her death. Threasa always regretted not going to high school, because it meant she could not be a registered nurse, a profession she dearly loved. Threasa lived a rather lonely life as she had lost her one great love; her fiance, Herman Folke Jr., was 25 years of age when he died in an auto accident. After training with Dr. Henneberger to be a practical nurse, she joined her brother Fred Andrew (Fritz) in Kentucky. She worked in a hospital there in Louisville. Then the war came and Fritz went into the Navy. So she went to Detroit, Michigan because she heard you could work in a factory to make more money. Later she went to the Detroit hospital working as a practical nurse. She was working at the hospital and lived in a fireproof apartment building. One day she came home from work at 4:30 AM.

Threasa as a Nurse

Her landlady was at the entrance and she asked her, "Would you call me at 7:00, I promised a nurse friend of mine to take her shift, so she could go to her sister's wedding. I'm so tired, I'm afraid I won't hear the alarm clock."

The landlady said, "Sure, I will call!"

Another woman across the hall had gotten up to go to work, she opened her door to see out the hall window. She wanted to know what was happening with the weather. She immediately heard Threasa's moaning and saw smoke coming from her door! She ran across the hall to try to get in, but the door was locked.

She ran to the phone, called the landlady: "Get the Fire Department, Smitty's (Threasa's nickname) apartment is on fire."

The landlady said, "She was just here!"

The fire department arrived at 5:10 AM. Threasa had tried to escape, was lying at the door, her hair burned off, and her right arm severely burned. The cause of the fire was never determined. The heat was so intense it melted her iron bed frame to the cement floor, and the medicine cabinet in the bath melted and ran down the wall.

My mother could not afford an autopsy and the best analysis of the cause was made by the fire department. The people in the unit knew that Threasa had a plastic bedspread, very popular in those days. They also knew that Threasa did not smoke. The fire department decided that she had an electric light cord that ran under the bed to a lamp on the opposite side. They felt the cord had a short and lit the spread and blankets on fire. That kind of plastic bedspread would burn rapidly, and since Threasa was so tired, she did not waken until she herself had caught fire. The family accepted that analysis.

When we arrived, the lady across the hall informed us, "Smitty was engaged to be married."

We never met the man she was engaged to, no one knew his name. The death notice did not bring any inquiries, so only God knows who he was, where he was, and if he ever knew what happened. A fire alarm today still brings shivers down my spine, and I always say *may she rest in peace*. She died on December 17, 1951 at the age of 40 years two months and 14 days. She was meeting her father; long awaited for time together, true companions as long as life lasted.

--

Annie Catherine was born on April 3, 1909, 14 years before me and we never saw each other. Annie died of diphtheria, a terrible disease. All the older children had to be vaccinated in the back. Dr. Henneberger came twice a day to check on all. The whole family was quarantined and could not leave the house. My father was operating the meat market and could only drop food at the door but could not come in. Annie lived 31 days through the illness and appeared to be recovering. She asked if she could go eat at the table with the rest of the family, and Ma let her. She ate and then told them she was tired. She was taken back to bed and that evening left the earth in her sleep, being held in her father's arms. She passed away on October 25, 1922. She was only 13 years of age, and *so* loved by her mother, sisters and brothers. Ma Schmid did all she could to console her family, even as her own heart was breaking. She told her brothers and sisters that they should picture her waiting in one of the ivory palaces looking out of a crystal clear window.

"We can see her beyond in the fields of fadeless flowers beside the steel waters. Our hearts cannot be comforted because the angel in our house is now gone. We know that we will see her again in Heaven. She is gone but not forgotten."

--

Frank and Fred's life was pretty normal for children of that vintage. They were fraternal twins. Each had his own personality. Fred was a little more stable emotionally, but pretty determined to do what he wanted to do. Frank on the other hand would display emotions when he didn't get what he wanted, or when he wanted people to recognize that he was somebody.

Fred Andrew (Fritz)

Fred (Fritz) moved to Kentucky after marrying Gertrude. He worked as a manager at the A & P store and took over the meat department. Gertrude worked at a hospital and found a doctor who pleased her better than Fritz and off she went. Now came the war, Fritz went into the Navy and met a woman named Alice Russell who was married and had a little girl, Carolyn. Her husband had been killed in the war. Fritz married her in 1957. Fritz and Alice had a little boy, Fred Jr., and they nicknamed him Butch. Butch and Carolyn grew up as real good friends. Butch, however, was similar to his Uncle Johnnie, he was so intelligent they didn't want to work with him in high school, so he was pushed along and graduated at the age of 13. He went to college and graduated from there at 16! He was so brilliant that he was offered a tremendous job with IBM in Indiana.

Fred Andrew (Fritz) in the Navy

His mother, Alice (my brother's second wife) became ill and died three years later of cancer. His father (my brother Fritz) married a third time to a woman named Frieda Ochs. She had a hard time coping with Butch. So Butch decided to take the job in Indiana and would come home on occasion for the holidays. Fritz noted, however, that he loved to drink wine. He also knew that Butch had been offered a Fulbright Scholarship. This is an exceptional scholarship offered by Oxford University in England to a very limited "selection of exceptional minds." Butch felt he did not need the extra education, so he never went forward with it. He was so bright he didn't need to.

Then one day a call came from Indiana, that the police had a problem with Butch. When Fritz got to Indiana, they told him a girl across the hall where he lived smelled a terrible odor coming from his apartment. They attempted to reach Butch but got no answer. They went to the door and broke in only to find him dead on the floor from an overdose of wine! He had been dead for several days.

When Fritz cleaned out the apartment he found un-cashed paychecks from IBM amounting to over $65,000. Fritz called my brother Paul, in Denver, and he immediately flew out to help him. Paul helped Fritz clean up the apartment, and was there to help him identify the body. After finding all the uncashed checks, they were very concerned that IBM would not honor the checks. Many of the checks were written years before. God was good to Fritz that day, as he went to IBM with the un-cashed checks and they honored every one!

They told Fritz, "Your son was so intelligent; we classified him as a genius."

Butch died on February 4, 1983, just 40 years, two months and four days old.

I truly believe, that IBM's token of kindness allowed Fritz to retire! Fritz died thirteen years after losing his son, on April 21, 1996, three weeks short of turning 82. Frieda is still alive today in 2010. No one ever knew where Carolyn (Fritz's step-daughter) went. We do know she married and had two children. Frieda retains Fritz's ashes in her present home. My brother Paul was there as Fritz went into eternity.

--

Frank became a great butcher, or 'butcherer' as he would always say. He would challenge any of his brothers to skin the animal as fast as *he* could. The boys always shared that job which usually took place in the early morning so Pa could take the meat off to market. They would shoot, skin, and clean a cow, a steer, a pig or a goat. Pa never allowed them to kill a sheep as he regarded sheep as 'sacred animals.' Before the war Frank left home to work at a slaughterhouse in North Platte, Nebraska. Meat market owners like my father would buy the meat already for them to sell. The slaughterhouse ran a contest and gave a large award to the person who could kill the animal, skin it, clean it, and send it down the line in the shortest time. Frank took the challenge and won! He knocked the cow in the head, stabbed it, skinned it with six swoops of the knife, cleaned it and sent it down the line in SIX MINUTES! Second place was won with a sixteen minute 'job-down,' 10 full minutes slower than my brother! Frank made the news in every state newspaper for his outstanding accomplishment. I don't know what the prize was for winning, but he merited plenty of publicity.

Frank George

He then married Milly Flood and moved to Chicago where he took another job, in another slaughterhouse. Then World War II started. He did not want to be drafted so he joined the Navy. He joined in Illinois and went on his way. As you have read, the war changed Frank's life and it ended in a very tragic way. There were some great blessings in the end. His sister Agnes and brother Jim brought him home to spend his last years in the same residence as the mother he loved so dearly. How much he knew after the surgery, I do not know, as I had long been gone from home. I remember Agnes writing that he was always looking for his daughter Joan to come see him. If he thought she was coming and then didn't show, he would cry for days!

Born, raised, baptized and confirmed a Catholic, Frank, through all his troubles, forgot to live up to his faith. Father Flavin was able to visit him on a weekly basis in the home and, like my brother Johnnie, he too was admitted back into the church by Father Flavin. He died having received his final graces on May 26, 1970. He was 66 years of age.

--

Verneda Frances

Verneda married Edwin Rippe on February 3, 1937. Ed chose to leave his family who refused to accept the fact that he wanted to convert to Catholicism. He was raised in the Lutheran religion. None of his brothers or sisters went to the wedding. His father and mother attended but did not resume any family relationship until many years later when one of his brothers died and

Ed helped them out with the funeral. In the end, the others reversed their thinking and resumed their connections with Ed and Verneda. Ed and Verneda were renting a farm near Herndon, Kansas and had seven sons, one daughter and Verneda was pregnant again in 1958.

Their older boys were helping in the harvest field one day when Bobby came home saying: "Mom, we need you, Dad is running the tractor and going around the field like crazy. We can't get him to stop! Come quick!"

They drove back to the field in the truck. When they got back to the field, they drove the truck alongside Ed on the moving tractor. Verneda was able to get onto the tractor by jumping off the moving truck! Ed was apparently having a heart attack. She stopped the tractor and Ed was rushed to the hospital.

He lived only six days. He died of a blood clot on July 14, 1958, at 48 years of age, leaving pregnant Verneda with an already large family. Verneda, heartbroken and forlorn, miscarried the child growing inside of her a few weeks following Ed's death.
Bobby had been trying to put himself through college, so he and Clarence made a deal that they would trade off taking care of the farm for their mother, Verneda. The next younger one, Richard was able to step in as well. Farmers recognized her hard work and determination and due to a letter submitted by her one daughter Carolyn, the McCook Gazette named her "Mother of the Year" in 1962.

After many, many hard years, the younger children went off to college, earning their own way. Eddie, the youngest one, did not want to go on, he wanted to stay on the farm. That was working out until one day in the middle of the morning, there was a terrible thunder and lightning storm. Verneda was making dinner at the cook stove, when the lightning struck the house and it went into full blaze! She was only able to grab her purse, and phone for help. But the house burned completely to the ground. There was no running water. Fires were fought with firewater trucks. The first truck arrived too late to save the house, and the truck ran out of water before the flames were extinguished. Only ashes, and many broken hearts remained.

Lightning fire consumes home

Lightning struck the home of Mrs. Verneda Rippe mid-morning Sept. 3 during a heavy thunderstorm between Ludell and Herndon, and was responsible for a fire which totally destroyed the house. It was speculated that wiring damaged by the lightning started the fire.

Verneda says the immediate impact sounded like a blast of dynamite. After checking the lights, she went to the porch to get the fire extinguisher. Smoke poured into the porch from the east wall where the fire started and prevented her from getting the extinguisher. Smoke was also accumulating in the kitchen so thick that she found it difficult to read the dial numbers on her phone. She called son Rich's place for help because she already knew the number.

Rich left right away with the tractor as the roads were extremely muddy, and his wife, Teresa called the sheriff's office for emergency fire assistance.

The new fire chief, Doyle Vrbas, says that the call was received at 9:57 a.m. and volunteer units from both Atwood and Herndon responded. Plenty of volunteers came to help including some of Verneda's neighbors, but it just spread too fast and was too far gone to control." The volunteer help arrived shortly after Rich did and the fire had spread from the east side around to the south of the house.

Verneda's son, Eddie, was using a saw in the hog building at the home place, and didn't hear her initial calls from the house. She turned off the electricity, and when he came outside to investigate he found out about the fire.

Eddie turned off the propane tank and used fire extinguishers from the pickup. In the meantime, Bernita had grabbed her purse and checkbook when she came out of the house, and she went to the basement garage to back out the car.

She and Eddie could see the rafters in the basement were already burning, and they hurried into the house to look for a metal box containing legal papers which could not be located because of the thick smoke.

Verneda says "I don't know why, but on the way out I just picked up the vaccum cleaner and the baby highchair, and Eddie grabbed a box of his machinery manuals." Everything else in the house was lost; the front steps and chimney are all that is left standing near the charred hole which was once a basement.

CHARRED REMAINS OF THE RIPPE HOME, eight miles east and two south of Atwood are the chimney, front steps and ruins of the basement. The Sept. 3 fire was started by lightning. CP Photo

Charlie, one of Verneda's younger brothers, took Verneda into his crowded home for a few weeks, when a family up near St. John's Church decided to donate a trailer home to her. The town of Atwood responded with a 'trainload' of clothing, housing supplies and assistance. She and Eddie were able to resume life until she settled her homeowner's insurance. My brother Paul in Denver came to her rescue and designed for her a new three-bedroom house with a basement. With his expertise, he was able to get the construction done as cheaply as possible. After many years of hardship, she finally had a home of which she was proud. Her son Richard had married and moved over into a house north of her, and again farming became their livelihood. Her son Eddie then found a girlfriend and decided to marry. Verneda did not want to be a burden to Eddie so her children rallied together, bought her a house up in Atwood, and visited her frequently to help her.

Originally, farmers were not able to have Social Security, so Verneda lived on the land and the products of her hard work. She sold eggs to the neighbors for 25 cents a dozen and would drive down the road to deliver them on a daily basis. She kept her chickens alive and fed, but when the products of the land became scarce, her quality of life depreciated as well. When she did receive Social Security in 1965 she received only $110 a month, not even enough to pay her utility bills. Then she discovered how people would save strips off the Minute Maid orange juice cans, and labels off cans of vegetables to send in for rebates. Verneda's basement was filled with boxes of these things. Anything that could be reused for a dollar here or a dollar there she would save. She took these boxes with her to her new home in town and every night she would co-ordinate and send off the required amount to the companies offering rebates. This was her livelihood for years.

Good hearted as she was, she would send the letters with my name as a contributor, or her kids' names as contributors and the refund would go to that address. She paid the postage but found when it got up to 10 cents that was costly. So when the refunds would come and there was a sizeable amount, I would send her the check with a little extra added. Her children did that as well. That is how she existed, that is how she kept herself alive. Then one day, someone disclosed to an authority that the refunds she was getting were unfair because she should have been limited in the amount that only one person could earn. After that the companies refused to accept her strips and wrappers. From then on, she was broken hearted, poor and discouraged. She felt betrayed, because she only wanted a decent way of life, without having to rely on her children. When we visited her, her refrigerator was empty 99% of the time. She never went out to buy groceries, so her children supplied her with meals.

The house in town was only about two blocks from the Sacred Heart Church and as long as she could walk, she would go to Mass every day. Then my high school friend, Martha, who lived across the street, would call her and take her in a car to church. Unfortunately, Martha was found dead in her living room in 1980 and so Verneda's method of travel was eliminated. The house that her son bought for her remained her home until she was placed at the Good Samaritan home for the elderly.

The children had placed her in the Good Samaritan home because one night in January in sub-zero temperature she awoke and for some reason went out the kitchen door in her nightgown. The door closed behind her and locked. She walked down the middle of the street freezing and crying. A neighbor two blocks away heard the cries and called the fire department. They found her almost dead from hypothermia. She never returned home. She was taken to the hospital and then into her new home, the Good Samaritan.

Verneda's Remaining Sons, 2000

Verneda went on into eternity on November 25, 2002 at the age of 86. Unfortunately, about two years before her death, her second son, Clarence died of cancer. A picture of her remaining sons was taken at his funeral: a masterpiece of a mother's care during a life of poverty.

--

Joseph Henry, as a result of the war, lost many years of a productive life. His wife Lottie was his soul mate from the first day they met until she died. Joe struggled with many hardships but became a well-known contractor in Denver, Colorado. He has struggled with his health all these years. Joseph was in the Infantry and was leading a company when he was assigned to the worst battle of World War II, the Anzio Beachhead. He was struck in the spine with a hand grenade and was diagnosed as a paraplegic and told he would never walk again. His story lies in the *Ravages of War*. His determination and his insistence on self-sufficiency, though successful, brought back to him a life of indescribable pain and hardship. He did walk again with a cane and made a life for himself, regaining notoriety as a contractor, but had many mishaps along the way. He used a walker when the cane was not enough, and only when he could not accomplish what he wanted on his feet, did the wheelchair become his locomotion. Proud of his family and never wanting to quit, but facing unsolvable health problems he had to face reality, he could not support the family. His wife, Lottie passed away, but he stayed at home taking care of himself.

Joseph Henry (Joe)

When I called him one day, he said he had just finished mopping up his kitchen floor.

Then I asked, "Joe, how did you do that?"

His answer: "Well, it took me four hours, but I did it from my wheel chair."

The neighbors were appalled but amazed how he would mow his lawn in a wheel chair, fertilize the land, plant vegetables and cultivate flowers, turning his home into a show place. How did he do it? Using his wheel chair, lying on the ground on his stomach, and doing all the work without counting on other people!

His finality of production arrived on a very cold winter day, the sidewalk was frozen with ice and he was concerned about the mail carrier, or a visitor falling on it as they were trying to reach his front door. He told me he had called a neighbor's son to come and clean up the walk, but that he didn't show. He went outside and chopped ice by himself for five or six hours. Exhausted, he took himself back into the house, climbed into a chair and fell asleep for some 10 to 15 hours.

When he awoke he was dehydrated and couldn't get out of his chair. He called Jimmy his son on the telephone. Jimmy called his sister, Marilyn who was in charge of the local Emergency Medical Team. She arrived and took Joe to the hospital. Joe went from the hospital to assisted living where he now resides.

He is adjusting to giving up his way of life but hoping and praying something will change so he will be allowed to go home. Perhaps with his life ebbing, he will view it from the skies above when our Lord and Savior takes him to eternity.

Joe was another tribute to Pa's philosophy in that he never went to high school, he was not allowed, but succeeded anyway. He felt that he was cheated because he didn't learn how to spell! But due to his ability of mind, his dedication to life and hard work, he became a man of accomplishment. He could always pay his own way and will probably leave an estate to his children and grandchildren. He, along with his brother Paul, became big name contractors in Denver. They built countless houses and were regarded with the highest esteem. World War II has never been forgotten; its impact on his life left indelible marks. The Purple Heart signifies the cost of his commitment, a loyal and true soldier.

--

Agnes, my next older sister, used to be a little different. She hated housework and she loved reading. Agnes and her friend Mable used to tolerate me going to school and having to keep me under their wings. There were no other girls in the school and I am sure she thought I was a pain in the neck. I know that I was a pain to her at home, because we both had assignments keeping up the house. One week one of us was in charge of the main house to keep it clean, do the cooking, and clean-up after. The other one had to clean the bunkhouses and the washhouse. In her week to do the bunk and washhouses, Agnes would quickly throw the beds together and quickly do the washhouse and then hide reading! When she was to do the main house, I used to get really uptight, because she would not do the work like she was supposed to. She would sweep the dirt under anything she could find so she would not have to scoop it up. She would not wash the dishes properly. So each week at exchange time, it would take me two or three days to get it all straightened away, so my job was really tough. I was old enough, however, not to complain to Ma because she had too much to do as it was. If I had complained to Pa, he would have disciplined her and I wanted her love, so I never squealed.

Agnes Elizabeth

As was true with her older brothers and sisters, she was not allowed to go on to high school. She was only 19 years of age when she met Steve Barenberg. He was eleven years older than she, had been married but lost his wife and baby when the wife passed away in childbirth. He was mourning her death and loved Agnes because she was so caring about people's sadness. She married him in January of 1938 and they moved to a farm 17 ½ miles south of Atwood. Because Ma and Pa never really talked about marriage, Agnes was appalled when she learned the expected intimacy of a man and wife. She resisted his advances and told me that on the night they were married, he wanted her to go to bed with him.

She said, "Get out of my bedroom, I am not going to bed with you."

Later she learned from someone what marriage was all about. From whom, I do not know, but I understand that after two weeks, the marriage was consummated.

She had a nightmare of the facts of life her first year of marriage because Steve would always call her Lilah, his first wife's name. That hurt her so deeply.

She would call me and cry: "Why does he do this to me?"

A younger non-experienced youth, I could only console her and tell her, "Just remind him that you are not her! Eventually, he will call you by *your* name."

How long it took, I do not know. Steve was not an aggressive farmer; Agnes would always be the one to be driving the tractor in the fields, plowing, mowing and planting. Her housework was never done, but somehow she did her cooking. That became her mark of distinction throughout the rest of her life.

An event I long remember was when the blizzards took over, food was scarce as the cows were thin and didn't give as much milk. That also meant less cream, the chickens did not lay as many eggs, and the only food to eat was salt pork, bread, and dill pickles which she had canned during the summer. I went to help her out when her third child was born. She had gotten home before the roads became impassable. Eating pork sandwiches with bread and dill pickles every morning, noon and night became a meal I have not repeated since. That is all we had to eat, the pork barrel was nearly empty, since after the storm you could not go anywhere until the roads were clear. Finally after about three weeks the neighbors all got together and shoveled their way to the main highway, which meant they could get into town for necessary items. This particular day, we were so anxious for Steve to come home thinking he would really bring us some great food! Our hopes were dashed as he entered the house with five pounds of coffee, 25 pounds of flour and a "fifth" of whiskey. A thunder or lightning storm could not have erased the flying words when the truth came out! Agnes went into her bedroom and locked the door and wouldn't come out.

Steve begged her, "Well, I only had $15 what did you expect me to do? You mean I couldn't have one small drink after all we went through?"

No answer! The next day I was able to go back to my other job at the Gatlins. How that fight ended, or when it ended, I was never informed. For sure, I did not have to eat pork sandwiches and dill pickles as a daily diet anymore. Oh well, another day, another dollar. Truth to tell, Agnes and Steve had barely a life of meager existence. They had to pay their landlady for half of the crops that were raised, and when there were no crops, the landlady would complain. In a five-year period at this time, four years of terrible hail storms destroyed half the crops! The difficulties of Steve's life built up as life went on.

There were three boys and three girls in the family. They all got to go on to high school, and some went on to college. In 1964, at the age of 56, Steve had a stroke and ended up at the Good Samaritan home where he stayed for many, many years. He passed away on August 31, 1989, at the age of 81. Tragedy came when their daughter Teresa died after having married and had two sons. She had a kidney removed at the end of October and then passed away from a heart attack in the next February, 1999. Her death took its toll on us all.

In 1968, it was not possible for Agnes to continue on the farm, and again my brother Paul came to her rescue. He designed her a house and had it built for a pittance so she was able to move to town. To my knowledge her daughter, Janis who became a truck driver was able to help her with the house payments all her life. Agnes started working in a restaurant waiting on tables, but was paid only meager dollars. When I visited her once, I lectured her because the restaurant was not paying her social security.

I told her to report them and she begged, "Laura, I need the job, if they have to pay my social security, they will let me go."

My reply: "So, you find a job that will pay your social security, what do you think you will live on when you get old?"

After several years, she finally went to work as a laundry worker at the Atwood Hospital and they paid the social security.

When she turned 70 years of age, she decided to take a job cooking for the senior citizens in the area. She would get up at 4:00 AM, go to the center, make homemade bread and prepare meals for 150 seniors. They had a truck to deliver 60 meals at 10:00 AM to another town. The other 90 were residents of Atwood and she had to have their meals ready by 12:00 noon! The state paid her for six hours a day, even though she would work 8 to 12 hours a day and was never paid overtime. Her children used to try to convince her to slow down, but she kept that job until she was 80 years of age!

Agnes in 1992

Did she stop cooking when she finally left that job? No! She was hired to make doughnuts for the Knights of Columbus in the town and she would make bread and donate it to anyone who asked her for a loaf. She also worked at the Good Samaritan center taking care of elderly people for a number of years. Time at home was not wasted cither, she quickly took up sewing dressing dolls that could be purchased and dressed. Her children marketed them in the towns where they lived and she managed to make dolls for all her nieces and anyone who married, making a bride doll for the new wife. She embroidered also, as long as she could see well enough to thread the needle. She was in the process of making a beautiful quilt for her daughter Janis, but left this world with one or two unfinished blocks.

Agnes had a goal to live for 100 years. That was her dream to live 100 years and to celebrate those years with her family at Christmas. Well, *the Lord never said life would be easy!* She always adopted her mother's acceptance of life's ups and downs.

Agnes went to visit Janis in Camp Verde, Arizona. Janis noticed stains of blood on her blouse!

She asked her what happened and Agnes said, "Oh, a pot fell off the shelf at work and hit me in the breast and it made a wound."

Janis insisted she go for a checkup and the doctor announced to her that she had breast cancer. She accepted the ultimatum that she must undergo chemo and radiation therapies. Janis kept her in her home, made sure she got to all the appointments and did what she was supposed to do. This went on for five years because she had to return for checkups. Then she and Janis returned to the doctor to get the 'good news.' Yes, there was some good news, but there was also bad news.

"Your breast cancer is cured, but you have a 15 pound malignant tumor on your lung that is also attached to your kidney!" said the doctor.

He suggested she go home and live as happily as possible until the end.

Agnes replied, "Tell you what, you operate and remove the tumor and the kidney and when I get home, in two weeks, I will cook you a real meal!"

The doctor said, "You really want to do this?"

"Of course, I am going to live to be a hundred."

She accomplished her goal of getting home and cooking the meal, but within two weeks she contracted pneumonia and fought hard to win the battle, but her life ended on February 7, 2007 at the age of 87. Her legacy of devotion, hard work, attitude and determination remains as a measuring stick of life to all who knew her. She did not make the 100 years, but in her 87 years she paved a hundred miles of love and hard work. Our brother Joe may reach her 100-year goal, as he is still alive at 91.

Agnes loved entertaining. She was always bringing in friends and family. Having her family in for holidays was a huge task as they numbered from 35 to 55 with all ages. Her older daughter

Bernardine, who lives in Colorado Springs, was always the handy lady to come help solve the work, cooking and cleaning! Her second son David, though he lived 100 miles away, still came by to do the yard work. Philip became a policeman of honor in Denver, and Stanley her oldest, still drives huge delivery trucks today and also owns an Ostrich farm in Hedville, Kansas. They gave her a final farewell with food from her house for all, knowing full well she would be unhappy if that food was not given to her friends. A large crowd of friends and relatives sent her on her way.

--

Paul Albert (Spuds)

Now comes Brother Paul, my pal Spuds. Did we ever fight? If we did I don't recall! We used to do a lot of things, some questionable, but we survived and took care of each other. When Spuds was a young man, he had to help out on the farm because the older boys had gone on their way. He never got to go to high school, and always regretted that. But as the years rolled off he knew *he could be somebody without that stuff!* And following World War II he did just that! Spuds would work at anything! He started carving wood and moved on to making furniture of all kinds for each member of his family and his own home. He became skilled enough to build impressive roll top desks. He hand-made all the cabinets in the house he built for his daughter Lorrie and her husband Mark. He also made a very large dining room table of solid mahogany for his son Buddy and Buddy's wife Charlotte.

Shortly after he left home for Denver, he would to come back to Atwood and take Charlie and I out to see what a city was like. One day Spuds and his wife Shirley introduced me to a morgue. I only saw the caretaker there and remember him leading me around. I remember how lonely and quiet the place was! I won a prize on the editorial I wrote my first year in college because I was so taken back to think they put bodies in a drawer! Soon I accepted what families felt they wanted to do.

Spuds ended up in World War II signing up with the Navy, and when he returned I had gone on to college and to a life of my own. Spuds became a provider of endless deeds. If a neighbor had problems, he would solve them. If the family came to Denver, he would provide for them and took countless numbers of nieces and nephews to Lakeside, a recreational park in town. Whenever any of the kids wanted to go fishing he would take them. He would drive endless hours up to the mountains for his family. He loved to cook and every Christmas he would hold a party in his home for 200 people! He would spend days shucking and stuffing barrels of Oysters. Each year when the party was over those oysters were all eaten. Where he purchased the oysters, I do not know. It was Denver's annual event: *Oysters with Spuds Schmid.*

A different side of him was that he loved nice things like collectibles. His favorite collectibles were Hummels. He would order every plate that was made, every figurine that he found, and he purchased for Shirley a magnificent large statue that was displayed in their living room as long as they lived. Spuds was clever and diligent in his various deeds. When he retired he would cut out grocery coupons, sort them and store them, keeping a file for 'double coupon days' at the local grocery stores. With little money he could stock his storeroom well for his children with all kinds of non-perishable food. He told me it was not at all hard to buy over a $100 worth of groceries on double coupon days and end up paying as little as seven or eight dollars! He used to laugh because he said the workers at the stores learned who he was and they would say "Not again!" when they saw him coming with a pile of coupons. Note that this was a man of integrity and honesty and would not cheat anyone even out of a penny.

His three children and anyone who came to visit, especially family were the benefactors of all this work. He always had lots of food for visitors and would do anything to make them comfortable. All would take home boxes of food that they could use. When Dan and I would go to my home in Atwood to visit, we would always stop in Denver to see Spuds.

And of course, "You've got to take food back!"

Many times we would have a trunk-full to take back to the family in Kansas.

When no one else was around, he would always make a trip home to make sure his mother never went hungry or had a desire for anything. When he went into eternity the families truly realized how much he had done for all of them. He, who had learned how to build houses from others while he worked as a lather. He purchased an apartment building early on. The rent provided him with cash to keep building. He designed houses for three of his sisters, myself included. Our home at 28 Fieldstone Drive in Stoneham was by far one of the most outstanding in the town in 1971. He even flew out to

Laura's House at 28 Fieldstone Drive, Designed by Her Brother Paul

check on the builder, and gave him a raking-over when he found the hard wood floor was not put in lying straight-way through two rooms! He made the builder re-do the foundation so the floor was laid right! The builder, Paonasa by name, was so impressed with his ability that he flew to Denver to meet with Paul (Spuds) and see some of the work he had done. He told us later that he was absolutely amazed that a guy who never went to high school or beyond could do what Paul had done.

At the time, Paul had designed a house for an owner of 'Dairy Queen' on the side of a mountain south of Denver. It was a hard, tricky job as he had to make sure the house would not slide off the hill. He also designed an electric floor with an interior pool under it, so the family could take a swim whenever they desired. The floor would revolve off into another area and the furniture would move off with it, uncovering the pool! He installed a fan to remove moisture from the pool as well, solving the main problem with the pool system before it caused difficulties with the family. In those days that home cost a mint. Today I am sure it is worth millions.

Paul Albert and His Wife Shirley in 1998

I doubt that Spuds ever missed a challenge. He felt if it could be done, he could do it. Spuds would go see his brother Joe because they both were doing the same thing, succeeding without ever having gone on to high school (the way Pa wanted it). In later years he saw Joe deteriorating as a result of the war and that he was not doing so well, so he would cook supper for both he and Lottie several times a week. Then, after Lottie passed away, he provided Joe with meals practically every evening. Spuds knew that loving deeds were the food of a good life. One day, he cooked Joe a meal and delivered it to him. The very next day Spuds dropped dead of a heart attack. It was September 13, 2001, two days after the World Trade Center disaster in New York City. Spuds was 79 years old.

In recreating what might have happened to Spuds, the family discovered he was severely stressed just before his death because he received some horrifying news. His youngest son, Paul Jr., asked him to go to the doctor with him a few weeks before. The doctor gave Paul, Jr. an alarming report that he (Paul Jr.) had a malignant brain tumor and it was not curable! Paul Jr. joined his dad in eternity one year and two weeks after his father's passing.

The Trade Center Disaster cancelled air flights, and so travel was not possible. I was unable to go home to say my last farewell to my brother Spuds. Time will come when we will re-unite. I have no concerns for that reunion. No one will ever forget this man who lived a life of dedication, love, and hard work.

--

My last three brothers were born at the end of our long family road and faced change of every kind. The dust storms had subsided, the depression had ended, but now World War II took away their older brothers. At this time Pa was very ill and passed away in 1943 after having closed his butcher shop in 1937. The farm was in complete financial disorder! This put Charlie, Louie and Andrew in charge of taking care of what remained. Louie however was drafted and went off to war. Charlie should have been taken, but they allowed Ma to keep him to take care of her. Charlie went up to the recruiting office and explained his mother's contribution to the service with six sons already on the list, five of them now in active service. They granted Charlie a reprieve and he remained to take care of his mother.

Spuds was my very best pal all the time we were growing up. As a young man he left, and after he did Charlie and I became the best of buddies. We hung out a lot together; we were so near in age. When Paul Albert (Spuds) went away, that left Charlie and I to figure out what had to be done to save the farm. Because I had a need to build a life of my own, I would be leaving soon so I was only there for Charlie to encourage him on the way. He would stay to do the work. He too, as all my brothers had been, was a devoted, hard-working, money-wise kid. He had to do the farming and he had to figure out how we were going to save Ma's home. Thank goodness, Occidental Life gave me credit for going to high school and for that reason decided to give us time to recoup the back-owed funds.

Charles Martin (Bushy)

Charlie had a drive that kept him going through these tough economic times. He had a tremendous deep faith and trust in God. He embraced that faith and trust through his life-long partnership in the catholic church. He joined the Knights of Columbus and lived up to their standards as well. When times got tough, Charlie started building a larger herd of cattle. Cattle prices were beginning to increase. The herds could be taken off to McCook, Nebraska to be shipped to Omaha for slaughtering. I never had much time to give, but on weekends I would go home to run the tractor in the fields. I would mow, plant, or plow. It wasn't much help; Charlie was left with most of the load. Then Andy grew to the age where he could be trusted driving horse-drawn mowers and rakes, and so he took a better chunk of the workload off of Charlie. Because Pa had two farms, Charlie had a lot of early mornings and late nights, and little rest or relaxation. As Andy grew older he took over the home place. Charlie was finally able to get a mortgage in his name and purchased the North Place. That left the farm Ma lived on to be taken care of by Andy. By the time I graduated from high school Charlie and Andy had become real partners and worked tediously together. Thank goodness the rains came, crops improved, cattle prices were up and the farm was redeemed. Both boys could now act on the individual places without relying too much on each other.

Charlie then met Rita and married her in 1954. I actually went home with our three children to make all the dresses for the wedding because I knew money was scarce. I was able to use Ma's sewing machine and made the bride's dress and three bridesmaids' dresses as well. It was an easy make, for I was one of the bridesmaids. Easy but time-consuming; it took me one month to get them all done.

Charlie and His Herd of Cattle

As the years rolled on, Charlie and Rita had nine children and lived in a four-room house (which he later expanded). He was able to borrow money from the bank to increase his herd of cattle and when we went home he was so proud of his white-faced steers. Well, nothing stays constant, and with time, the crops began to fail again, the price of cattle deteriorated, and he fell behind with payments to the bank (who had encouraged him to borrow too much money).

One day when he was out in the field, Rita went to town and left the four children in the house alone. At noon Charlie went home to get something to eat and, low and behold, there was a fire in the kitchen! He managed to get the children out safely, but by the time the fire engines got the flames out, most of the house had been burned. Charlie needed to rebuild. One of his neighbors brought him a big trailer to attach to the remaining rooms in the house.

Rita got a job driving a truck, which took her away from the family for days and sometimes weeks at a time and from then on, life was a terrible task for all. The older children did what they could to be self-sufficient. They had to walk a mile to catch a bus to go to school. The youngest daughter Mary was born deaf because her mother had measles while she was pregnant. Each kid had an assignment to do. The older kids packed the school lunches and helped the younger ones get dressed.

Mary, Marty, Tim and Tom were a year or two apart. Time did not change any of the problems. Charlie remembered all the problems Ma had encountered raising 15 children and remembered how she managed, so this gave him the courage to keep the family and farm together despite a non-participating spouse. Rita, however, decided to leave Charlie and moved into a trailer in town. A divorce was filed and because it was the 1970's the children were assigned back to Rita. Tom at 15 refused to stay with his mom and went to his father with a lot of anxiety for all. Tony, the oldest, was working for another farmer and lived away from home. Cathy, the older girl, had married and moved out. Her sister Anita got a job and moved out of the trailer in town to live in an apartment. The others lived in the trailer with their mother in the town of Atwood. Ted and Tim, 9 or 10 years of age, were in charge of watching and taking care of Marty and Mary whenever Rita would leave on a trip.

One day, they put the wash in the dryer, didn't know enough to clean the lint trap and went off to school. Yes, another fire, the trailer burned down and Tim's dog was burned to death! It was a good thing that the children had all left for school or they would have been hurt or killed! Now it came down to *where to from here?*

The children went back home to Charlie, and Rita took a room off the side of his house and nailed the door into the main house shut, so she could have her privacy. She lived there alone (by choice), and had little to do with her adjacent family.

From then on Charlie was happy that the kids were home again, and as Charlie said, "At least their mom is here, if they need her."

On one visit back home Charlie told us that he had found a sand pit in the pasture and that if it contained enough sand the highway department was going to pay him a lot of money, which would give him enough cash to support his family at the North place, *and* help Andy with the home place. He tested the sand pit and the results were good, there was a lot of sand! But again misfortune struck. The bank put a lien on the property so Charlie could not have the money. He lost his farm in 1979, but the new buyer allowed him to live in the house, as he bought the property only for the use of the land. That meant the children could finish school without having to change homes again.

Charlie then got a job at the Elevator in Ludell. He was in charge of receiving grain that was brought in by farmers who needed storage or wished to sell. He told us he had been battling a terrible pain he had in his right arm, and that the doctor thought it was rheumatism. One year, when we were visiting, he said he really had a tough time at the Elevator because he could no longer handle moving the grain, so they gave him a job doing the paper work. We left for home and then the news came that Charlie had a chest pain at the Elevator and put himself in the car, and drove 50 miles to the hospital in Colby.

The doctor examined him and announced, "Charlie you have just had a major heart attack, I am going to have to air-flight you to Colorado Springs."

Charlie said, "Hold it, not just yet, I have something I have to do. I am going back to Atwood and will call you when I'm ready."

The doctor went bonkers: "You will die driving that car back! Charlie, you can drop dead at the wheel!"

"Well, if I do, the Lord will know what I wanted to do."

He made it back to Atwood. What was his mission? He wanted to go to confession, so he went to the Sacred Heart Rectory to see Father Flavin.

He asked Father Flavin, "Can you hear my confession now?"
Father Flavin answered him, "Of course I can!"

He gave him absolution, and Charlie thanked him and said, "Good-bye!"

When he got to the car, he called the doctor. The doctor arranged the air-flight to take off from Atwood and to land in Colorado Springs. He was committed to Memorial Hospital there and within several days underwent bypass surgery. This was very new in the medical field. They did *seven* bypasses. He survived and was in the hospital for many weeks, then sent home. He was to return for a checkup in late August.

Dan and I made plans to go home to see him with our family. We were there from mid-July to mid-August and we were able to spend time with him. His attitude was great. He was determined to get back to work. We left around August 14 and his checkup was to be August 16. When we got home he called to tell us they said he could go back to work by mid-September as long as he did no lifting and worked at first for only a few hours a day. That he did, but sometime in October, he began to not feel well. He went to the doctor only to find out that the bypasses had failed. He was hospitalized in Atwood but departed his life at 58 years of age on December 12, 1982.

This was heart-breaking news as we had thought he truly was going to survive. The ONLY thing he wanted was to live. At this time, I was elected as President of the Eastern Middlesex Board of Realtors, and was being installed that evening, December 12 at a formal dinner dance. Now, I needed to get plane reservations so I could go home to say good-bye. The plane was leaving at 2:00 AM on December 13, so when the installation was over, my family took me to the airport to make the flight. It was indeed an emotional and traumatic time for us all, as he was such a great character. He could whistle like you couldn't believe. He was always pulling funny jokes on everyone and would smile and wink on a daily basis. Returning years later I visited his grave to read his lifeline:

I've lived my life, and fought the good fight.

For sure, he did, leaving his sister, Laura with sorrow and pain.

Several years later, my brother Spuds (who was very upset about how Charlie died) found an article in the Denver paper stating that the doctor who had done the bypasses for Charlie had his medical license cancelled. The article stated that there was a rule that no more than four bypasses could be performed at one time. Charlie had been given seven and had been in surgery some ten hours. The news did not give us back our loving brother, Charlie.

--

My brother Louie who had gone to war, returned home having married, had a hard time re-adjusting to life. He had seen the ravages of war, had to use his gun and received injuries from the enemy. He was unable to adjust back to life and started drinking.

Louis Frederick

He really did not like farming. Aunt Cora was an angel in his life, asking him to help her out with a house she owned in Beardsley. He lived there working for her and after nine years he moved to Denver to work in an auto body shop. His wife and four children were there.

Then alcohol again took over his life, the family fell apart and he moved to somewhere in Arizona. His life ended from a gunshot wound on October 5, 1977, at 51 years, 6 months and five days old. No one really knows how he died. It was accepted as a suicide, because no one requested to have a criminal check made.

My younger brother Andrew, one of Louie's most devoted family members, always claimed the gunshot wound was such that he could not have done it himself. He was laid to rest alongside his Mother, Father, and sisters Threasa, and Annie in St. John's Graveyard. He left to meet his master in eternity. Hopefully, he found peace. He left behind his wife, Elaine and four children, Eva, Michael, Patrick and Susan.

--

Andrew, my youngest brother, grew up with lots of attention. He was probably the cutest, and probably more spoiled than I, Laura. My mother was 45 years of age when he came to this earth. He, Louie and Charlie were very near in age, so they had a great camaraderie growing up together. Pa gave them two ponies, Bill and Don, and they spent hours of every day riding the ponies. When they were old enough they were sent to get the cows out of the pasture on those ponies. They built a wagon as well and that meant they could have a good time taking the neighbor kids for a ride, as well as their older brothers' and sisters' children, when they came to visit. Charlie and Louie would ride their ponies three miles up to town every day to serve Mass for Father Hubert. The ponies were a part of their lives.

The boys give pony-wagon rides to the local children

Andrew was fourteen in 1943 when Pa passed away, and immediately entered into adulthood because of the financial situation at the time. Ma counted on the three boys to help run the farm. Then Louie was drafted. Charles and Andy were left to provide for her. Andy was just a kid, and loved to pull tricks on the other kids. I remember him always trying to pull off something to make everyone laugh.

Andrew Bernard

One time after I left home and was married, I returned for a visit. Andy hung a bucket of water over the porch door, so when I opened the door to go in, the bucket would tip and shower me with water. Another time he put corn flakes between the sheets and folded the bottom sheet up so when you got into bed, you could only go so far and got all this crappy food all over you. He would laugh like crazy but would never admit he did it.

After a few of these anomalies, my friend Evelyn, whom I had taken to Kansas for a trip, and I decided we would get even with Andy. We arranged that Ma connect the hose from the water tank to the hose from the garden, so we could turn on the water from the garden spout. There was a hole in the roof of the outdoor closet because it was so old, so Evelyn and I got the hose up to the roof and put it inside the hole, just enough to hold it in place. Ma had told us that Andy got up every morning at 5:00 AM and would go to that closet and sit there with the door open to read awhile before he came to her house for coffee. Ma told us she would call us to get up when she saw him make his way to the closet. We had a camera; Evelyn was assigned to sneak out around the bunkhouse so she could snap a picture of whatever happened. I, Laura, not to be outdone sneaked around to the faucet in the garden and once we were stationed, I turned on the faucet full force!

"HOLY ..... WHAT THE...?" yelled Andy from the closet!

He came running out, pulling up his pants and Evelyn caught the whole picture. Of course the three of us were laughing like crazy. The end result: he knew from then on to watch his tricks. The last time I saw him, we laughed about the event. I don't think he ever truly changed. He loved fun.

Andy's home life on the Kansas farm at that time really was the true essence of poverty. He had no money to buy anything other than what was absolutely needed. They lived off the products of the farm, eating meat, potatoes, gravy, pancakes and eggs. Day in and day out their menu changed very little. The only money they would have would be from delivering eggs, cream or milk to the neighbors, or in town for people who could afford to buy them. However this did not stop him or his family from managing since loyalty, hard work, commitment and dedication to family were his "A+" grades in life.

He loved taking the kids fishing or hunting. You could fish in the lake built by the C.C.C. (Civilian Conservation Corpse) during the war. You were allowed to hunt rabbits on your own land. These were the family's outings their whole life through. On a Sunday, he would get in the car and drive to Trenton, Nebraska 35 miles away to the lake there. They would hope and pray they would catch a washtub full of catfish and that was their food for days or weeks. As long as he survived, the fishing trips were never abandoned.

When Ma went into the Good Samaritan Home, the farm had to be sold and Andy was asked to leave. He had to get rid of all the unused junk in the remaining buildings. He found a two-bedroom home down in Colby that had a back yard and a garage. That's where the "memorials of the Butch Schmid farm of Atwood, Kansas" were taken. Going back to Kansas during the years that followed, all that was left to see were the remains of most of the buildings. Then the new owners destroyed them all.

Andy's youngest son took over the house in Colby and lives there today. Andy and Maryellen moved on to Hays, Kansas for a better life. He worked at car repair, then health problems took over and he had to be treated for heart problems. He loved Maryellen dearly and one year he wanted to buy her a birthday gift. He had no money so he took the battery out of his truck and sold it. He used the money to buy Maryellen a gift.

On October 5, 1991, the family experienced the accidental death of their son Brian. He had gone out with a friend to a dance in Colby, Kansas, about 100 miles from Hays. When the dance was over he said to his friend he was too tired to drive home. He knew there was an empty garage down town where he could just pull in and take a nap; then he would start home. Evidently it was a cold night and no blankets were in the car. He must have started the motor to heat the car and that was the end of his life. He died of carbon monoxide poisoning! His body was taken home to the prairie in Atwood and there he lies beside other family members.

Andy, suffering from the heart condition, decided he needed to retire. Maryellen, who had worked all her life, continued to work in a restaurant as the main cook and is still there today. In order to help with finances, Andy decided to take up making dollhouse furnishings, making wooden yard adornments, and anything that he could design and tool to sell at fairs. He gave me a set on one of my visits and, of course, they are the pride of my displays. He made a boy and a girl on swings and gave them to me to hang in our tree in our yard. They hung there until we left Fieldstone Drive. To my knowledge he had to have heart surgery. He had been doing well after a long time of recuperation. Years passed and again he became ill. He went to the doctor one evening to find answers.

The doctor told him, "We need to do a by-pass tomorrow. I need to take you into the hospital now."

Andrew, wanting to make peace with his Savior, asked if he could go out for a little while. He went to the local parish church, was able to see the priest and went to confession. He called Maryellen and told her he was being admitted into the hospital.

Maryellen called me and told me, "Andy is undergoing serious surgery tomorrow morning. This is his number if you would like to talk with him."

I immediately called the number, the hospital answered and I asked to speak to Andrew Schmid.

The nurse in the room replied, "I think you should call his wife, she has information for you."

I thought, *hmm, that's odd, why wouldn't they let me talk to him? Well, maybe he was undergoing tests.* I immediately called back Maryellen and she answered the phone.

When I told her what happened, she started to cry and said, "Laura, no sooner had Andy checked in, they took him to his room and he started to undress, but dropped dead."

Only minutes, only time, and life changes! No notice. No introductory lessons. What is, is! Was it a birthday gift to me, his youngest devoted sister? He passed away April 9, 2002. Will I forget? Never!

Now the family is all gone except for two of us. No one can erase in any way shape or form the memories of a large family devoted to following rules, regulations, livelihood, kindness, honesty, integrity and charity. Poverty to us was not halting our life in any way. Poverty was education, poverty brought kindness, poverty required caring, and to live with poverty was persevering.

All who experienced this life left many friends, families and relatives with love and enduring memories. Until death does one *live!* A measuring stick of life: live each day as if it may be your last. It may not be easy, but time proves *you can be what you want to be.*

I, Laura, have not forgotten!

The Wolves – written by Andy at about 9 or 10 years of age. He won an award for it and was presented with a plaque:

Upon the frozen moonlit lands,
With head raised high, the gray wolf stands
To send his call of silver tone,
To distant lands so far unknown.
Out on the plains far and wide,
Two wolves travel side by side,
To meet the pack, to fight and kill
The big Bull Moose upon the hill,
And then with heads raised to the sky,
The wolf pack gives the victory cry.

IN APPRECIATION

I wish to extend my sincere appreciation and gratitude to my only remaining brother, Joe, for his participation in my book project. Joe was five years older than I and therefore experienced many happenings that were unknown to me. Joe, you recorded on tapes your memories and did a magnificent job. Our grand niece, Wendi Schmid, grand daughter of Paul (Spuds), spent many hours typing the tapes for me, then spent many days and hours checking town libraries for evidence to insure that the memories were as recorded. My love and sincere thanks to you both. I, Laura, love you both!

Editor's note: After completion of this book Joseph Henry Schmid, Laura's brother Joe, passed away on May 2, 2010, at the age of 92. He died of natural causes; he did not succumb to the crippling injuries he had sustained in the war 67 years ago. Also on that day, Laura's husband Daniel William Hogan passed away of widespread cancer. He was 89. Before he died he asked his wife to say goodbye to his children, because he knew May 2 would be the day of his passing.

Schmid Family Tree

Place of Birth	Date of Birth	Marriage Date(s)	Rest In Peace
Martin Schmid			
Solbock, Germany	February 17, 1872	October 13, 1872	October 25, 1943
Eva Marie Haller			
Haubstadt, Indiana	July 4, 1884	October 13, 1872	January 25, 1976
SCHMID OFFSPRING AND THEIR SPOUSES			
James Paul Schmid			
Ludell, Kansas	August 11, 1904	September 27, 1932	September 7, 1975
Nina Lintner			
Atwood, Kansas	March 26, 1908	September 27, 1932	January 3, 2006
Katherine Mary Schmid			
Ludell, Kansas	January 21, 1906	October 12, 1937	April 5, 1993
Walter Conant			
Orleans, Nebrask	May 10, 194	October 12, 1937	February 28, 1978
John Joseph Schmid			
Ludell, Kansas	October 17, 1907	March 1, 1932 January 26, 1936	May 24, 1963
Olive Hatch			
		March 1, 1932	
Opal Blakely			
	October 11, 1902	January 26, 1936	November 24, 1992
Annie Catherine Schmid			
Ludell, Kansas	April 3, 1909		October 25, 1922
Threasa Louise Schmid			
Ludell, Kansas	October 3, 1911		December 17, 1951
Frank George Schmid			
Ludell, Kansas	May 10, 1914	May 3, 1937	May 26, 1970
Mildred Flood			
Trenton, Nebraska		May 3 1937	
Fred Andrew Schmid			
Ludell, Kansas	May 10, 1914	?? ?? October 18, 1958	April 21, 1996
Gertrude Shattuck			
		??	September 1932??
Alice Russell			
Printes, Indiana	1911	??	August 16, 1957
Freida Ochs			
	August 4, ??	October 18, 1958	

Place of Birth	Date of Birth	Marriage Date(s)	Rest In Peace
Verneda Frances Schmid			
Ludell, Kansas	May 24, 1916	February 3, 1937	November 25, 2002
Edwin Rippe			
Ludell, Kansas	April 1, 1910	February 3, 1937	July 14, 1958
Joseph Henry Schmid			
Ludell, Kansas	March 22, 1918	May 28, 1942	
Lottie Peachey			
Coloroado	July 21, 1917	May 28, 1942	July 25, 2002
Agnes Elizabeth Schmid			
Atwood, Kansas	July 1, 1991	January 5, 1938	Grbruary 7, 2007
Stephen Conrad Barenberg			
Herndon, Kansas	November 26, 1908	January 5, 1938	August 31, 1989
Paul Albert Schmid			
Atwoood, Kansas	Gebruary 15, 1922	April 5, 1942	September 14, 2001
Shirley Jones			
Colorodo	January 15, 1921	April 5, 1942	December 25, 2006
Laura Margaret Schmid			
Atwood, Kansas	April 9, 1923	June 14, 1947	
Daniel William Hogan			
Wakefield, Massachusetts	January 6, 1921	June 14, 1947	May 2, 2010
Charles Martin Schmid			
Atwood, Kansas	September 20, 1924	August 16, 1964	December 12, 1982
Rita LeBow			
McDonald, Kansas	August 27, 1933	August 16, 1964	
Louis Frederick Schmid			
Atwood, Kansas	March 29, 1926	December 24, 1945	October 5, 1977
Dorothy Elaine Johnson			
Perth??, Louisiana	Aprill 22, 1926	December 24, 1945	May 12, 1992
Andrew Bernard Schmid			
Atwood, Kansas	October 1, 1929	April 25, 1959	April 9, 2002
Mary Ellen Jackson			
Atwood, Kansas	August 31, 1938	April 25, 1959	

Gone – but not forgotten!
As the years roll by, we must say good-bye, but remembering we
will, we love them still!

Name	Nickname or Relation	Cause of Death	Date of Death
Annie Catherine Schmid		Diptheria	October 25, 1922
Olive Hatch Schmid	Johnnie's 1st Wife	Cancer	January 6, 1934
Martin Schmid	Pa	Stomach Cancer	October 25, 1943
Threasa Louise Schmid		Accident – Fire	December 17, 1951
Alice Russell Schmid	Fritz' 2nd Wife	Cancer	August 13, 1957
Edwin Rippe	Verneda's Husband	Blood Clot	July 14, 1958
John Joseph Schmid	Johnnie	Heart Attach	May 24, 1963
Joseph Walter Conant	Joker, Toots' Son	Auto Accident	December 4, 1965
Evelyn Schmid Porterfield	Johnnie's Daughter	Breast Cancer	June 26, 1968
Frank George Schmid	Frankie	Brain Tumor	May 26, 1970
Jared Martin Conant	Jerry, Toots' Son	Auto Accident	November 2, 1970
James Paul Schmid	Jim	Heart Failure	September 7, 1975
Eva Marie Schmid	Ma	Heart Failure	January 25, 1976
Louis Frederick Schmid	Louie	Accident	October 5, 1977
Walter Conant	Toots' Husband	Kidney Cancer	February 23, 1978
Charles Martin Schmid	Charlie, Bushy	Heart By-Pass Failure	December 12, 1982
Fred Schmid, Jr.	Butch, Fritz' Son	Alcohol Overdose	February 4, 1983
Stephen Conrad Barenberg	Agnes' Husband	Heart Condition	August 31, 1989
Brian Andrew Schmid	Andy's Son	Carbon Monoxide	October 5, 1991
Elaine Johnson Schmid	Louie's Wife	Cancer	May 12, 1992
Opal Blakely Schmid	Johnnie's 3rd wife	Congestive Heart Failure	November 24, 1992
Elizabeth Conant Heimer	Toots' daughter	Breast Cancer	November 26, 1992
Katherine Schmid Conant	Toots	Congestive Heart Failure	April 5, 1993
Fred Andrew Schmid	Fritz	Heart Attack	April 25, 1996
Clarence F. Rippe	Verneda's Son	Cancer	May 22, 1998
Teresa Barenberg Baes	Agnes' Daughter	Kidney Cancer	February 13, 1999
Mildred Schmid Arendt	Millie, Frankie's Wife	Unknown	September 27, 1999
Paul Albert Schmid	Spuds	Heart Attack	September 14, 2001
Andrew Bernard Schmid	Andy	Heart Attack	April 9, 2002
Paul Albert Schmid Jr.	Spuds' Son	Brain Tumor	September 29, 2002

Gone – but not forgotten!
As the years roll by, we must say good-bye, but remembering we
will, we love them still!

Name	Nickname or Relation	Cause of Death	Date of Death
Verneda Schmid Rippe		Congestive Heart Failure	November 25, 2002
Nina Lintner Schmid	Jim's Wife	Congestive Heart Failure	January 3, 2006
Shirley Anne Schmid	Spuds' Wife	Congestive Heart Failure	December 25, 2006
Agnes Schmid Barenberg		Pneumonia	February 7, 2007
Daniel William Hogan	Laura's Husband		May 2, 2010

Family Members List for picture on page 78:

The Family (Except for Annie Catherine) in 1932:

Back Row, Left to Right:

James, Fred, John, Laura, Frank, Joseph, Paul

Front Row, Left to Right:

Verneda, Katherine, Louis, Eva, Andrew, Martin, Charles, Threasa, Agnes